David Cox

1783–1859

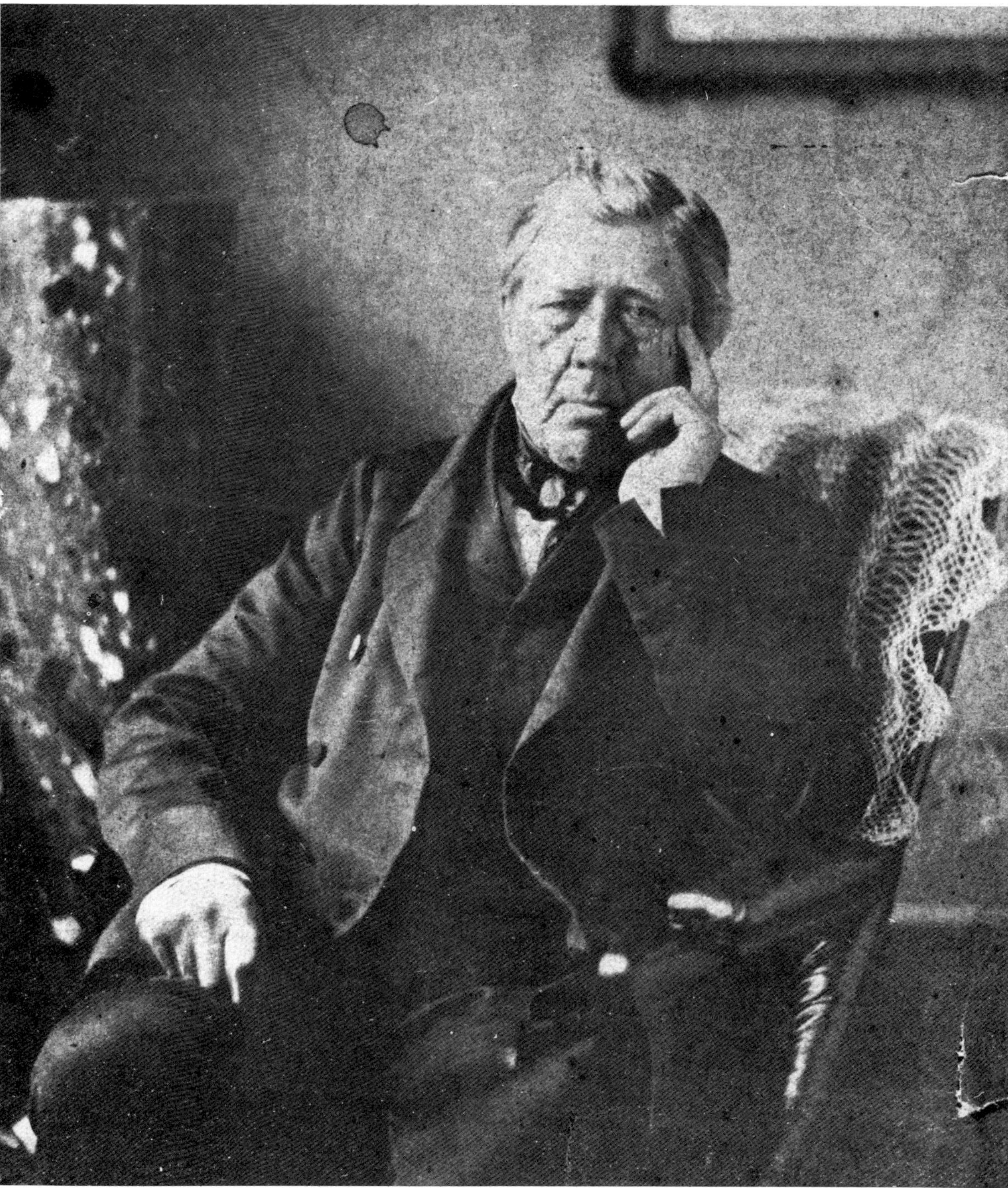

David Cox

1783–1859

Selected and catalogued by Stephen Wildman

Introductory essays by

Richard Lockett and John Murdoch

With 80 monochrome illustrations and 16 pages of colour

Birmingham Museums and Art Gallery

David Cox, 1783–1859. A Bicentenary Exhibition
Birmingham Museums and Art Gallery, 26 July–14 October 1983
Victoria and Albert Museum, London, 9 November 1983–8 January 1984

First published in Great Britain in 1983

ISBN 0 7093 0114 6

Produced by the South Leigh Press Ltd, Chilcroft Road, Kingsley Green,
Haslemere, Surrey GU27 3LS. Tel. 0428-3459
Distributed by A. Zwemmer Ltd, 26 Litchfield Street, London WC2H 9NJ
Printed in Great Britain

Contents

Foreword

David Cox was a contemporary of Turner and Constable, and features in all the standard surveys of British painting. However, there has been no significant publication on his work since Sir Trenchard Cox's volume in 1947, and no major exhibition since that held here in Birmingham, his birthplace, in 1959.

Birmingham's Cox collection, numbering some five hundred items, is easily the largest anywhere. It seems therefore appropriate that we should mount a major celebration of one of our best-loved sons to mark the bicentenary of his birth.

The exhibition shows the whole range of Cox's work, including the hitherto neglected oils, and has been selected and catalogued by Stephen Wildman, Deputy Keeper of Prints and Drawings. Richard Lockett, Keeper of Fine Art, and John Murdoch, Deputy Keeper of Paintings at the Victoria and Albert Museum (formerly of Birmingham Art Gallery) have contributed introductory essays to the catalogue.

To all of them my sincerest thanks are due for much hard work and a notable achievement. I would also like to thank the Victoria and Albert Museum, and particularly Michael Kauffmann, for giving the exhibition a London showing, where indeed it will be the first large watercolour exhibition in the newly-refurbished Cole building.

A special word of thanks must also go to Messrs Harper and Tunstall, of Wellingborough, who have provided generous financial assistance towards the costs of initial research and publication of this catalogue and towards the Exhibition itself; and especially to Ewan Harper, an enthusiastic champion of Cox's work.

All exhibitions of this kind depend heavily on the generosity of public and private owners, and once again it gives me great pleasure to place on record our thanks for the remarkable goodwill of a great many lenders.

MICHAEL DIAMOND
Director, BMAG

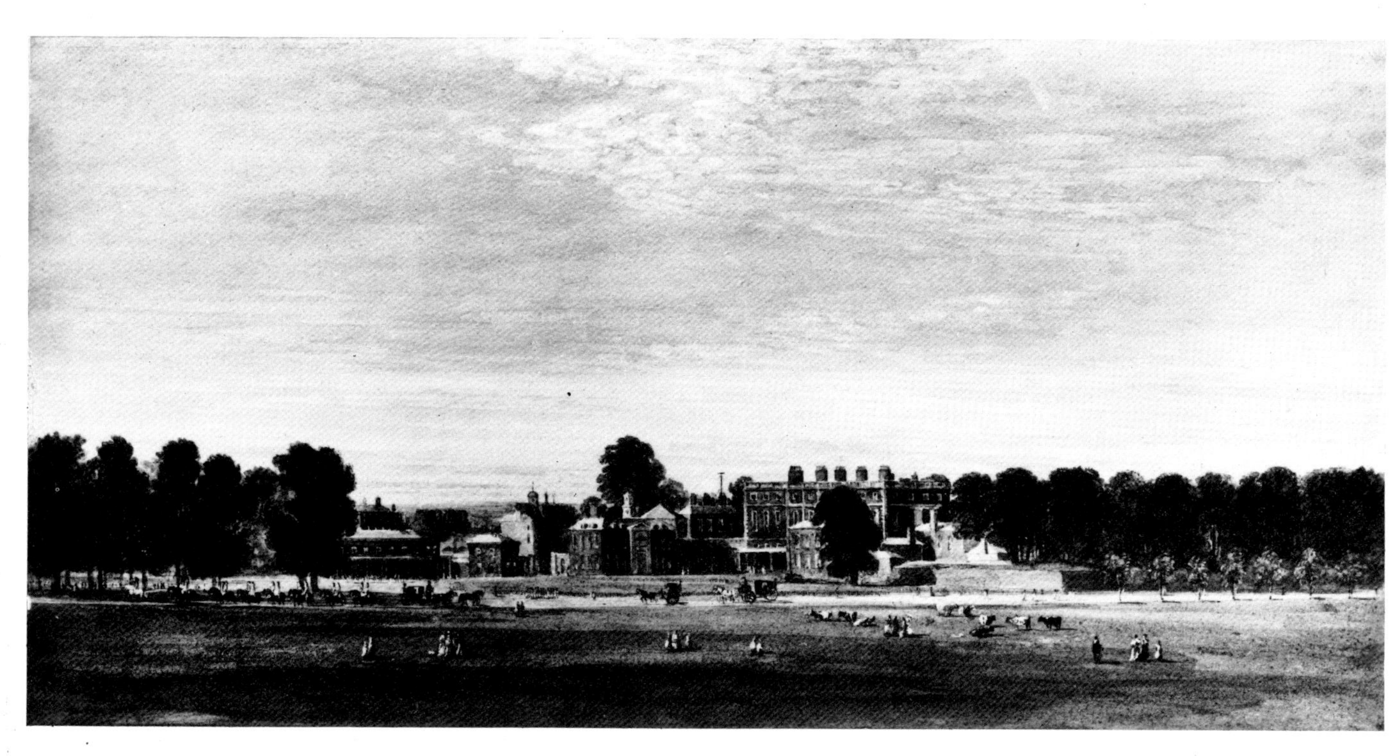

Buckingham House from the Green Park 1825 (cat. no. 30)

Cox: Doctrine, Style and Meaning

It should hardly need saying that Cox belonged to the aesthetic culture of the late 18th century, and, put like that, the statement seems only mildly odd in relation to an artist who died in 1859. But since the time of the biographies in the last century, and in the mainly critical accounts that have appeared since 1900, Cox has been treated in an exclusively 19th-century manner, as the isolated genius who produced work from the recesses of his own most personal insights by means of his least conditioned impulses. Cox was of course a romantic, and some of this romantic view of him is therefore quite apt. Yet as a romantic he belonged ineluctably to a culture which determined his career and work. We recognise, correctly, the importance of upbringing, of a person's relation to the social hierarchy and the means of production, as determinants of opportunity and achievement. In this essay I want to look at the theoretical and doctrinal conditions of Cox's art – those factors which lie more profoundly in the creative process than 'influences' from other artists, and more immediately to hand than objective sociological conditions.

The basic terminology of late 18th-century aesthetics in England was that of Edmund Burke,[1] whose approach to the subject had important similarities with that of the natural scientists. Working on a formal division of aesthetic experience between the Sublime and the Beautiful, he sought to establish clear aesthetic species through a rigorous taxonomy of the relevant experiences. Crucially, what he examined were the properties of objects, those qualities such as size, colour, texture, etc, that were sensorily accessible, and related them constantly to the sensations they aroused. Thus, properties such as smallness, smoothness, lightness were conducive to the sensation of Beauty, and properties such as vastness, ruggedness, and darkness provoked the sensation of the Sublime. Burke's analysis (whatever its apparent drawbacks, especially in such a summary) is usually called 'sensationist', which means that it was in fact rigorously empirical. His philosophy is thereby very different from that of the idealist Emmanuel Kant (to whom the word and perhaps the concept of aesthetics is attributable) and it is importantly different also from that of other British writers. Archibald Alison for example pointed to the role of association in the causing of aesthetic experience, claiming that it was 'when we are absorbed in this powerless state of reverie, when we are carried on by our conceptions, not guiding them, that the deepest emotions of beauty or sublimity are felt'.[2] But Alison, whose insight is of particular relevance to the descriptive verse of Scott or Byron and to the landscape painting of Cozens and Turner, was building on the categories established by Burke; and part of Burke's importance came thus from the way in which his austere method provoked enlargement and improvement. In England, his *Enquiry* was fundamental, its method profoundly congruent with British empiricism, and with the whole intellectual ethos of the cultural elite.

Against this background, I find David Cox especially interesting because he seems to have matched in rigour the basic sensationism of British aesthetics.

The point was not lost on Burke's modern editor, J. T. Boulton, who found in Cox's *Treatise on Landscape Painting* unmistakable allusions to the *Enquiry*. Cox's opinions that beautiful cottage scenes ought to project 'pleasure without astonishment', that ruin scenes, marked by awful sublimity, should create a 'reverential and permanent impression', that 'sublime ideas are expressed by lofty and obscure images', certainly do derive from Burke and they make the point that there is a direct correspondence between the qualities of the object or image and the resulting experience. Cox does not say that a landscape needs to refer to any outside ideas: its own physical make-up creates the impression. Thus, as Professor Boulton observes, *Buckingham House from the Green Park* (no. 30) deploys the technical constituents of Beauty: 'the colours – predominantly green, brown and pale blue – are what Burke would call clear and fair' not 'strong'; the lines are 'even and horizontal', which Cox believed would produce 'serenity'; and there is a general 'smoothness' about the whole picture, especially in the broad area of grass in the foreground and the large background of sky.[3]

What we have here in the iconography of landscape is a non-symbolic system: it creates the specific and intended sensation of Beauty without outside reference, with no allusions to poetry or romance, but by the inherent qualities of the objects depicted and by the ways in which paint is applied to the paper. This is not to say that it excludes association. Here there might be associated ideas of prosperity or plenty, both functionally related to the Beautiful in Burke as well as in the rational economics of Adam Smith. But there is in pictures of this sort a simplicity of diction, a directness of correspondence between the painted image, the object itself and its intended significance, without the spread of association, which is fundamental to the Enlightenment and ties Cox firmly into the English tradition of the 17th and 18th centuries.

The approach to the Sublime is similar, though the imaginative stimulus is of course much stronger. Cox's most eloquent images in this category are those which use the principal motif like a simple statement, placing the bull in the foreground, or the horse and the steam train in antithetical compositional balance (e.g. *On the Moors, Bettws-y-Coed* (no. 102) or *The Night Train* (no. 79)). Burke of course did not discuss the aesthetics of the steam train, but its sublimity in the strict sensationist definition (its vast power, outpourings of opaque smoke, hellish fiery glimmers of furnace and steel, and sudden frightful noise) would certainly have seemed typical. For Burke, the horse illustrated one type of Sublimity, and the point of Cox's picture rests in the contrast of the natural and the artificial, the past, the present and the future, between darkness and illumination, as they arise precisely out of the painted image.

The bull of course is definitively Sublime: 'the idea of a bull is therefore great, and it has frequently a place in sublime descriptions, and elevating comparisons'. The moor is dark, extended apparently towards infinity; the bellowing and the storm 'awaken a great and aweful sensation in the mind'.[4] Also, I think, Cox's *drawing* itself is Sublime, while in the *Buckingham House* it had the graphic qualities of the Beautiful. Here his palette is characterized by the 'privation' of colour and

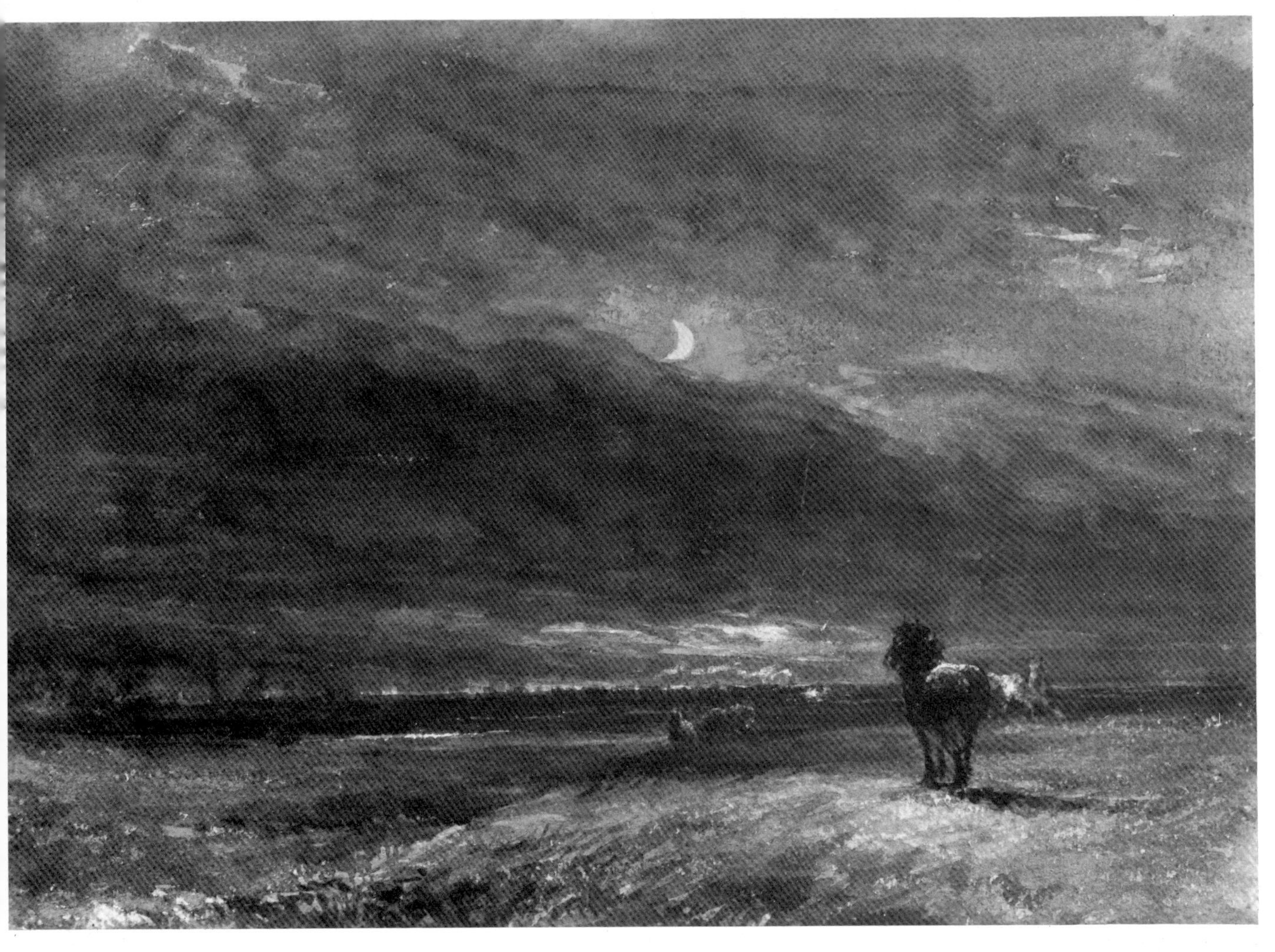

The Night Train (cat. no. 79)

light, and the dark colours are applied in such a way as to confuse outlines and to create that difficulty of exact perception which is essential to the Sublime. Cox's power to do this lies in his cultivation of an anti-linear graphic idiom. He works without outline, in dashes that are themselves usually without relevant form and which build up an image of accumulated obscurity. It is the most direct and 'literal' approach to the problem of achieving or discussing the Sublime in the small compass of a drawing: the workmanship possesses the same qualities as the subject, and both are Sublime in the same strict sense.

This perception can direct our understanding of Cox's drawings in the third great taxonomic division of late 18th-century aesthetics. The Picturesque was not defined by Burke but easily its most coherent formulation was that expressed by Uvedale Price,[5] an avowed follower of Burke. He proposed that Picturesque landscape was an additional and intermediate category, the sensations it aroused being caused by a quite distinct set of qualities in objects. These were identified as intricacy, sudden variation, partial concealment, roughness, etc, qualities that resulted usually from the operations of unassisted nature working through long periods of time. I believe that Price's publications, printed and reprinted at intervals from the 1790s through the 1840s, were of general importance in the ideology of British romanticism, and had a particular part in clarifying the aesthetic significance of naturalism and historicism. We will return to these aspects of his doctrine shortly, but here I mention simply his advocacy of a strict sensationism in the Picturesque.

From about 1820 the Picturesque became increasingly his main concern, both as a teacher and as an exhibiting professional artist. Significantly he went off to live and teach in Herefordshire, not with any *mens rea* for the Picturesque, but it was the county of Uvedale Price and it was from the landscapes of that period that his first work in the 'broken tint' style of the '20s and '30s emerged. For his pupils he formulated the 'look' in *The Young Artist's Companion*,[6] illustrated in the highly appropriate medium of soft-ground etching. The subject of *Cottages in Herefordshire* (fig. 1) is specifically picturesque: the broken sandy bank, the decrepit and irregular fence, the cottage with its rough thatch and dormer windows, especially the extension implying an organic relation between the house and the increasing needs of its occupants for space, are all qualities itemized by Price. The very title of the plate proclaims its attachment to the doctrinal Picturesque. The version reproduced here is the drawing, and in it are evident Cox's interest in the variegation of tones in the graphite, and in the capacity of short linear flicks of the pencil to denote a shifting dappled reflectiveness of foliage. In the published image soft-ground etching reproduced the quality of Cox's pencilling and made the point for all to see that the graphic medium itself, as well as the subject of the drawing, was instrumental in causing the sensations of the Picturesque. Soft-ground etching, in the period before the general employment of lithography, was the medium par excellence for reproducing picturesque drawings, for transmitting and even improving the 'broken tint' quality of graphite lying on a more or less rough paper surface.

In the finished watercolours, the *Lugg Meadows near Hereford* (Victoria and Albert Museum, 74–1885) or *The Aqueduct* (Birmingham, 292'25), the deployment of a direct painterly language of

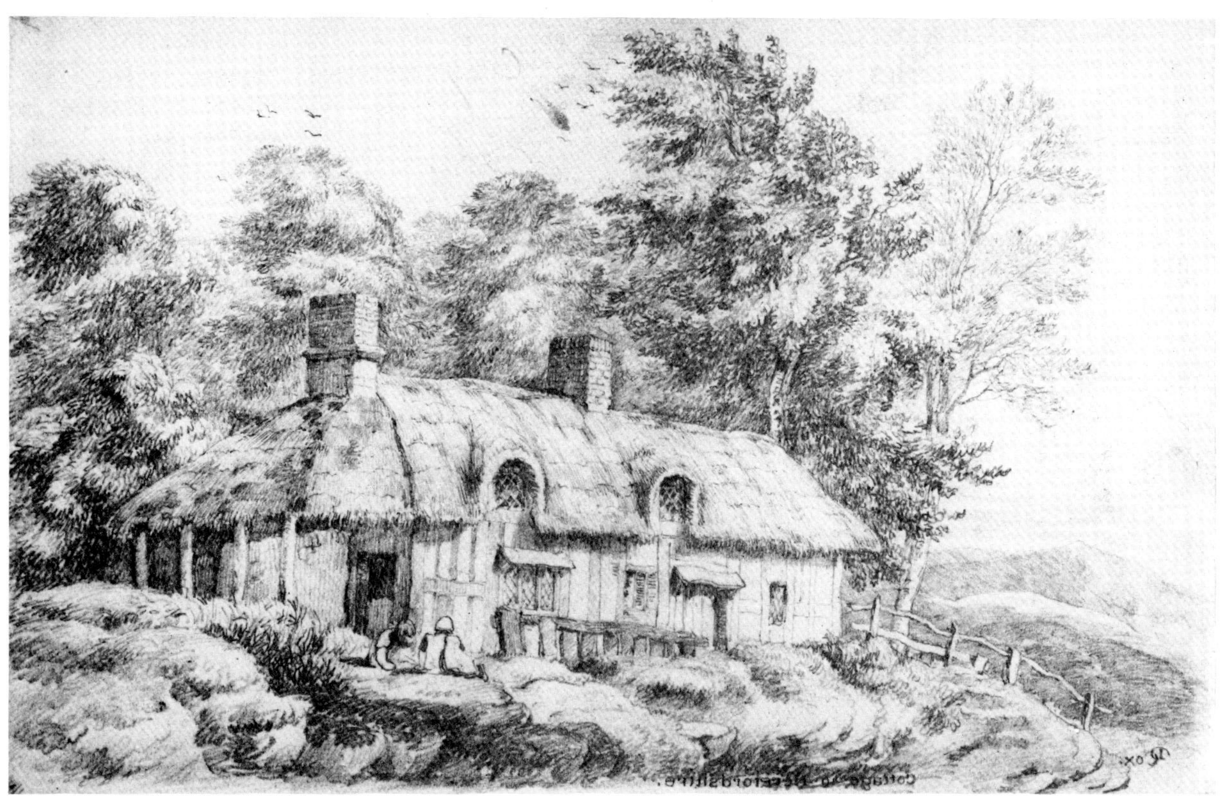

Fig. 1 *Cottages in Herefordshire* Private Collection

the Picturesque is equally evident. The two drawings are separated by ten or more years; *Lugg Meadows* represents the Picturesque at its interface with the Beautiful, and *The Aqueduct* verges on the Sublime, but in both Cox's main interest as a technician is in achieving an adequate way of describing the particular sensory qualities of the Picturesque. In the earlier he treats the broken lights by reserving areas of paper, by removing colour probably with a fine rolled chamois-leather point, and by cutting the surface of the paper; in the latter drawing he makes a bravura attack with the brush point, working with flamboyant and conscious mastery to create the broken, variegated, shifting and intriguing surface that was the certain stimulus for the Picturesque.

Cox worked out this way of painting in short overlaid strokes in order to achieve the Picturesque. It is often still said that he was some kind of 'Impressionist' – 'the first true Impressionist'. Of course, this is nonsense. His aesthetics have nothing whatsoever to do with Impressionism and his technique arises from the application (remarkable and original only in its fundamentalist strictness) of the sensationist doctrine. As Price would have put it, Cox's drawings 'excite the eye', according to the inevitable function of Picturesque qualities in any object.

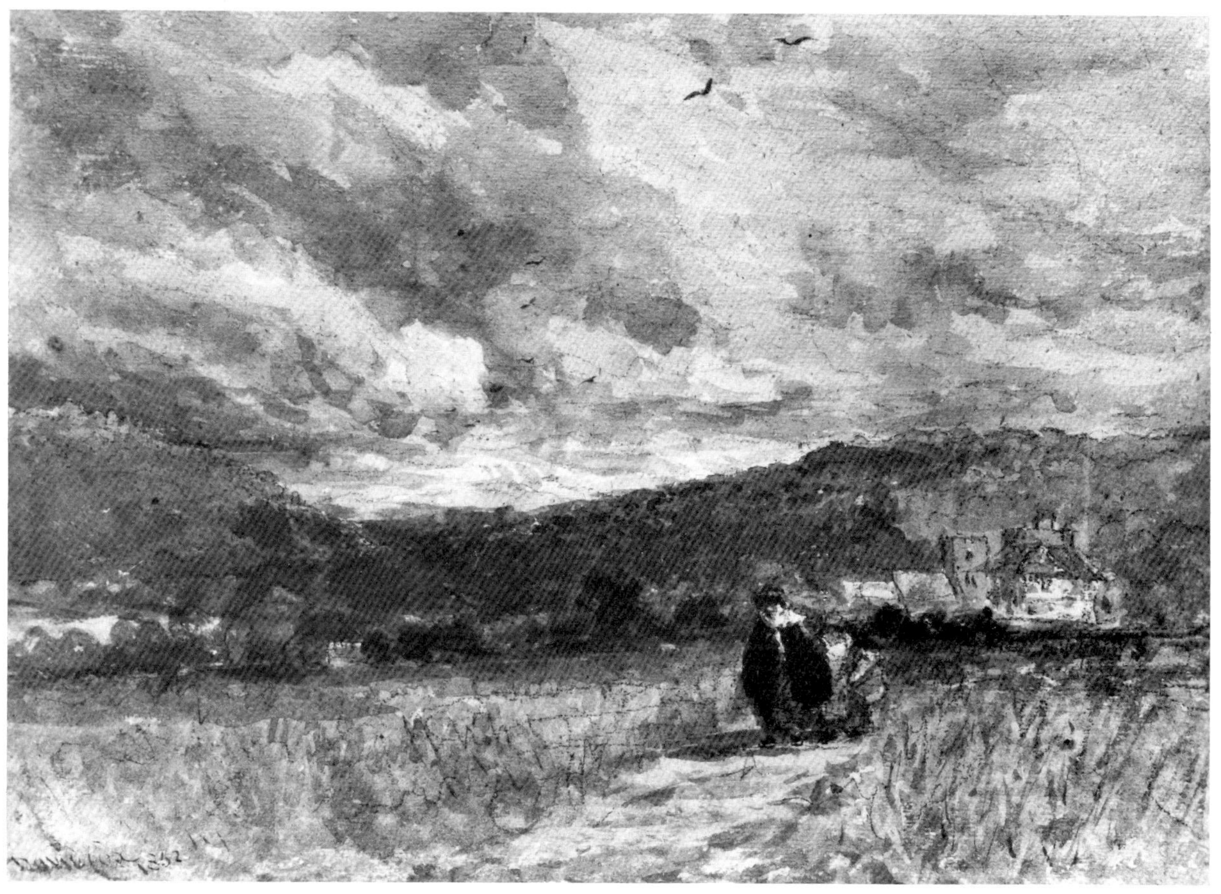

Stokesay Castle (cat. no. 98)

All of these landscapes are peopled. The figures are of no special significance, at least they are not enacting any scene from history or mythology, and they are not really such as Turner and others used earlier in the century to mark the different classes of landscape art.[7] Their presence proclaims basically that they, as human beings, belong in the natural order. Cox, Varley and other practical writers on pictorial aesthetics deploy on this point the useful concept of 'keeping' – the unity of sentiment in a work of art which is, in Varley's words 'one of the main sources of lasting impressions' especially in cottage landscapes. 'The figures best suited to a scene, are those which generally would be suggested by the view of such a place, or, of themselves might suggest such a scene.'[8]

But there is more to it than that. The Picturesque proclaims the role of the peasant[9] as a subject for art at the highest aesthetic level; it proclaims that the most admirable landscapes are those that represent the interaction of man and nature at a level close to, or not artificially elevated above, subsistence. This is the doctrine manifest in landscape painting after about 1780, a period marked generally by a move away from the cult of Sentiment and the neo-pastoralism of Ramsay, Mackenzie or Goldsmith. David Cox, however, a painter who tended to conservatism or a relatively slow response to trends, persisted with neo-pastoralism as in the *Lugg Meadows*, adapting the theme to the modern Picturesque by his technical inventiveness, and falling in by chance alongside the mystics and anti-rationalists of the Blakeian group in the later '20s. There is no evidence either in documents or in the drawings that Cox was even aware of Blake, still less attempting to follow his lead, but we know that Cox looked attentively at the annual exhibitions for sources of inspiration and it seems likely that he was confirmed in his sense of what was pictorially current at this period by the exhibited work of F. O. Finch and the younger Barret, the leading popularizers of the Blakeian-Virgilian aesthetic.

More wholly original and recognisably more the authentic voice of the mature David Cox were the later landscapes where the figures, as in the view of Stokesay (no. 98), have none of the Virgilian associations of the pastoral pictures. The composition is a paradigm of the Picturesque (the combination of low wooded hills, the sandy path, the village and church tower seem like incidents from Payne Knight's *Dialogue*) and the whole presents an image of apprehended organic unity between man and nature that is perhaps the principal ideal of the high Picturesque. Yet Cox's treatment presents the theme as dynamic and almost violently full of moving things; a subjective, momentary landscape, not at all the sort of still, reflective, slightly dispassionate view of the classical landscape tradition.

It may well be true that Cox studied his subjects directly, drawing his landscapes even out of doors, and studying figures especially of the Welsh upland peasantry from particular models. The Picturesque, in recommending the sophisticated aesthete to look closely at the actual peopled environment, gave impetus and doctrinal authority to romantic naturalism. Drawings such as this are therefore considered statements, not merely celebrations, as the critics sometimes put it, of wind, rain and the scent of woodsmoke. They are themselves icons of a recommended relationship between man and the world, and are of course, within the very texts of the aesthetic doctrine that informs them, consciously moral and political. They represent Cox's contribution to the culture of Tory neo-feudalism, a direct empirical study of the provincial peasantry in its ordained place, the image bringing the concept within the compass of a comprehensive aesthetic, moral and political approval. This is what Price said on the radical/idealist approach which he opposed:

> The destruction of so many picturesque circumstances by the prevailing passion for levelling, is mentioned with regret in many parts of this essay; the term itself may suggest regrets and apprehensions of a more serious kind. To level, in a very usual sense of the word, means to take away all distinctions; a principle that, when made general, and brought into action by any determined improver either of grounds or governments, occasions many mischiefs, as time slowly, if ever, repairs; and which are hardly more dreaded by monarchs than painters.

And here is his credo:

> A good landscape is that in which all the parts are free and unconstrained, but in which, though some are prominent and highly illuminated, and others in shade and retirement; some rough, and others more smooth

and polished, yet they are all necessary to the beauty, energy, effect, and harmony of the whole. I do not see how a good government can be more exactly defined; and as this definition suits every style of landscape, from the plainest and simplest to the most splendid and complicated, and excludes nothing but tameness and confusion, so it equally suits all free governments, and only excludes anarchy and despotism. It must be always remembered however, that despotism is the most complete leveller; and he who clears and levels everything round his own lofty mansion, seems to me to have very Turkish principles of improvement.[10]

His biographers refer only casually to Cox as a Tory, but the point is essential: his Toryism is a function of the same process of self-identification and doctrinal alignment as the work that concerns us here. The values advanced by his painting are Tory values.

Historicism in the early 19th century was a crucial part of the deep structure unifying aesthetics and ideology. In Picturesque doctrine it emerges as a belief in the virtue of time as the principle of creativity and renewal in the landscape. Thus the Picturesque placed a supreme value on the visible and accidental effects of time, for the 'broken tints' of weathered rock and masonry, and the rhythmic creativity of growth and decay in nature. It recognised the power of time to dignify and integrate even the most egregious and interventionist attempts by men to 'improve' landscape. Thus it proclaimed a special sympathy for the architectural gardening of the 16th and 17th centuries, for the Italianate Renaissance style and even for the 'Dutch' gardening of the era after 1688;[11] Price, in conservationist mood, admitted the excessive zeal of his own early destruction of a 'Dutch' garden, and it was these passages of his book particularly that underpinned the gathering antiquarianism and Jacobean revivalism of the culture. In Cox, this bent emerges from his treatments of the houses and gardens of Haddon, Hardwick and Knole where his imagery of life in the landscape is not of the present, but proclaims the qualities of freedom with order, sensuous richness and variety, to be distinctively inherent in the heritage of the past. Cox was very aware of George Cattermole as the leader among the professional watercolourists in historicizing landscape:

The exhibition appears deficient in real works of art – but my friend Cattermole has a large landscape with troopers fighting upon a bridge. The trees and figures are of the finest conception – indeed I do not know any painter who could have executed so fine a work . . . The mind of the man is greater than any.[12]

The troopers fighting on the bridge were probably a subject from *Old Mortality*, and Cattermole, who illustrated the Waverley Novels, was evidently the main conduit of influence from Scott to Cox. But so pervasive by the 1830s and '40s was this idealization of the past that it makes little sense to think of it as anything but a wholly authentic conviction in any artist. And though certain manifestations of it can seem sentimentally imprecise about period and overly interested in the leisured elegance of patrician life, the culture of Tory neo-feudalism did have its realistic aspect. In Cox or Scott this shows in the hard empirical readiness to study the actual inhabitants of particular places, and it leads on to the Tory revulsion against the human effects of untrammelled liberal capitalism. Georg Lukacz' sense of the descent through Scott of a genuinely determinist and realistic world-view, gives the clue to interpreting the historicism of the arts in the second quarter of the 19th century, to understanding its enormous importance to people like Cox at the time, and to grasping its relevance now.

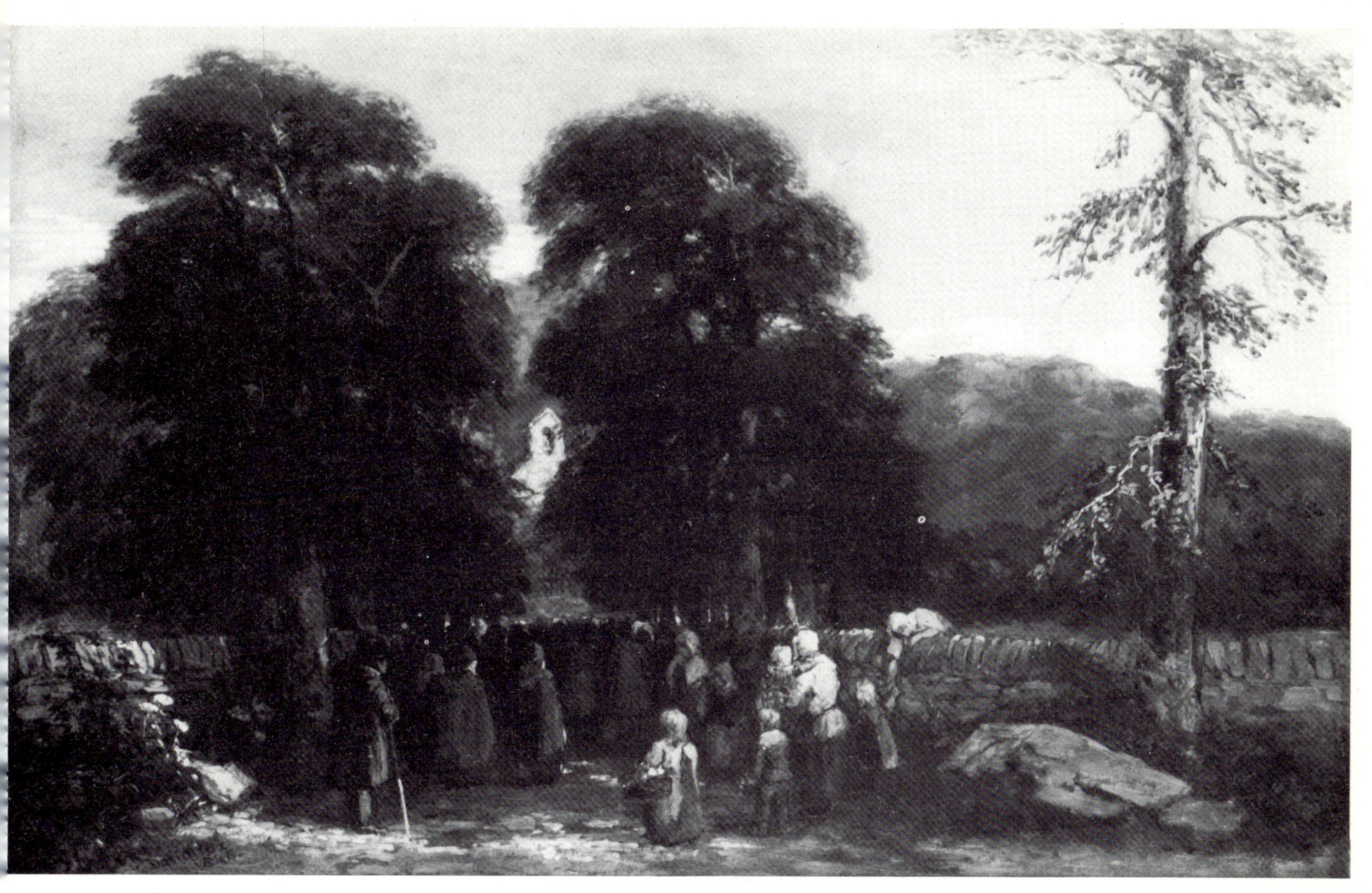

The Welsh Funeral 1848 (cat. no. 115)

In this perspective it is easier to see Cox as a special, eloquent member of his society and culture. One slightly invidious comparison will, I hope, show the delicate poise of his relation to the values of his time. When Constable suddenly contributed finished watercolours to the Academy in the mid-1830s he chose subjects that were, perhaps at one remove, historicizing. His *Old Sarum* and *Stonehenge*[13] were certainly intended as historic landscapes, using, as he carefully pointed out in the letterpress that accompanied the plates of *Landscape Scenery*,[14] the associationist mode of exciting aesthetic response. Both subjects are Tory in general sentiment, the *Old Sarum* being also an explicit Tory-political prophecy of disaster from the passing of the 1832 Reform Act. Constable seems, at the end of his life, to have fallen victim to this sort of cosmic Tory gloom, an aesthetic pessimism related, as Louis Hawes has suggested, to events in his private life,[15] but widespread also as a form of fashionable melancholy. Cox participated in this mood, adapting its idioms for subjects like *On the Moors, Bettws-y-Coed* (no. 102), and for the *Welsh Funeral* pictures painted outside the churchyard at Bettws (nos. 115–117). In Cox however the mood amounts to one of solemnity, a bleak comfortless respect for the world and its inhabitants who struggle against the rain and storms and come inevitably to the grave. The insight is linked to historicism because it depends on a sense of the present as a function of the past, and the future as a determined outcome of the omissions and commissions of the passing moment. It is an insight that places a burden of lonely responsibility on the individual, and it is typical, in the mid-19th century, of those whose adult morality grew from an early education at the evangelical end of the Anglican spectrum – Ruskin, George Eliot, even Matthew Arnold. There seems little doubt that Cox similarly drew on the severe Biblical culture of his mother, and probably beyond that on the non-conformist tradition in the Birmingham industrial and craftsman class. His encounter with the Welsh landscape and with its church or chapel culture was thus specially sympathetic – and possibly too solemn even for those whose morality and capacity to interpret the iconography of landscape enabled them to understand Cox's late work most sharply. Ruskin's comment on the telling juxtaposition of Cox's moorland landscapes with J. F. Lewis's *A Frank Encampment in the Desert of Mount Sinai* at the Watercolour Society of 1856,[16] shows how in the 1840s and '50s intellectual progressivism was excited by the bright liberating potential of gospel historicism and was tending to relegate the 'gloom and power' of the older Protestant tradition. Cox, an old man, did not participate in the Ruskinian-scientific optimism of the 1850s, but neither was he, as Constable had been, an iconographer of the religious reaction. His solemnity, his Toryism, his religious sense of the power of God made manifest in his works, were intimately related to the intellectual turmoils of the culture in which he exhibited his pictures, and yet at the same time they were not a sectarian part of them. What I think they were, and what I think his art finally amounted to as a statement about the world and about man's place in it, was an outgrowth of the basic Burkeian perception of the Sublime.

Cox complained, towards the end of his life, that he did not have the recognition that he felt he deserved. The complaint was barely justifiable, but Cox probably sensed accurately that the metropolitan elite did not respect his work very much, and did not, in the '40s and '50s, feel that it was engaging the vital concerns of the time. Cox's reputation in fact was always strong in the West

Midlands, and it came back strongly in London from about the 1870s, partly in the normal course of revaluation of artists at a safe distance from their death, and partly under the influence of Solly's biography.[17] More profoundly perhaps, the requirement among some intellectuals, thoroughly acquainted with scientific empiricism and with the challenge to religious fundamentalism that came from the Higher Criticism and from evolutionary theory, that there should nevertheless be grounds for faith and awe, brought back an interest in the artists of the Burkeian Sublime. The particular validity of the Burkeian tradition in a century dominated by scientific positivism was that it was itself so strict, so positive in attributing great emotional and aesthetic effects not to anything magical or mysterious, but to precisely knowable sensory causes.

JOHN MURDOCH

[1] Edmund Burke, *A Philosophical Enquiry into the Origin of our Ideas of the Sublime and Beautiful* 1757; ed. J. T. Boulton 1958.

[2] Archibald Alison, *Essays on the Nature and Principles of Taste*, 1790; enlarged edition 1810.

[3] Burke/Boulton, loc. cit. Introduction p. cxvii.

[4] ibid pp. 65, 66, 82.

[5] Uvedale Price, *An Essay on the Picturesque, as Compared with the Sublime and the Beautiful*, 1794; enlarged edition 1810; also, *A Dialogue on the Distinct Character of the Picturesque and the Beautiful*, 1810.

[6] Published in 16 parts to 1825.

[7] In the *Liber Studiorum*.

[8] J. Varley, *Treatise on the Principles of Landscape Design*, 1821, 'General Observations', unnumbered pages.

[9] This term is used by Picturesque writers to refer to people living close to subsistence in the country, partly labouring and partly living on the remaining feudal rights such as the gathering of firewood 'by hook or by crook' and by running cattle on common land.

[10] Price, loc. cit. I, 374–75.

[11] ibid II, 147.

[12] Autograph letter to William Roberts, 20 April 1844; ms. Birmingham Museums and Art Gallery.

[13] Victoria and Albert Museum.

[14] *Various Subjects of Landscape, Characteristic of English Scenery, From Pictures Painted by John Constable R.A.;* published in five parts, 1830–32. Usually referred to as *English Landscape* or *Landscape Scenery*.

[15] Louis Hawes, *Constable's Stonehenge*, V & A 1975, p. 5.

[16] 'Notes on some of the Principal Pictures exhibited in the Rooms of the Society of Painters in Watercolours, 1856' *Works of John Ruskin*, ed. Cook and Wedderburn, XIV, 76–8. The Lewis watercolour is now at the Yale Center for British Art.

[17] N. Solly, *A Memoir of the Life of David Cox*, 1873.

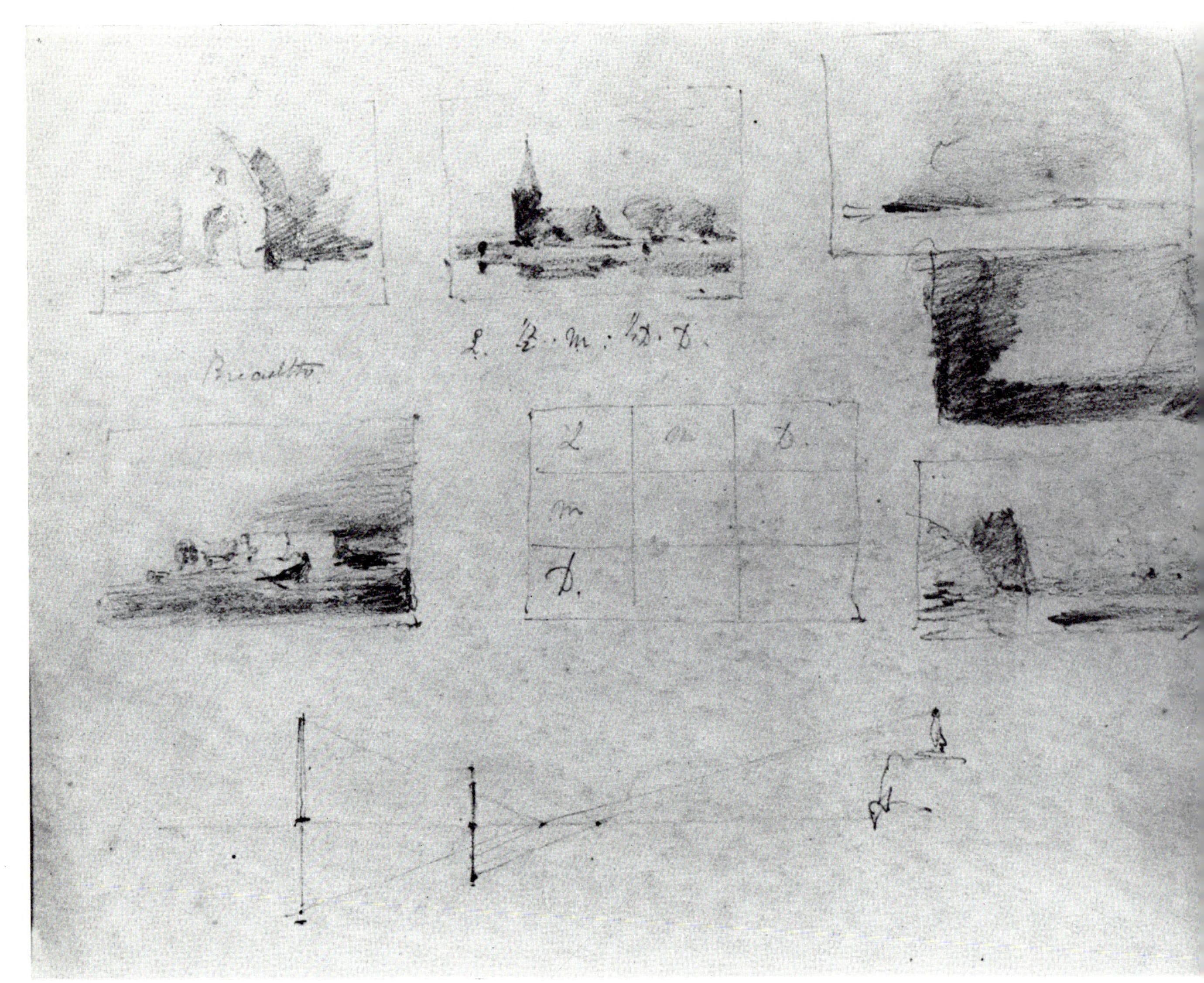

Studies in composition method (cat. no. 12)

Cox the Drawing Master

Cox's activity as a drawing master and as the author of drawing manuals was typical of his age, the first half of the 19th century. These more humdrum aspects of an artist's life were chronicled by Hall and Solly, who had access to account books most of which now seem to be lost. About 1810 Cox was only charging five shillings a lesson. He was persuaded then to raise his fee to ten shillings or half a guinea, a rate that he maintained into the 1820s. Cox only reached the quite usual rate of a guinea a lesson after returning to London from Hereford in 1827.

An adequate income was hard to make at these modest fees, but Cox eventually learned to augment his earnings by selling drawings, even those made during the lesson itself, to his pupils or their families. He would get five or ten guineas for such drawings and he continued to sell even much of his exhibited work at this modest level well into the 1830s.

Cox's pupils were to be found amongst the upper ranges of society by the time of his move to Hereford in 1814, a move that was in fact financed by one of his pupils, Lady Arden. Cox's move is a little surprising in view of his minor but established position in his profession. He had already been chosen by three leading publishers to help them supply the demand for drawing books and he had been elected a Member of the Society of Painters in Water Colour. Nevertheless Cox decided to take on a two days a week teaching job at Miss Croucher's school in Hereford (The Gatehouse, Widemarsh Street), an appointment that he kept until 1819.

If Solly is correct in his statement that a memorandum in Cox's account book dates the move to October 1814, then his successful application for a teaching post as 'military draughtsman' at the Staff College (then at Farnham, Surrey), implies that he did not originally plan to stay in Hereford. If such a problem existed it was resolved by the fact that Cox only held the Farnham job for five weeks in April/May 1815 (Hardie 1979) and he was able to take on other teaching jobs in Hereford concurrently, at the Grammar School, Miss Poole's and Miss Croucher's. He also taught at schools elsewhere, such as at Leominster. Teaching was one of the activities that enabled him to move from small to larger rented accommodation and finally to a house that he built himself and which turned out to be an excellent investment. It is known that Cox took boarding pupils at seventy guineas a year, but only a sight of his account books would show how many such pupils he had and how many of them, like J. M. Ince, became professional artists. None of his pupils appears to have achieved any real distinction.

The early biographers provide more information about Cox's informal teaching, the advice that he would have given to his sketching tour companions, such as old fellow students of Joseph Barber's evening classes in Birmingham (Charles Barber and S. R. Lines) or patrons such as

William Ellis (London) and William Roberts (Birmingham). Cox seems generally to have sketched in company at Haddon and elsewhere and his annual sketching tours from the 1840s at Bettws-y-Coed had a summer school atmosphere.

David Cox's move from Kennington to Harborne in 1841 was motivated partly by a desire to give up teaching. During the 1830s Cox senior increasingly involved his son in his teaching practice. Cox junior was of course his father's pupil and frequent sketching companion. In 1834 the father even exhibited watercolours of Scottish subjects made after his son's sketches. At this time they were both contributing illustrations to the same travel books and to later editions of one of Cox's drawing manuals, of which the son should probably be described as editor. They maintained a close and affectionate correspondence in which Cox senior kept his son up to date with any technical innovations – 18 November 1842: 'Try by lamplight a subject in charcoal, and don't be afraid of darks, and work the subject throughout with charcoal in the darks, middle tint and half, and with some spirited touches in parts to give a marking. When you have done all this, have your colours quite soft, and colour upon the charcoal. Get all the depth of the charcoal, and be not afraid of the colour. When you look at it by daylight, and clean it with bread, you will find a number of light parts which have been left when the colour will not exactly adhere over the charcoal. For a distant mountain I have used cobalt and vermilion, and in the greyer part I mix a little lake and a small quantity of yellow ochre with the cobalt.' (Solly, pp. 118–19)

One would expect the advice which Cox offers at sixty as an established professional to differ from that given to young students in the drawing manuals published when he was thirty. In 1812, he would have recommended a pencil outline fleshed out with ink washes through which to learn the control of light and shadow, before going on to master working in full colour, perhaps laid over a wash or neutral tint foundation. The lights would be produced not by happy accident, but by deliberate tinting or 'taking out', lifting colour already laid by wetting and then blotting the paper. The master would never have suggested working in colour by artificial light or by different light sources at different stages in the creation of a watercolour drawing. Cox's choice of pigments however remained relatively unchanged as documented from 1811 to 1845 through differing editions of *A Series of Progressive Lessons intended to elucidate the Art of Painting in Water Colours*. There was nothing unusual about Cox's palette and the only addition to it mentioned in the quotation, cobalt, was a substitute for the notoriously impermanent Prussian blue.

Cox had begun to supply recipes for monochrome wash drawings soon after reaching London in 1804 and he sold them for two guineas a dozen to printsellers, Simpson in Greek Street and Palser in the Westminster Road, for resale to country drawing masters. The similarity of such drawings to those of many contemporaries belies the varied nature of his own training. This conventional early style can be seen through the sepia aquatints of *Ackermann's New Drawing Book of Light and Shadow in Imitation of Indian Ink*, first issued in 1809–10. Although the plates generally acknowledge the aquatinters (Sutherland and Bluck), they only once give the artist's name: a view of Battersea is by 'Evans', probably the copyist Richard Evans with whom Cox shared digs when he first came to London. The attribution of the remaining plates to Cox must rest on biographical evidence. Who else but David Cox would have supplied Ackermann with a selection of sketches made in North Wales, Montgomeryshire, Harborne, Kenilworth and London, including three of Dulwich where Cox lived?

This book is not, as its title suggests, a drawing manual since the author, who is clearly not the artist, does not explain the process of making a drawing in ink wash. He prefers to draw analogies between the plates and the Old Masters or masters of the modern British school such as John Varley 'whose skilful display of his art, in many small pictures of river scenery, is above all praise'. At one point he detaches himself completely from editorial control: 'It would be an advantage to the work before us, were some of the plates coloured, as the lights upon certain parts are too sudden, which a thin wash of colour would subdue, without injuring the sunny appearance.'

A Series of Progressive Lessons, first published by Thomas Clay in 1811, supplies this defect and is a genuine drawing book that begins right at the beginning with the choice of pencils, the setting of the paper on a drawing board and so on. The difficult matter of perspective, dealt with in a number of other available treatises, is passed over in a sentence or two with one single illustration. Wash and watercolour painting are well covered and the rather miniature plates have a finely-grained aquatint that faithfully expresses the quality of washes. The sepia aquatints of the Ackermann book are very coarse-grained by comparison. The Clay publication sounds one contemporary note: 'Indian ink has for some time been very properly exploded in the preparation of a Landscape for colouring, notwithstanding it is equally susceptible of force, as it is of delicacy; but it is found to give too great a degree of opacity under many circumstances . . .'

The teaching method is to proceed straightforwardly via models of increasing sophistication: from drawing (soft-ground etching) to monochrome washes (aquatint), to full watercolour (coloured aquatint). Exactly the same method is followed in J. H. Clark's *Practical Essay in the Art of Colouring and Painting Landscapes* (1807), J. Bryant's *Treatise on the Use of Indian Ink and Colours* (1808), W. H. Pyne's *Rudiments of Landscape in a Series of Easy Lessons* (1812), and S. Prout's *Rudiments of Landscape in Progressive Studies* (1812). The last two were both published by Ackermann in the same year, an indication of the strength of the market.

Most of these titles share with Cox's *Series* the idea of 'progressing' a repeated landscape design through several stages from pencil outline to finished watercolour. John Laporte's *Progress of a Water Colour Drawing* (*c.*1802) gives fourteen such progressions with four devoted to the sky alone! This is the only instance that I have seen where text and hand-coloured plates really allow the student to follow the artist's every brush stroke. Both Clark and Cox attempted to provide similar help through simpler means. Clark, by placing a strip of coloured boxes in a numbered sequence along the bottom edge of the illustration, and Cox by including patches of colour within the text to his illustrations. David Cox may have been the first to employ the latter system, one that proved popular with other authors.

A Series went through nine editions between 1811 and 1845, being taken over by Ackermann from Clay in 1841. Its popularity no doubt came from its advertised 'simplicity', copying step by step a progression of illustrations with a closely related text. A rare example of a more general approach reads: 'Enlarging now and then a subject, four or six times the original, gives scope for boldness, and freedom of hand; reversing the lights, placing the breadth of light on the foreground, as in the Abbey, on the middle, as in the Sea View; or on remoter parts as in the Ruin, are studies of considerable consequence to the learner, they induce the mind to exert itself and excite the desire to sketch from nature.'

As the decades passed, the text remained remarkably unaltered but for minor rearrangements and the addition, early on, of 'three plates and several pages upon the Rudiments of Perspective'. The illustrations, on the other hand, constantly change and thereby reflect the development of subject matter and style within Cox's oeuvre. *View near Dinas Mouddy* and *Marine Subject*, in the 1823 edition, are very close to Samuel Prout. The 1828 edition has a *Hayfield* and a *Windsor Castle* which are far more characteristic of Cox. For this edition he made partial use of the fashionable medium of lithography which he otherwise rarely exploited. The 1838 edition reflects a tour of the Continent in 1826 with *Dutch Boats on the Scheldt, Off Antwerp*, and, with *Scene near Balquidder, North Britain*, a journey to Scotland by his son in 1834.

Progressive Lessons on Landscape, published by S. and J. Fuller in 1816, was not Cox's next contribution to the drawing-book list, but was announced as introductory to a *Treatise on Landscape Painting and Effect* (1813–14) which was. Unlike the *Series* and *Treatise*, *Progressive Lessons* contained no aquatints or coloured aquatints. Instead there are twenty-four excellent soft-ground etchings (for which he was paid £63) with a very brief preface as text. Like the earlier etchings in the *Treatise*, these show Cox as a mature artist for the first time in the medium of the print, first through 'detached parts of nature' (Bryant) and then through landscapes equalling the best work of his contemporaries in this medium. He gives 'the youngest students' the full vocabulary of the picturesque landscape painter: chimney pots and stiles, castles, cottages, trees, chickens, sheep and cows (fig. 2). The book is altogether reminiscent of Prout's *Progressive Fragments for the Use of Young Students* published in the same year.

A Treatise on Landscape Painting and Effect in Water Colours: from the first rudiments to the finished picture: with examples in outline, effect, and colouring was published in twelve parts beginning in March 1813. The publisher's puff places the author firmly among the leaders of his profession: 'The abilities of Mr Cox, as a Painter in Water Colours, have been long established; and his Knowledge of Effect is equal to that of any artist of which the age can boast. His pencil drawings are in the boldest style, and the etchings, in imitation of lead pencil and chalk . . . will be marked by a peculiar character of fidelity, and derive an additional value from the circumstance of their being executed by himself . . . In the progress of this work, the Author will introduce a variety of imitations of his drawings, in sepia and colours, from all the most striking effects in Nature; the plates from which will be executed by the finest aquatinta engraver in London; and the subjects appropriated to this department of the work, will be so selected as to display an unusual variety of the most picturesque scenes in England and Wales.'

Cox's original drawings and Reeves's transcriptions of his sepia drawings into aquatint merit this advertisement and persuaded Hardie (1906, p. 118) to pronounce this 'the best and most important

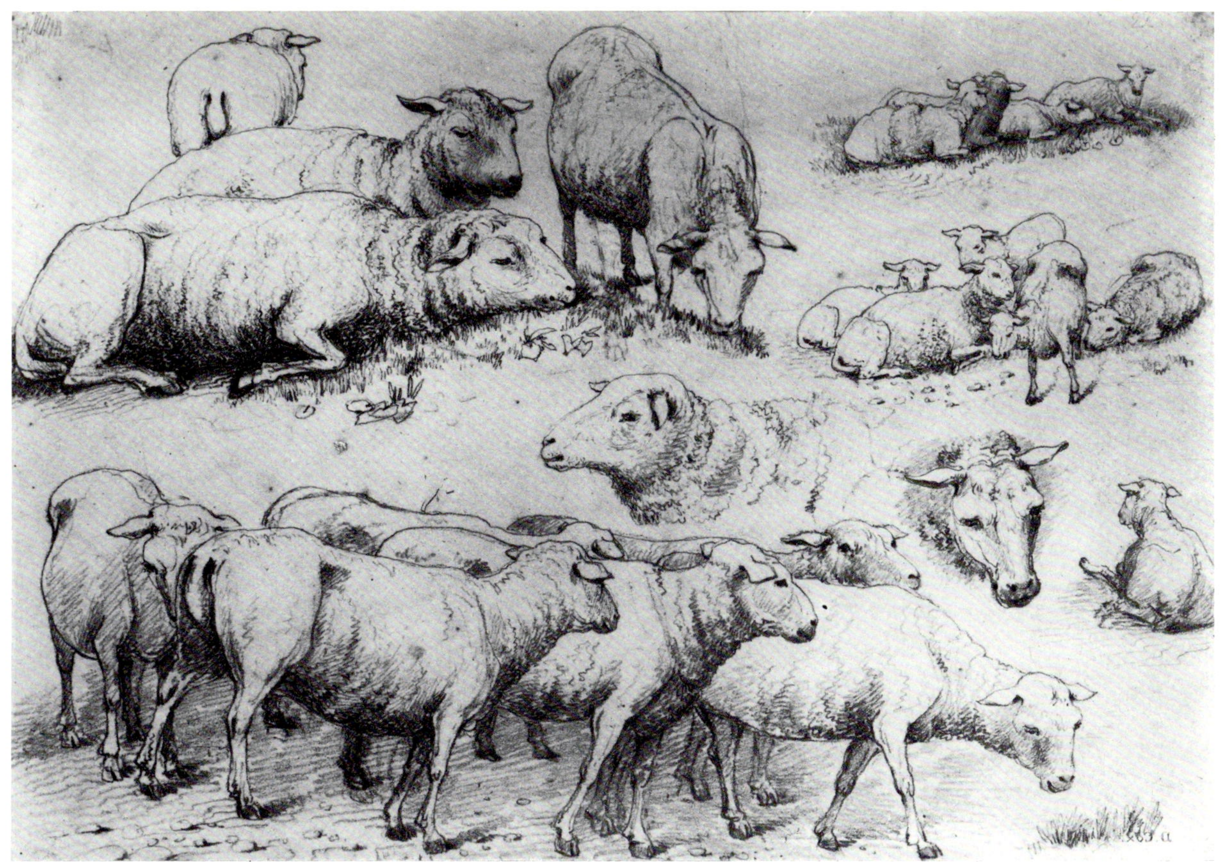

Fig. 2 Studies of sheep for *Progressive Lessons on Landscape*, Fitzwilliam Museum, Cambridge

of all the early drawing-books, in view of the position that their author now holds in public esteem'. Cox was a master of sepia and provided Reeves with models of the highest quality (cat. no. 18). The care with which the aquatints were thought out is revealed by impressions which have not received the colour washes usually added by a team of colourmen after models prepared by the artist himself. Such impressions do not in fact make sense without this colour; they can be seen in volumes made up of the plates of the *Treatise* as republished in 1840–41 together with the plates of *The Young Artist's Companion* (1821–25) which have been printed on pages of the same size. The latter plates do make sense, i.e. were not so carefully calculated for the needs of the drawing manual to which they originally belonged.

The *Treatise* differs markedly from the *Series*: it is larger, more expensive (£5 10s), has David Cox's name as author for the first time, and has a relatively long and theoretical introductory text. Cox is said to have been assisted in the writing by a more literary gentleman than himself, possibly a clergyman. The tone, however, is unassuming when compared with that of more ambitious theoretical works, such as Edward Dayes's posthumously published *Essays on Painting* (1805) or Francis Nicholson's *Practice of Drawing and Painting Landscape from Nature in Water Colours* (1820). One quotation will indicate that Cox was probably aware of the Revd William Gilpin's addition of the Picturesque to Burke's more ancient aesthetic categories of the Beautiful and the Sublime: 'Abrupt and irregular lines are productive of a grand and stormy Effect; while serenity is the result of even and horizontal lines, where no roughness or intersections appear, to invade the mild harmony of beauty.'

The introductory discussion 'On Light and Shade' is made up of a long quotation 'extracted from a celebrated work'. For Cox's own words we must turn to the notes that he made for Miss Frances Carr, sometime between 1827 and 1841 (Cundall 1909). These notes, which, incidentally, quote Gilpin, accompany eight pen and wash progressives of an imaginary Rhine view, a landscape that Cox never saw but which his pupil was about to visit. The artist demonstrates how lights can be managed to produce quite different landscapes from the same view, an idea first illustrated in print by Alexander Cozens in the 18th century. The idea, but not the expressive style of Cozens and Cox, appears more formally in treatises such as those by Nicholson and John Varley.

Around 1807 or 1808, Cox was but one of many distinguished watercolour artists who received instruction from John Varley, 'that admirable professor of watercolour painting' (Ackermann 1809). His teaching practice and his connection with the colourmen must have made his technical and theoretical ideas widely known before the relatively late appearance of his manuals from about 1816. Another drawing-master author, George Hamilton, tells how Varley, in 1812, 'has obligingly favoured us with a list of the colours used by him in drawing, together with the mixtures prepared under his direction . . .'. Varley's illustrations are mostly sepia aquatints so that light and shade and compositional analysis displace discussion of tints. Varley's concern in landscapes labelled 'Epic', 'Pastoral', 'Sunshine' and 'Twilight' is for 'the unity of sentiment', the prevailing effect.

Varley's style is elevated and one of Cox's grander statements in the *Treatise of Landscape Painting and Effect* matches it: 'The principle of Landscape Painting consists in conveying to the mind the most forcible effect which can be produced from the various classes of scenery; which possesses the power of exciting an interest superior to that resulting from any other effect . . .'. The sepia aquatints *Twilight, Warwick Castle* and *Morning, Windsor Castle* are equal in composition and mood to Varley's best work.

The term 'effect' was understood by Varley and Cox to mean both the general and the particular or transient effect. This one aspect of landscape painting was the subject of J. H. Clark's *A Practical Illustration of Gilpin's Day*, 'representing the various Effects on Landscape Scenery from Morning till Night in thirty designs from Nature, by the late Rev Wm Gilpin, A.M.' (1811). The author wished, apparently, to repair Gilpin's failure to supply landscape effects in colour; Gilpin had in fact chosen to sketch and publish in monochrome, a prejudice that Clark's six varieties of sunset might have confirmed. Cox's transient effects in the *Treatise* (*Rainbow Effect, Moonlight Effect, Snow Scene*) are far more subtle than Clark's *Freaky Sun-Set* and the most successful, *Afternoon, A View in Surrey*, is

Turneresque. By 1813 Cox had not developed a distinctive technique with which to produce really novel landscape effects. His personal contribution to the landscape of effect came with his broken surfaces and 'constant *repetition of touches*' (Solly, p. 174).

These technical developments were still in the future when Cox published a smaller and cheaper volume (£2 2s), *The Young Artist's Companion, or Drawing-Book of Studies and Landscape Embellishments*, in 1819–20. This attractive poor relation of the *Treatise* is quite well-known on account of the coloured frontispiece showing the artist's studio (col. pl. 8). The *Companion* used the same introductory text as the *Treatise* and repeated the method of illustration: soft-ground etching, aquatint, coloured aquatint. The addition of three examples of still-life (cat. no. 22) did not, in the event, herald a new genre in Cox's exhibited work.

RICHARD LOCKETT

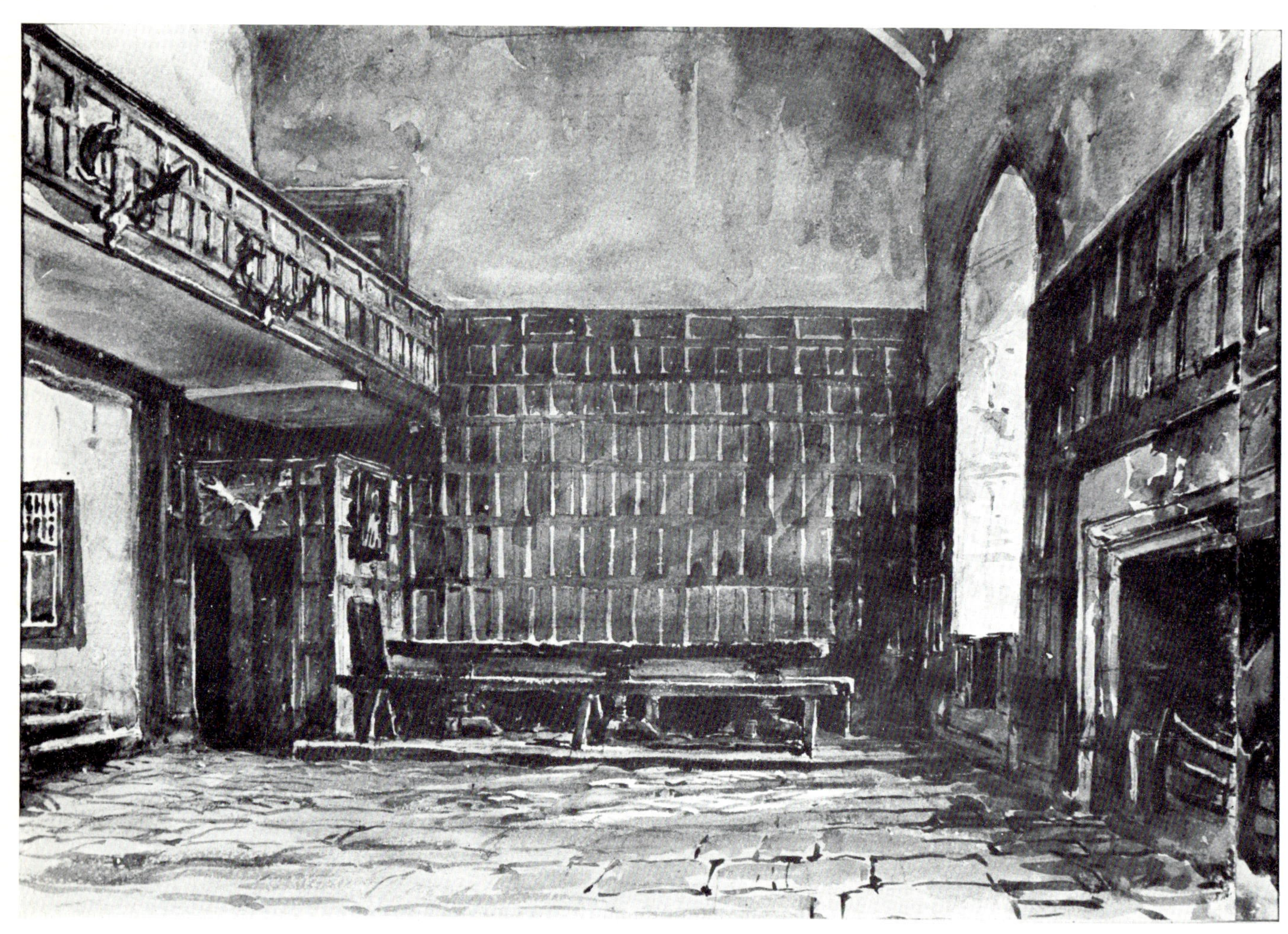

The Great Hall (cat. no. 107)

'Dear Old Haddon'

'For many years, beginning with 1831, I find a series of visits recorded to Haddon Hall, Hardwick Hall, Bolsover Castle, Bolton Abbey, and the neighbourhood of Lancaster.' (Solly, p. 61) Solly's evidence included a letter of 28 August 1831 from Cox to his friend and patron William Roberts who had been at the Rowsley Inn with himself and David Cox junior shortly before. 'I hope by the end of the week to see you in Birmingham, there to show you a few additional sketches of this delightful old Haddon; and, as it will be utterly impossible for me to make all the subjects which I see and feel pleased with, I must defer it until another year . . . We have visited the Hall each day since you left. Today we had Mr Severn's car and went to Chatsworth, and round by Bakewell, but did not see anything striking; but I do not expect to be much pleased with anything this country can afford after my favourite old Haddon. Indeed, that alone is quite enough for one summer. The weather has been very fine until yesterday afternoon, when we had heavy rain and thunderstorm, but got home dry in the evening, and it afterwards turned out fine. Today it has been beautiful for the *effects*.' Cox then refers to the sketches that Roberts and H. H. Lines had made at Haddon a few days before. Cox and his sketching companions would often apparently have their midday meal sent over to the Great Hall from the Peacock Inn. This facility was a valuable one; the weather was so bad in May 1845 that indoor sketching was all they were able to accomplish.

Interiors and garden terraces must have been the two most distinctive aspects of the five Haddon views exhibited at the Old Water Colour Society exhibition in 1832. Cox never gave quite the same prominence to any one location except Bettws-y-Coed in the 1850s, with the exception of Powis Castle in 1838 and Hardwick Hall in 1838–40. The latter two represent an extension of interests first awakened by Haddon, which he visited in 1831, (?) 1835, 1836, 1837, 1845 and 1850. George Proctor acquired as many as twelve Haddon views in 1837 including the majority of those exhibited in 1832, and Cox was commissioned to make another series for his sketching companion on the 1845 visit, William Ellis. Solly later saw in Ellis's portfolios sketches 'powerful and admirable in arrangement and colour . . . evidently very rapid, but nothing is wanting, except more finish, to make very lovely and powerful drawings.' A quick pen sketch of the Haddon courtyard has, noted on its reverse, the titles for nine out of a series of eighteen Haddon subjects (fig. 3).

Such a degree of concentration upon one place was matched by two books published in 1836 and 1842, S. Rayner's *History and Antiquities of Haddon Hall* with thirty-two tinted lithographs by George Cattermole, and D. Morison's *Views of Haddon* with twenty-five plates and a title page vignette, all in tinted lithographs by the author. Morison's book is a splendid imperial folio containing exterior and interior views many of them reminiscent of Cox, although executed in a style closer to that of

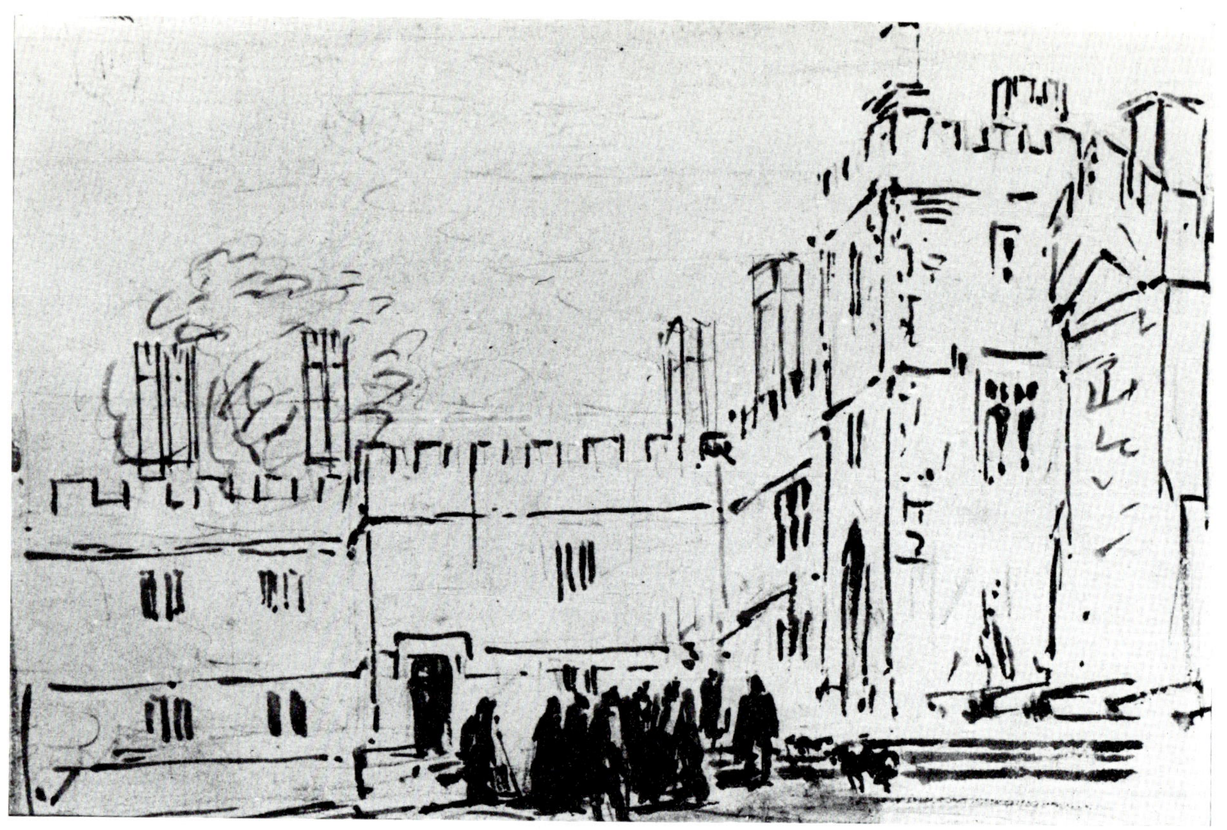

Fig. 3 *Courtyard of Haddon Hall*, Birmingham Museums and Art Gallery

J. D. Harding, the leading lithographic landscape artist. Morison shortly afterwards won the interest of the Prince Consort for a similar book on the Palaces and Hunting Lodges of Saxe-Coburg and Gotha. However, in 1891 Roget thought that Morison's book was spoilt by an unfortunate anachronism, 'representing the building in its modern state of picturesque dilapidation, and peopling it with residents of its palmy days'. (Vol. II, p. 294)

Such a criticism could not be levelled at the five lithographs of Haddon in Joseph Nash's *Mansions of England in the Olden Time* (1839; he featured Hardwick in volume 2), whose object was 'to present them [the mansions] in a new and attractive light; not as many of them now appear, gloomy, desolate, and neglected but furnished with the rude comfort of the early times of "merry England".' Calling Haddon 'that deserted mansion of the Vernons', Nash illustrates the Hall with minimum furniture, almost as bare as Cox's rooms, but after a spring clean. The Long Gallery 'is represented as occupied by a family party in the costume of Charles I. It was probably used as a ballroom, as well as for promenading; and from hence we may suppose Dorothy Vernon eloped with her lover on the day of her sister's nuptials.'

The Long Gallery had been used as a ballroom, if not for elopements, more recently. Although the Manners family had abandoned Haddon in favour of Belvoir in the early 18th century, they had kept their Derbyshire seat in a basic state of repair and used it occasionally for festivities such as the celebration of the Peace of Amiens in 1802 and the then owner's coming of age in 1809. The 5th Duke survived to welcome the Archaeological Association to Haddon in 1851. The peculiar interest of the Hall as an untouched survival of a late medieval/Tudor house, the character and domestic arrangements of which had withstood 16th-century embellishments, had been established in a paper, published in the antiquarian periodical *Archaeologia* in 1782, by Edward King entitled 'Observations on Ancient Castles'. King's hope that no modernising hand would interfere was piously repeated by all later writers including Rayner in 1836. The fully furnished rooms of Hardwick (no. 47) contrast with the stark interiors of Haddon (nos. 107–108).

Nash's *Mansions* characterises two cultural strands which, woven together, explain the appeal of Haddon to Cox when he first saw it and indeed the fascination of the house to us today. By 1830 the antiquarian interest in ancient architecture had developed to the point when the different periods of architectural history and style were understood in their outline. The High Victorian obsession with earlier Gothic had not yet ostracised late medieval and Tudor. Henry Shaw's *Elizabethan Architecture*, published in 1839, which contained two illustrations from Haddon, was symptomatic of a period that replaced the Houses of Parliament, destroyed by fire in 1834, with Barry and Pugin's stupendous creation.

Nash's and Morison's depiction of the rooms and terraces of Haddon with figures from the 16th and 17th centuries (it is not always quite clear from which century they come) represents another strand, that spun from the historical novel. *Peak Scenery* by E. Rhodes, published in 1818–19, suggested that Haddon had assisted Mrs Ann Radcliffe in producing her immensely popular Gothic novel *The Mysteries of Udolpho*, first published in 1794. Trenchard Cox (1947) hinted at the prevailing atmosphere breathed in by David Cox: 'It is evident . . . that he was impressed by the feudal way of living; and the drawings reflect a subjection to contemporary romantic fashion which suggests that the novels of Sir Walter Scott figured among the books which Mrs Cox used to read aloud to her husband when at work.' Scott's *Peveril of the Peak* (set in an earlier time) was first published in 1822. The legend of Dorothy Vernon's elopement with the first of the Manners family to own Haddon was told in W. Bennett's *The King of the Peak*, published the very next year. That Haddon had become an established romantic spot is signalled by the appearance of a poem by H.B. in the *Bijou* of 1828:

> No hunter's horn is heard to sound;
> No dame, with swan-like mien glides by,
> Accompanied by hawk and hound
> Or her fair palfrey, joyously.

Morison's *South West View from the River* supplies the dame on her fair palfrey, and Cox's *Return from Hawking* (see no. 106) the rest of the vanished scene (Joseph Nash's cast is much too prosaic to fit the bill). The pictures exhibited in 1834 and 1839 signal that David Cox was attracted by the idea of historical romancing at this time: *The Lady of the Manor* and *A Castle in the Olden Time*. This latter title might have been suggested by Nash or by a two-shilling guidebook published in Derby and London in 1838: *A Visit to Haddon Hall in 1838: or, 'a description of a Baronial Mansion of the Olden Time', by G.V.* (in Gothic lettering taken from a detail in the house).

G.V. refers to the tourist to Rayner's more expensive *History* which was enlivened by Cattermole's lithographs. Cattermole was a specialist in historical romance and naturally introduced figures from the past into the Haddon scene. Rayner tells his readers that 'the discovery of the picturesque beauties of Haddon may indeed be a circumstance of rather modern date'. He claims to have introduced Haddon 'to my friend Mr Cattermole' who 'presented [his sketches] to me without any remuneration, at a time when more than one publisher was negotiating for the purchase of them'.

It is a nice point as to whether Cattermole or Cox could claim to have discovered Haddon in the sense of bringing it to the attention of the London public. Cattermole was exhibiting views of Haddon at the Old Water Colour Society in 1831 and 1832. It is coincidental that his landscape style was influenced by that of Cox. 'In this department the works of Cattermole bear a marked resemblance to those of David Cox, who on divers occasions evinced a warm appreciation of his brother artist's talent' (Roget, II, p. 63).

Unlike Cox, Cattermole moved in exalted political and literary circles associating with members of the Young England set to which Lord John Manners (younger son of the then owner of Haddon) belonged. Cattermole would have been the ideal artist to have recorded the Eglinton Tournament of 1839. In Rayner's *History* George Cattermole's romantic fancies took second place to the castellated mansion and his illustrations are matched by those of Nash and Morison and, when he introduces costumed figures, by those of Cox. But in *Evenings at Haddon Hall* by the Baroness de Calabrella, published in 1846, both author and artist cut the traces. 'The title is merely a vehicle for the collection of a series of tales written to explain a number of Cattermole's drawings supposed to be in a portfolio, turned over by a birthday party, confined to the House at Haddon by the snow.' (Roget II, p. 73). Lady Eva's guests make little attempt to link any of Cattermole's twenty-four drawings to their Derbyshire venue and the book's only Haddon illustration is the frontispiece – Victorians on a moonlit Haddon terrace.

David Cox and George Cattermole were friends and apparently admired each other's work in the distinct genres of picture-making in which they each specialised. Haddon Hall was a subject that they both shared but which did not, as far as is recorded, bring them together either as sketching companions or as fellow contributors to the same publication. To imagine such a publication we have to look at Thomas Roscoe's *Wanderings and Excursions in North Wales* (1836) 'with 51 engravings by Radclyffe from drawings by Cattermole, Cox, Creswick, etc.' in which Cox's *Caernarvon* accompanies Cattermole's *Caernarvon Castle*, entered by soldiers of the middle ages.

Rayner's 1836 preface claims that Haddon had within a very few years been popularised: 'Within the last five years especially its attractions have been generally felt and acknowledged; and lying as it does between those frequented watering-places Matlock and Buxton, visitors have frequently been drawn thither by the interesting character of the building, and the charms of the surrounding scenery on the banks of the Wye.' Princess Victoria in 1832, like Cox in 1831, got there just before the rush. Artists played their part in disturbing the peace: 'Cattermole, Lewis, Cox and others of equal celebrity in the world of art', G.V. tells us, 'have at various times enriched their sketchbooks with scenery in this part of the country, and through the exhibition of their beautiful works, its attractions have been generally felt and acknowledged.' The 1838 Guide advises visitors: 'The Banquetting Hall is perhaps better adapted than any other part of this ancient mansion to call forth associations connected with by-gone times. Here parties bringing their own provisions, may gratify a taste for antiquity, by dining off the same long table which has often groaned . . . ere the luxury of forks' and, we could add, the dinners sent from the Peacock by Mr and Mrs Severn for David Cox.

RICHARD LOCKETT

David Cox: A Chronology

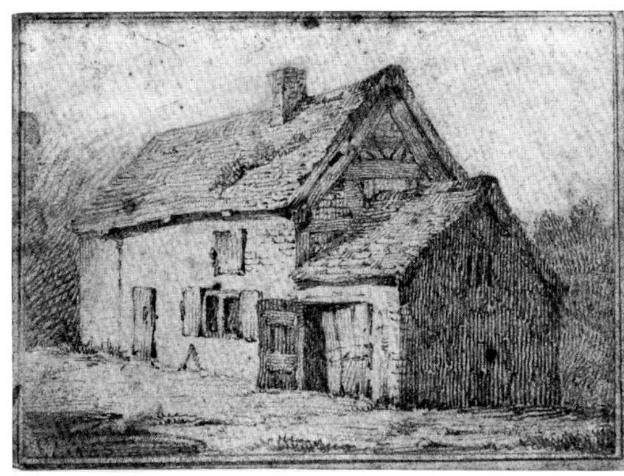

Fig. 4 Samuel Lines, *Birthplace of David Cox*, Birmingham Museums and Art Gallery

1783 29 April: born in Heath Mill Lane, Deritend, Birminghan, second child and only son of Joseph Cox, blacksmith, and Frances Walford.

*c.***1798** At fifteen, apprenticed to a miniature painter named Fieldler.

*c.***1800** Fieldler commits suicide; engaged as assistant to theatre scene-painter.

1804 Engaged as scene-painter with Astley's Theatre and moves to London; abandons this work for art; takes lessons with John Varley some time between this date and 1808.

1805 First trip to Wales, with Charles Barber; earliest dated watercolours; first exhibits, at Royal Academy.

1806 Second trip to Wales.

1808 Marries Mary Agg, rents cottage on Dulwich Common; paid for scenery for Wolverhampton theatre; receives first pupil (future Earl of Plymouth).

1809 9 July: birth of only child, David junior; *Ackermann's New Drawing Book* (first edition) published.

1810 President of Associated Artists in Water Colour.

1811 2 March: death of mother (buried at Aston, Birmingham); *A Series of Progressive Lessons* (first edition) published.

1812 Collapse of Associated Artists; elected Associate of the Society of Painters in Water Colour (i.e. Old Water Colour Society); visits Hastings.

1813 Elected Member of the Old Water Colour Society: exhibits every year (except 1815 and 1817) until his death; *Treatise on Landscape Painting* (first edition) published.

?1814–15 Appointed drawing-master at Military Staff College, Farnham; appointed drawing-master at Miss Croucher's girls' school, and takes up residence in Hereford, in cottage at Ailstone Hill; later, moves to George Cottage, Hereford.

1816 *Progressive Lessons on Landscape* published.

1817 Moves to Parry's Lane, Hereford.

1818 Journey to North Wales; represented in Hassell's *Aqua Pictura.*

1819 Journey to Devon; Ann Fowler employed as maid; *Young Artist's Companion* (first edition) published.

1820 *Six Views of the City of Bath* published.

1822 Makes lithograph of County Hall, Hereford; 22 June: in London, records embarkation of George IV from Greenwich.

1824 Moves to Ash Tree House, Hereford.

1825 Journey to Wales, with Edward Everitt; *Young Artist's Companion* (second edition) published.

1826 Takes son on trip with brother-in-law to Belgium; tour extended with friends into Holland.

1827 Provides illustrations for *The Hereford Guide*; leaves Hereford for London, taking up residence at 9 Foxley Road, Kennington Common.

1829 Contributes to *Graphic Illustrations of Warwickshire*; travels with son to France, forced by minor accident to draw mostly in Paris; exhibits for first time with revived Birmingham Society of Artists.

1830 First journey to North of England.

1831 26 June: death of father (buried at Aston, Birmingham); 1 August: records opening of new London Bridge; late August: first visit to Haddon Hall, Derbyshire; exhibits for first time at Liverpool Academy.

1832 Final continental journey, to north coast of France.

1834 First visit to Lancaster and Ulverston Sands, with William Stone Ellis.

1836 Visits Wales, to make illustrations for Roscoe's *Wanderings and Excursions in North Wales*; on one of occasional visits to Birmingham, sketches *Porch of St Philip's Church*; discovers Scotch wrapping paper as drawing material.

1837 Illustrations to Roscoe's *Wanderings and Excursions in South Wales*; journey to North Yorkshire.

1838 Accompanies wife to Seabrook, near Hythe, and sketches in Kent; visit to Hardwick Hall, makes drawings of Long Gallery.

1839 Two watercolours bought from OWCS exhibition by Marquis of Conynham for Queen Victoria; takes lessons in oil painting from W. J. Müller.

1840 *Treatise on Landscape Painting* re-issued; visits Blackpool with William Roberts.

1841 March: visits Birmingham, to look for house; in summer, leaves London for Greenfield House, Harborne; buys painting by W. J. Müller.

1842 Journey to Wales, with son.

1843 Severe illness in summer, stays with sister at Sale to recuperate; on recovery, works hard at oil painting.

1844 Two oils exhibited at Royal Academy; June: journey to North Wales, with Harry Johnson, stays for two weeks at Royal Oak inn, Bettws-y-Coed; September: journey to Bolton Abbey and Knaresborough.

1845 Ninth and last edition of *Series of Progressive Lessons* published; returns to Bettws-y-Coed (and every summer until 1856), contemplates buying property there; last important visit to Haddon Hall; 23 November: death of Mary Cox, aged 74.

1846 Visits Bolton Abbey.

1847 Repaints signboard at Royal Oak.

1848 Stay at Bettws-y-Coed spoiled by wet weather.

1849 Death of young girl at Bettws-y-Coed occasions painting of *The Welsh Funeral*.

1850 Praised by Thackeray in *Sketches after English Landscape Painters*.

1851 Probably visits Great Exhibition in London.

1852 Visits Ludlow, Stokesay and Powis Castle.

1853 March: suffers severe attack of bronchitis; 12 June: suffers stroke; health never fully recovers.

1855 Represented by watercolours at Paris Universal Exhibition; subscribers commission portrait by Sir John Watson Gordon; 13 August: journeys to Edinburgh for sittings; 19 November: portrait presented to Cox at Metchley Abbey, Harborne.

1856 Portrait exhibited at Royal Academy; 24 May: to London to sit for second portrait, by William Boxall; 16 August: introduced to Rosa Bonheur, on her visit to Birmingham.

1857 Deterioration of health, including eyesight.

1858 2 August: makes will, including £500 legacy to Ann Fowler, maid and housekeeper since 1819; exhibition of work arranged by Conversazione Society, Hampstead.

1859 April: retrospective exhibition at German Gallery, Bond Street, London, well received; 7 June: died at Greenfield House, with son at bedside; 14 June: buried beside wife in Harborne churchyard.

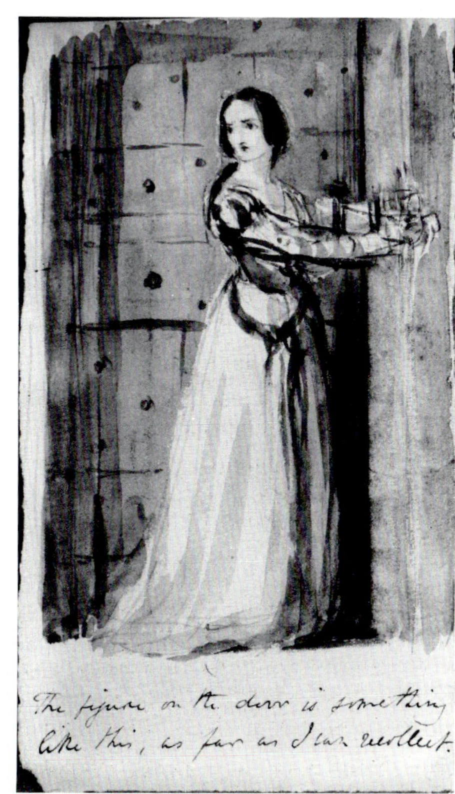

Fig. 5 Elizabeth Barber (?), copy of Cox's fresco *Catherine Douglas barring the door* at the Royal Oak Hotel, Bettws-y-Coed; Royal Society of Painters in Water-Colours

Checklist of Books by, or with Illustrations by, David Cox

This is a revised resumé of part of Margaret Rooker's *Bibliography on David Cox*, unpublished typescript, 1955. Those items marked * are not listed in that work.

THE DRAWING BOOKS

Ackermann's New Drawing Book of Light and Shadow, in Imitation of Indian Ink R. Ackermann, Repository of Arts, London, 1809; 1812.
24 aquatints.
Cox is nowhere credited in the book, but it has always been acknowledged to be his work. Copies of this scarce work have been found bearing the dates 1809 and 1812.

A Series of Progressive Lessons intended to elucidate the Art of Painting in Water Colours T. Clay, London, 1811.
2 soft-ground etchings, 11 aquatints (6 coloured).

A Series of Progressive Lessons 2nd edition; T. Clay, London, 1812.
'The rapid sale of the first edition of this work induces a presumption that it has so far been acceptable and useful. A second edition is accordingly submitted in a revised state.'

A Series of Progressive Lessons 3rd edition; T. Clay, London, 1816.
'A Third Edition of this Work being demanded, it is presumed to have passed the ordeal of public investigation; the whole has notwithstanding undergone a revision, in which many particulars have been added, and others expunged, as the proposed clearness of direction appeared to require. There have also been new designs introduced upon the principles of those contained in the preceding editions.'

A Series of Progressive Lessons 4th edition; T. Clay, London, 1820.
3 engraved 'Introductory Illustrations on Perspective' added.

A Series of Progressive Lessons . . . with Introductory Illustrations on Perspective and Drawing with Pencil 5th edition (larger format); T. Clay, London, 1823.
3 engravings, 4 lithographs, 11 aquatints (8 coloured).
'The original intent of the series of Progressive Lessons was, that it might be found of utility in the absence of a good Drawing Master; but how far this end has been accomplished is evinced by the demand for a fifth edition . . . In the present edition new exertions have been made towards improvement, it has undergone a careful revision; the subjects of the preceding editions have been cancelled: new ones, (all drawn from nature) substituted, with others added and treated progressively in Pencil, Indian Ink, Seppia, and Colours.'

A Series of Progressive Lessons 6th edition; T. Clay, London, 1828.
Minor alterations to plates.

**A Series of Progressive Lessons* 7th edition; T. Clay, London, 1838.
3 engravings, 4 lithographs, 11 aquatints (9 coloured); 4 of the plates by David Cox junior.
'In order to explain the system adopted in the present improved state of the Art, it was necessary to discard the preceding work altogether, and to produce another entirely new.'

A Series of Progressive Lessons 8th edition; Ackermann and Co., London, 1841.
Unchanged; Ackermann's name substituted for Clay's throughout.

A Series of Progressive Lessons 9th edition; Ackermann and Co., London, 1845.

A Treatise on Landscape Painting and Effect in Water Colours S. and J. Fuller, London, 1813–14 (issued in twelve parts, in paper wrappers).
24 soft-ground etchings, 32 aquatints (16 coloured).

A Treatise on Landscape Painting and Effect in Water Colours S. and J. Fuller, London, 1840–41 (re-issue in monthly parts, in paper wrappers, of 1813–14 edition).
Plates inscribed 'Re-published 1840 by S. and J. Fuller'.
Solly (pp. 56–7) quotes a letter of 31 January 1840 from Sam Fuller to Cox, regarding this edition:
'It is now six-and-twenty years since we published your work, "A Treatise on Landscape Painting and Effect" and during this time a new family and many aspirants to the art have appeared, and many are forthcoming, so that I think if your work was to appear again there are many who would be inclined to take it. With this in view, we propose to re-publish it, in monthly numbers again, the first number to appear next March. The plates have been proved, and found to be in good condition, particularly the soft-ground, which I consider as good as ever. The sepia or shadow and effect will want some little attention, and which I shall thank you to be so good as to look over; but I believe that I am in possession of some proof impressions that may assist the engraver. As I propose to advertise this to the world, it will give an interest and a demand for the art again. I have no doubt but you will be surprised to find that it is twenty-six years since you commenced this work. Time has passed away and many changes have taken place, but I do not think myself that anything has been added by those who have brought out similar publications.'

Progressive Lessons on Landscape for Young Beginners S. and J. Fuller, London, 1816 (issued in six parts, in paper wrappers).
24 soft-ground etchings (no text).

The Young Artist's Companion S. and J. Fuller, London, 1819–20 (issued in sixteen parts, in paper wrappers).
40 soft-ground etchings, 24 aquatints (12 coloured).

The Young Artist's Companion S. and J. Fuller, London, 1825.
Frontispiece added (coloured soft-ground etching).
The introductory text is the same as that of the *Treatise*, to which notes on the twelve coloured plates are added.

? Liber Studiorum (projected)
Two related volumes exist of compilation of plates from the 1840 *Treatise* and *The Young Artist's Companion*, possibly 'proof' sets of a projected *Liber Studiorum*, which title appears on the spine of one of the volumes (Birmingham collection).

WORKS CONTAINING ILLUSTRATIONS BY AND AFTER COX

(Number of identified works by Cox given in brackets).

John Hassell, *Aqua Pictura*, (?) 1813 (1); 1818 (1).

Six Views of the City of Bath, 1820 (6).

*Lieut. J. Moore and Capt. F. Maryat, *Rangoon Views*, 2nd series, 1826 (1).

*W. J. Rees, *The Hereford Guide*, 3rd edition, 1827 (12).

Alexander Blair, *Graphic Illustrations of Warwickshire*, 1829 (6); 2nd edition with facsimile plates, 1862.

**Watering Places of Great Britain*, pub. I. T. Hinton, 1831 (8).

Fisher's Drawing Room Scrap Book, 1832 (1); 1834 (1).

Robert Elliot, *Views in the East*, 2 vols., 1833 (3); re-published as *Views in India, China, etc.*, 1835 (and see below 1846, 1857).

**Gallery of the Society of Painters in Water Colours*, 1833 (1).

The Gallery of modern British artists, 1836 (3).

William Hawkes Smith, *Dudley Castle*, 1836 (?9).

Thomas Roscoe, *Wanderings and Excursions in North Wales*, 1836 (31); 2nd edition, 1853.

Thomas Roscoe, *Wanderings and Excursions in South Wales*, 1837 (18); 2nd edition 1844.

*Thomas Roscoe, *The Book of the Grand Junction Railway*, 1839 (3).

*Thomas Turner, *Narrative of a Journey, associated with a fly, from Gloucester to Aberystwith, and from Aberystwith through North Wales*, 1840 (8); from Roscoe 1836 and 1837.

Louisa Anne Twamley, *The Annual of British Landscape Scenery*, 1839 (8); from Roscoe 1837.

**The Fashionable Guide and Directory*, *c.* 1840 (1).

Heath's Book of Beauty, 1840–45 (1 vignette for each year).

Countess of Blessington (ed.), *The Keepsake*, 1841 (1), 1842 (1), 1843 (1).

Robert Elliot, *Hindostan*, 1846 (3): same as Elliot 1833.

Louis Marvy, *Sketches after English Landscape Painters*, with short notices by W. M. Thackeray, 1850 (1).

*Thomas Compton, *The Cambrian Mountains*, 1851 (7); plates dated 1822–28, ? from earlier unrecorded edition.

*R. M. Martin, *The Indian Empire*, after 1857 (3): same as Elliot 1833.

John Tillotson, *Beauties of English Scenery*, 1860 (4); from *Watering Places of Great Britain* 1831.

Etchings by Edward Radclyffe, from drawings by the late David Cox, Art-Union of London, 1862–63 (12).

Cox Liber Studiorum (engravings by Edward Radclyffe), Liverpool Art Club, 1876 (3).

Bibliography

and Abbreviations used in Catalogue

WORKS ON DAVID COX

	Thomas B. Brumbaugh, 'David Cox in American Collections' in *Connoisseur*, February 1978, pp. 83–88.
	Cyril Bunt, *David Cox: Painter of Nature's Moods*, 1949.
Cox	Trenchard Cox, *David Cox*, 1947.
	Trenchard Cox, *David Cox 1783–1859*, Museum and Art Gallery, Birmingham, [1955].
Cundall	H. M. Cundall, 'David Cox as a Drawing Master' in *Art Journal*, 1909, pp. 177–180.
	J. Dafforne, 'David Cox' in *Art Journal*, February 1860, pp. 41–3.
Drawings	A. J. Finberg, *Drawings of David Cox*, [1906].
Hall	William Hall (with additions by John Thackray Bunce), *A Biography of David Cox*, 1881.
Long	Basil Long, 'David Cox (1783–1859)' in *The Old Water-Colour Society's Club Tenth Annual Volume*, 1932–33, pp. 1–19.
Oppé	A. P. Oppé, *The Water Colours of Turner, Cox & de Wint*, 1925 (includes catalogue of exhibition, Agnew's, 1924).
	Thomas Oldforde, 'Charcoal drawings by David Cox' in *Studio*, vol. 34, February 1905, pp. 38–43.
Redgrave	Gilbert Richard Redgrave, *David Cox and Peter de Wint*, 1891.
	Margaret Rooker, *Bibliography on David Cox, Landscape Painter, 1783–1859*, submitted in part requirement for University of London Diploma in Librarianship, unpublished typescript, 1955.
Roe 1924	Frederick Gordon Roe, *David Cox*, 1924.
Roe 1946	Frederick Gordon Roe, *Cox the Master; the life and art of David Cox, 1783–1859*, 1946.
Solly	Nathaniel Neal Solly, *Memoir of the Life of David Cox*, 1873; facsimile reprint, with index and new plates, 1973.
	Whitworth Wallis, 'David Cox forgeries', in *Connoisseur*, May 1905, pp. 55–56.

DAVID COX EXHIBITION CATALOGUES [IN DATE ORDER]

Burlington 1873	Burlington Fine Arts Club, *Drawings and sketches by the late David Cox and the late Peter de Wint lent by John Henderson*, 1873.
Liverpool 1875	Liverpool Art Club, *Catalogue of the loan collection of the works of the late David Cox*, 1875 (Preface by William Hall).
BMAG 1890	Birmingham Museum and Art Gallery, *Catalogue of a special collection of works by David Cox*, 1890 (Compiled by Whitworth Wallis and A. B. Chamberlain, with introduction by J. Thackray Bunce).
	Graves Gallery, Birmingham, *Water Colour Drawings, Charcoal and Pencil Sketches by David Cox*, November 1907.

	Birmingham Museum and Art Gallery, *Collection of works by David Cox: Mr J. Arthur Kenrick's gift, 1925, and earlier gifts and bequests*, 1925.
	Birmingham Museum and Art Gallery, *Catalogue of the permanent collection of works by David Cox*, 1926 (Introduction by A. B. Chamberlain).
	Catalogue of the Travelling Collection of drawings in water-colour, pencil and charcoal, by David Cox, lent by the City of Birmingham Museum and Art Gallery, 1926.
Hereford 1926	Hereford Art Gallery and Museum, *Supplement to Catalogue of Exhibition of Drawings by David Cox, opened July 14th 1926.*
Hereford 1928	Hereford Public Library, Museum and Art Gallery, *Catalogue of a Loan Exhibition of the Works of deceased Herefordshire Artists*, 1928.
Swansea 1953	Glynn Vivian Art Gallery, Swansea, *David Cox (1783–1859)*, Summer Exhibition 1953.
BMAG 1959	Birmingham Museum and Art Gallery, *David Cox 1783–1859: Centenary Exhibition*, 1959.
Lyon 1966	Musée de Lyon, *Peintures et aquarelles anglaises 1700–1900 du Musée de Birmingham*, 1966.
Bourges 1970	Maison de la Culture de Bourges, *'David Cox et son Temps': l'aquarelle anglaise au XIXe siecle*, 1970.
	Wren Gallery, Blackheath and C. P. Stockbridge, Cambridge, *David Cox 1783–1859: an exhibition of his works*, 1973.
	Anthony Reed, London and Davis & Long Company, New York, *David Cox drawings and paintings*, 1976.
	Dudley Art Gallery, *David Cox and his contemporaries*, 1976.
	Manchester City Art Gallery, *David Cox 1783–1859*, 1982 (typescript catalogue on occasion of display of permanent collection. Compiled by Jane Farrington).
	Davis & Langdale Company, New York and Anthony Reed, London, *David Cox 1783–1859*, 1983.

IMPORTANT CATALOGUES OF MAJOR COLLECTIONS

Sale Bequest	Mildred Berkeley, *Catalogue: Sale Bequest of Water Colours*, Victoria Institute, Worcester Corporation Art Gallery, [1918].
Binyon	Laurence Binyon, *Catalogue of Drawings by British Artists . . . in the British Museum*, vol. 1, A–C, 1898.
	A. E. Whitley, *Catalogue of Drawings*, Birmingham Museum and Art Gallery, 1939.
BMAG Oils	*Catalogue of Paintings*, City Museum and Art Gallery, Birmingham [1960].
	Randall Davies, 'Water-colours in the Birmingham Art Gallery', in *The Old Water-Colour Society's Club Sixteenth Annual Volume*, 1938, pp. 1–36 (includes appreciation and catalogue section on Cox).
Grundy	C. Reginald Grundy, *A Catalogue of the Pictures and Drawings in the collection of Frederick John Nettlefold*, 4 vols. 1933–38 (Vol. 1, A–C, contains works by Cox).
Hibbert	James Hibbert (ed.), *Catalogue of the Pictures & Drawings of the Newsham Bequest in the Corporation of Preston*, 1884.

Lambourne — Lionel Lambourne and Jean Hamilton, *British Watercolours in the Victoria and Albert Museum: An Illustrated Summary Catalogue*, 1980.

Bury 1901 — Whitworth Wallis and A. B. Chamberlain, *Illustrated Catalogue of the Wrigley Collection of Paintings*, Bury Art Gallery 1901.

STUDIO MAGAZINE SPECIAL NUMBERS

Masters of English Landscape Painting: J. S. Cotman, David Cox, Peter de Wint, 1903 (ed. C. Holme).

The 'Old' Water-Colour Society 1804–1904, 1905 (ed. C. Holme).

The Development of British Landscape Painting in Water-Colours, 1918 (ed. A. J. Finberg and E. A. Taylor).

Studio 1922 — *A Treatise on Landscape Painting in Watercolours by David Cox*, 1922 (Text plus selection of plates, with preface by A. L. Baldry).

Masters of Water-Colour Painting, 1922–23 (ed. H. M. Cundall).

OTHER WORKS

Scenery of Great Britain and Ireland in aquatint and lithography 1770–1860 from the library of J. R. Abbey, 1952; reprinted 1972.

Life in England in aquatint and lithography 1770–1860 from the library of J. R. Abbey, 1953; reprinted 1972.

Travel in aquatint and lithography 1770–1860 from the library of J. R. Abbey, 2 vols. 1957; reprinted 1972.

David Bell, *The Artist in Wales*, 1957.

Michael Clarke, *The Tempting Prospect: A Social History of English Watercolours*, 1981.

Trevor Fawcett, *The Rise of English Provincial Art*, 1974.

Joan Friedman, 'Every Lady Her Own Drawing Master', *Apollo*, April 1977, pp. 262–67.

Colonel M. H. Grant, *A Chronological History of the Old English Landscape Painters*, 2nd ed., 8 vols., 1957–61.

Hardie 1906 — Martin Hardie, *English Coloured Books*, 1906; reprinted 1973.

Hardie 1967 — Martin Hardie, *Water-Colour Painting in Britain: Vol. II The Romantic Period*, 1967 (Chapter XII is on Cox).

Hardie 1968 — Martin Hardie, *Water-Colour Painting in Britain: Vol. III The Victorian Period*, 1968.

Hardie 1979 — ibid, 3rd impression, 1979; Appendix I, *Drawing-Masters*, revised Ian Fleming-Williams.

Joseph Hill and Walter Midgley, *The History of the Royal Birmingham Society of Artists*, [1928].

C. E. Hughes (revised J. Mayne), *Early English Water-Colour*, 3rd ed., 1950.

Basil Hunnisett, *Steel-engraved Book Illustration in England*, 1980.

Esther Moir, *The Discovery of Britain: The English Tourists 1540 to 1840*, 1964.

S. T. Prideaux, *Aquatint Engraving*, 1909; reprinted 1968.

Roget — John Lewis Roget, *A History of the 'Old Water-Colour' Society*, 2 vols., 1891.

F. Schmid, *The Practice of Painting*, 1948 (esp. Chapter V, 'Water-Colour Books in England from 1750–1850').

Hammond Smith, *Peter de Wint 1784–1849*, 1982.

N. Neal Solly, *Memoir of the Life of William James Müller*, 1875.

Frederick Wedmore, *Studies in English Art*, 2nd Series, 1880.

Williams — Iolo Aneurin Williams, *Early English Water-Colours*, 1952.

Andrew Wilton, *British Watercolours 1750 to 1850*, 1977.

EXHIBITION CATALOGUES

Arts Council (Wales), *Art in Wales*, Swansea [1962].

J. Baskett and D. Snelgrove, *English Drawings and Watercolours 1550–1850 in the collection of Mr and Mrs Paul Mellon*, Pierpont Morgan Library, New York 1972.

Bayard — J. Bayard, *Works of Splendor and Imagination: The Exhibition Watercolor 1770–1870*, Yale 1981.

Bicknell — P. Bicknell, *Beauty, Horror and Immensity*, Cambridge 1981.

M. Butlin and A. Wilton, *Turner 1775–1851*, Tate Gallery 1975.

Colnaghi & Co., *John Linnell and his Circle*, 1973.

P. Conisbee, *Painting from Nature*, Cambridge and R.A., 1980–81.

K. Crouan, *John Linnell: A Centennial Exhibition*, Cambridge and Yale 1982–83.

K. Crouan, *John Linnell: Truth to Nature*, Martyn Gregory Gallery 1982.

Decade — J. Gage, *A Decade of Naturalism 1810–1820*, Norwich and V & A 1969–70.

RBSA 1968 — F. Greenacre, *Royal Centenary Retrospective Exhibition*, Royal Birmingham Society of Artists 1968.

G. Hedley, *The Picturesque Tour in Northumberland and Durham*, Newcastle-upon-Tyne 1982.

A. D. F. Jenkins, *The Romantic Traveller in Wales*, Cardiff n.d.

F. Owen and E. Stanford, *William Havell 1782–1857*, Reading 1982.

L. Parris, *Landscape in Britain 1750–1850*, Tate Gallery 1973.

L. Parris et al, *Constable*, Tate Gallery 1976.

M. Rajnai et al, *John Sell Cotman 1782–1842*, V & A, Bristol and Manchester 1982–83.

Scrase — D. Scrase, *Drawings & Watercolours by Peter de Wint*, Cambridge 1979.

M. Spencer, *R. P. Bonington*, Nottingham[1966].

C. White, *English Landscape 1630–1850: Drawings, Prints & Books from the Paul Mellon Collection*, Yale 1977.

Catalogue

Measurements are in centimetres, with inches given in brackets; height precedes width.
Dates, if given, are those inscribed on the surface of the work by the artist.

Abbreviations:
BMAG Birmingham Museums and Art Gallery; OWCS Old Water Colour Society; RA Royal Academy

PROV Provenance; EXH Exhibitions; LIT Literature

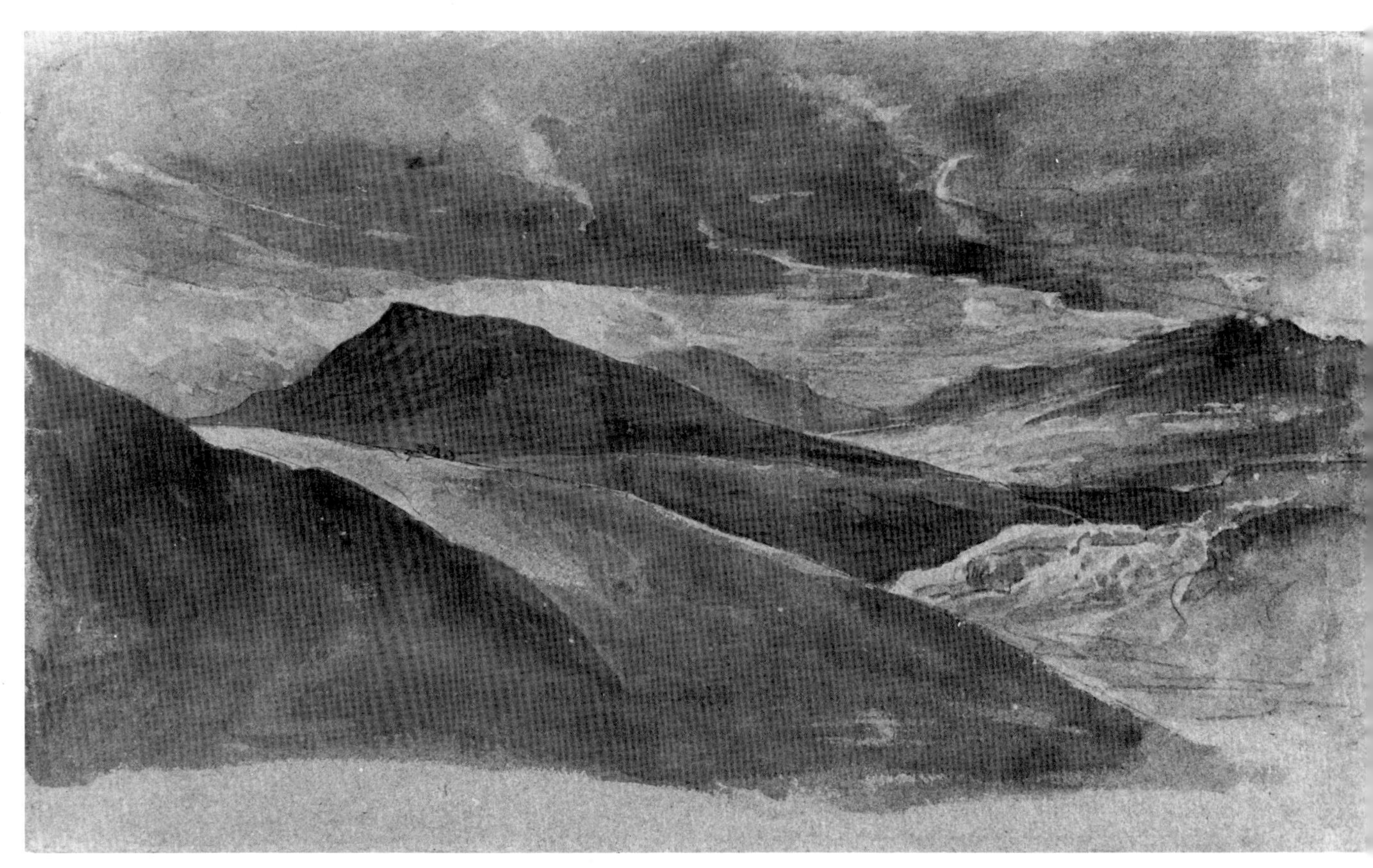

Mountains (cat. no. 6)

1. Birmingham and London 1783–1815

No juvenilia of any kind survive, and no works from either Cox's early tuition by Joseph Barber, or his career as a scene-painter. This is perhaps not surprising in view of the essentially ephemeral nature of that art. Some reminiscence of grand architectural back-drops, however, can possibly be detected in the larger views of London (nos. 1 and 9) and Kenilworth Castle (no. 3).

Cox's staple works in the early London years consisted of drawings sold to dealers, such as Palser and Simpson, for amateurs' scrapbooks or tuition copies. The two little London views (nos. 7 and 8) may afford a glimpse of that drudgery, but infused with a fresher observation of Thames-side life afforded through contact with the circle of young artists who formed around John Varley, from whom Cox was also happy to take lessons. The little Herefordshire Lane *(no. 4) is a charming study in the Varley manner, complete with an early example of Cox's awkwardly individual figure drawing.*

He made the long journey into North Wales (presumably via Birmingham – which he also visited on the later westward excursion of 1810) as early as 1805, and apparently repeated it in the following year. 'A Welch tour is surprisingly grand,' recommended the Birmingham publisher William Hutton in 1803; 'Nature is seen in extreme. The lofty, rough and barren mountains opposed to the beautiful and fertile valleys is a charming contrast.' Cox's own reactions are not, alas, recorded, but there is no reason to think that they would have been any less than those of another member of the Varley circle, John Linnell, who remarked that 'one month's stay supplied me with material for life'.

Although still not free of the need to supplement his income by occasional scene painting (as late as 1808), Cox must have achieved some standing as an artist, to become a member and then President of the Associated Artists in Watercolour (where he might have shown exhibition pieces such as no. 9). He must have been equally resilient to withstand that society's sudden demise, and go on to be accepted into the ranks of the Old Water Colour Society, in 1812. The movement to include oil paintings in the Society's exhibitions (an experiment which ran from 1813 to 1821) may have been the spur for Cox's own few attempts at the medium on a trip to Hastings in 1812 (nos. 10 and 11).

1. Old Westminster 1805

Pencil and watercolour on coarse paper 26.1 × 38.5 (10¼ × 15⅛)
PROV: presented by subscribers 1907 (347'07)
EXH: Arts Council, *English Romantic Art* 1947 (49); Swansea 1953 (3); BMAG 1959 (2).
LIT: *Drawings* pl. II; Roe 1946, pl. 13; Cox, p. 29 and pl. 3.
Birmingham Museums and Art Gallery

The inscribed date of 1805 may have been added by Cox to reinforce the faint pencil inscription, and remind himself of one of his very earliest works, made soon after arriving in London. It is tempting to deduce the artist's experience as a scene-painter from the unusual composition, contrasting grand and humble architecture, whilst also recognising an instinctive skill with the pencil and brush.

2. On the road from Pont Aberglaslyn to Maentwrog

Pencil and watercolour on four joined leaves of a sketch-book 15.1 × 94 (6 × 37).
PROV: bequeathed by J. R. Holliday 1927 (719'27).
EXH: BMAG 1959 (3); *Landscape in Britain*, Tate 1973 (255, repr.); *British Drawings and Watercolours for China*, British Council 1982 (49).
Birmingham Museums and Art Gallery

Inscribed by the artist in pencil with the title and names of two mountains, *Moel Hebog* and *Snowdon*; on the reverse are two slight landscape sketches in pencil and watercolour. This delightful panorama must be a product of one of Cox's first two visits to North Wales in the footsteps of Varley, in 1805 and 1806. Hall (p. 16) describes such early Welsh drawings; one, cited by him, of 17 July 1805 and another, *On the Road to Dolgelly*, of 19 July 1805 (Private Collection) are the earliest recorded drawings by Cox.

The trial of deliberately contrasted techniques (the watercolour section reveals no visible pencil under-drawing) is most revealing of the young artist's self-tuition through direct observation of landscape.

3. Kenilworth Castle

Watercolour over traces of pencil 36.2 × 50.8 (14 × 19¾).
PROV: presented by subscribers 1907 (323'07).
EXH: Swansea 1953 (1); BMAG 1959 (4); Bourges 1970 (1, repr.).
LIT: Solly, p. 16; Hall, p. 15; Cox, p. 26, repr. p. 27.
Birmingham Museums and Art Gallery

Solly and Hall both recount how, in 1806 or 1807, Cox made a copy (in watercolour) of a painting by Gaspard Poussin seen in the dealer Simpson's shop in Soho, and how he then attempted a watercolour of his own, 'about 16 by 20', in emulation. There seems no reason to believe that this is not that work, rather than an unfinished sketch, as hitherto described. The 'ghostly' figures are surely intentional and not incomplete, producing a visionary Arcadian effect akin to that sought by Cotman in such works as the *Classical Dance* (Norwich Castle Museum). Cox produced a few other 'classical' works in the style of Barret, Glover and Finch (notably *Carthage – Aeneas and Achates*, OWCS 1825; untraced) but they were not successful. The watercolour of 1807, *In Windsor Park* (V & A, P. 24–1948, repr. Hardie 1967, pl. 184), is an orthodox re-working of the same composition; and there is a version of *Kenilworth Castle*, dated 1830, in the Lady Lever Art Gallery, Port Sunlight (repr. Solly, p. 15).

4. A Herefordshire Lane

Watercolour 27 × 18.6 (10⅝ × 7⅝).
PROV: presented by the Misses Pritt 1925 (68'25).
EXH: Lyon 1966 (32).
Birmingham Museums and Art Gallery

Probably from the late 1800s, during Cox's pupillage with Varley. It is comparable in style with the work of William Havell, a close friend of the early London years. This is one of twenty-two drawings presented to Birmingham by the grand-daughters of Charles Barber, Cox's fellow pupil and lifelong friend, who settled in Liverpool as a drawing master; most of the drawings in the Pritt collection were given by Cox to Barber or other members of the family.

5. Sheet of studies: A Cornfield; Clouds

Soft pencil touched with white on blue paper 31.5 × 26.7 (12⅜ × 10½).
PROV: presented by subscribers 1907 (408'07).
Birmingham Museums and Art Gallery

One of a number of sheets of studies on 'grocer's paper', presumed to have been made on a journey from London to Birmingham in 1810. Several are illustrated by Finberg *(Drawings)*, who seems to refer to an intact sketch-book; the sheets in the Birmingham collection are all separate. These landscape studies are of great interest, foreshadowing the keenly-observed details of staffage in the *Treatise*, and demonstrating Cox's early fascination with the 'incidents' and 'effects' in landscape which are essential parts of his mature work. There is perhaps a hint of a knowledge of W. H. Pyne's 1806 *Microcosm* illustrations of such details here, but just as much personal observation.

6. Mountains

see p. 46

Grey wash over pencil on blue paper 28.4 × 46.5 (11¼ × 18¼).
PROV: presented by Augustus Walker 1910 (3326).
The Syndics of the Fitzwilliam Museum, Cambridge

A fine early study, probably of Welsh mountains, demonstrating the effectiveness of the simplest means. In true 'pure' watercolour tradition, the whiteness of the paper (albeit in this case blue) is retained for the highlight of the composition, dominated by a lowering sky.

7. On the Thames

Watercolour with stopping-out and scratching-out 13.3 × 26 (5¼ × 10¼).
PROV: bequeathed by J. R. Holliday 1927 (749'27).
Birmingham Museums and Art Gallery

8. London from the Thames above Westminster

Watercolour with scratching-out 13.5 × 29.2 (5¼ × 11½).
PROV: bequeathed by J. R. Holliday 1927 (669'27).
Birmingham Museums and Art Gallery

Both dating from about 1810, these slightly stiff but charming watercolours are typical of the large number of small works Cox is known to have made for his regular income, sold for small sums to dealers

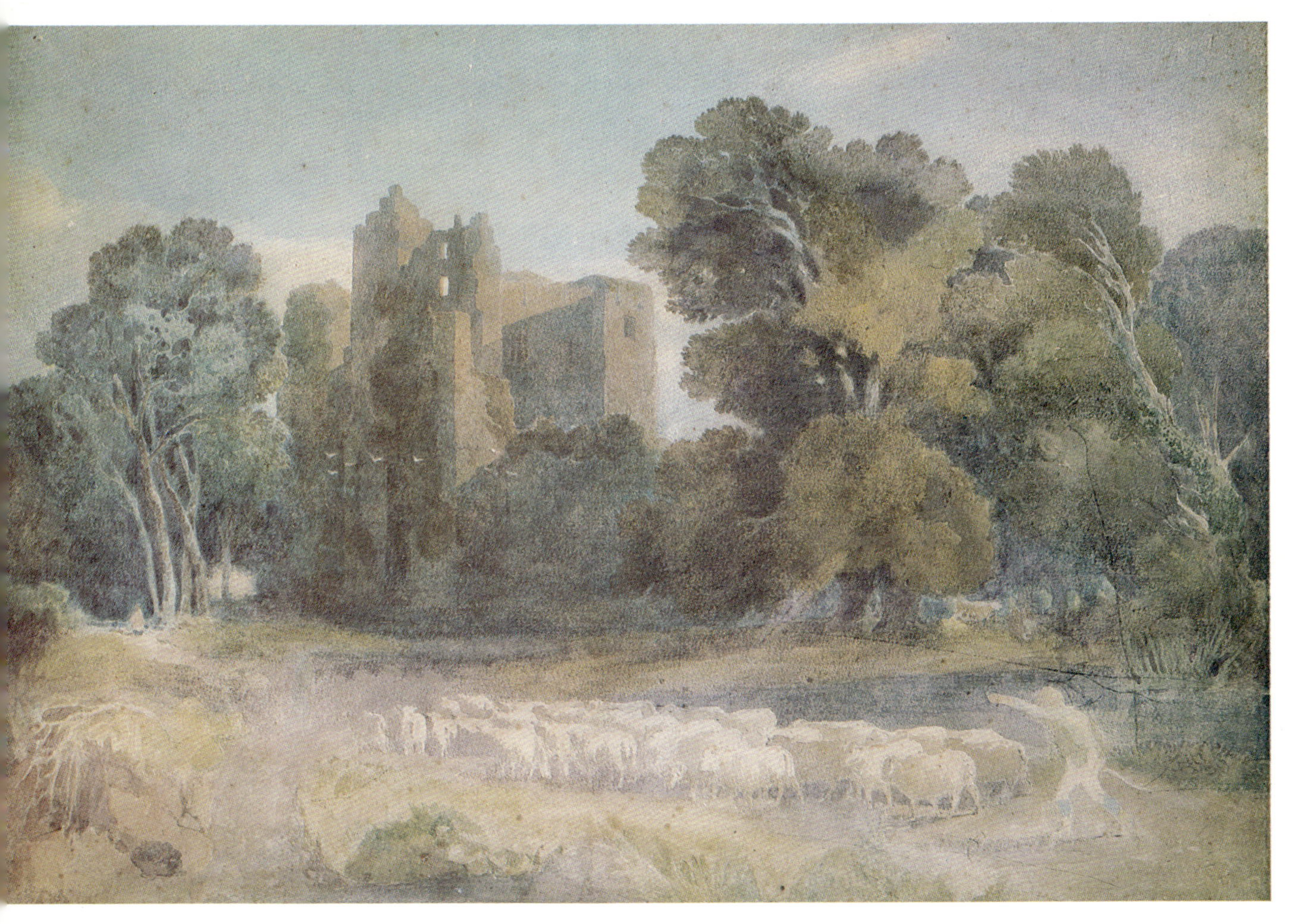

. *Kenilworth Castle* (cat. no. 3)

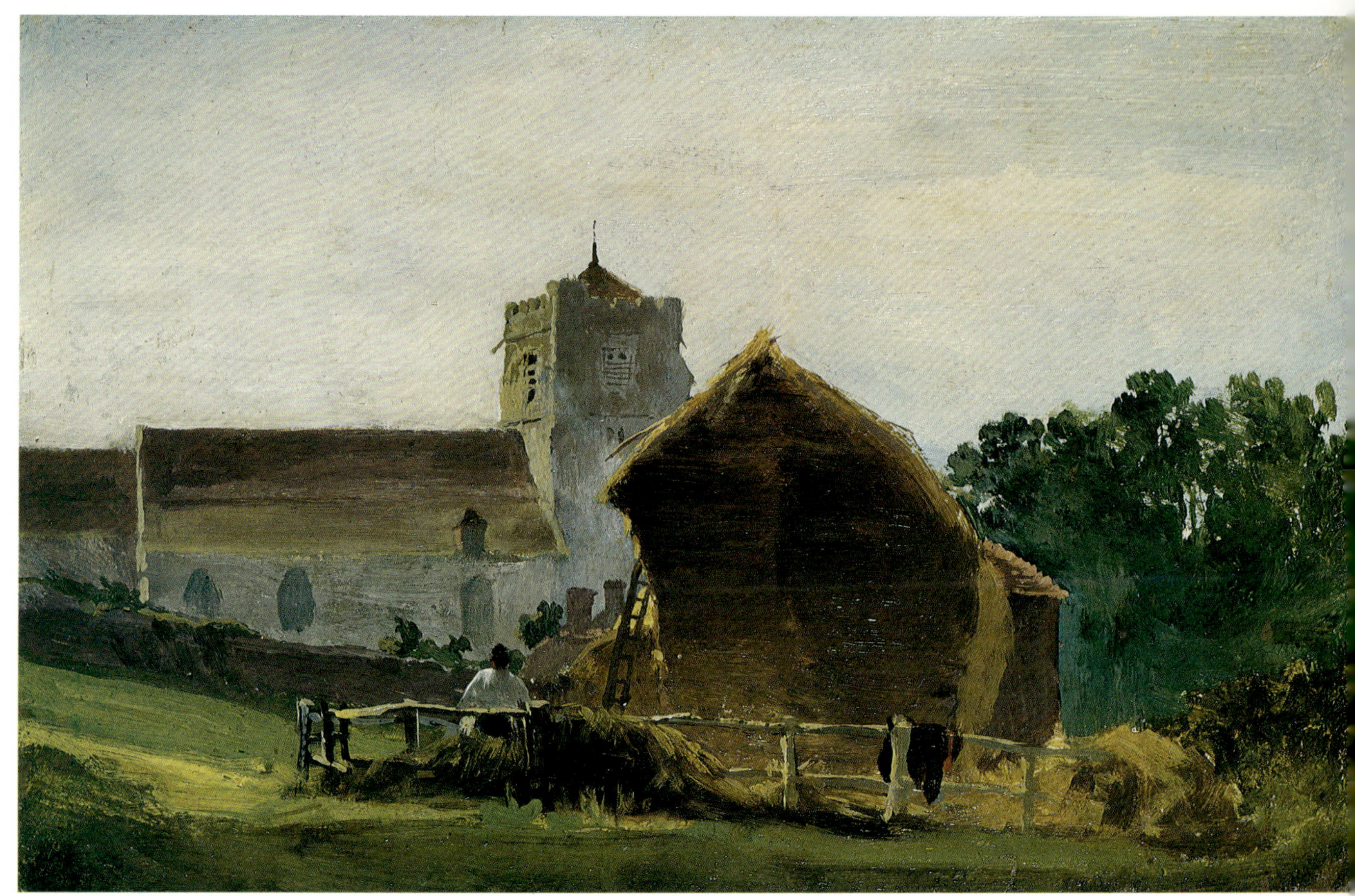

2. *All Saints' Church, Hastings* (cat. no. 11)

3. *A Herefordshire Lane* (cat. no. 4

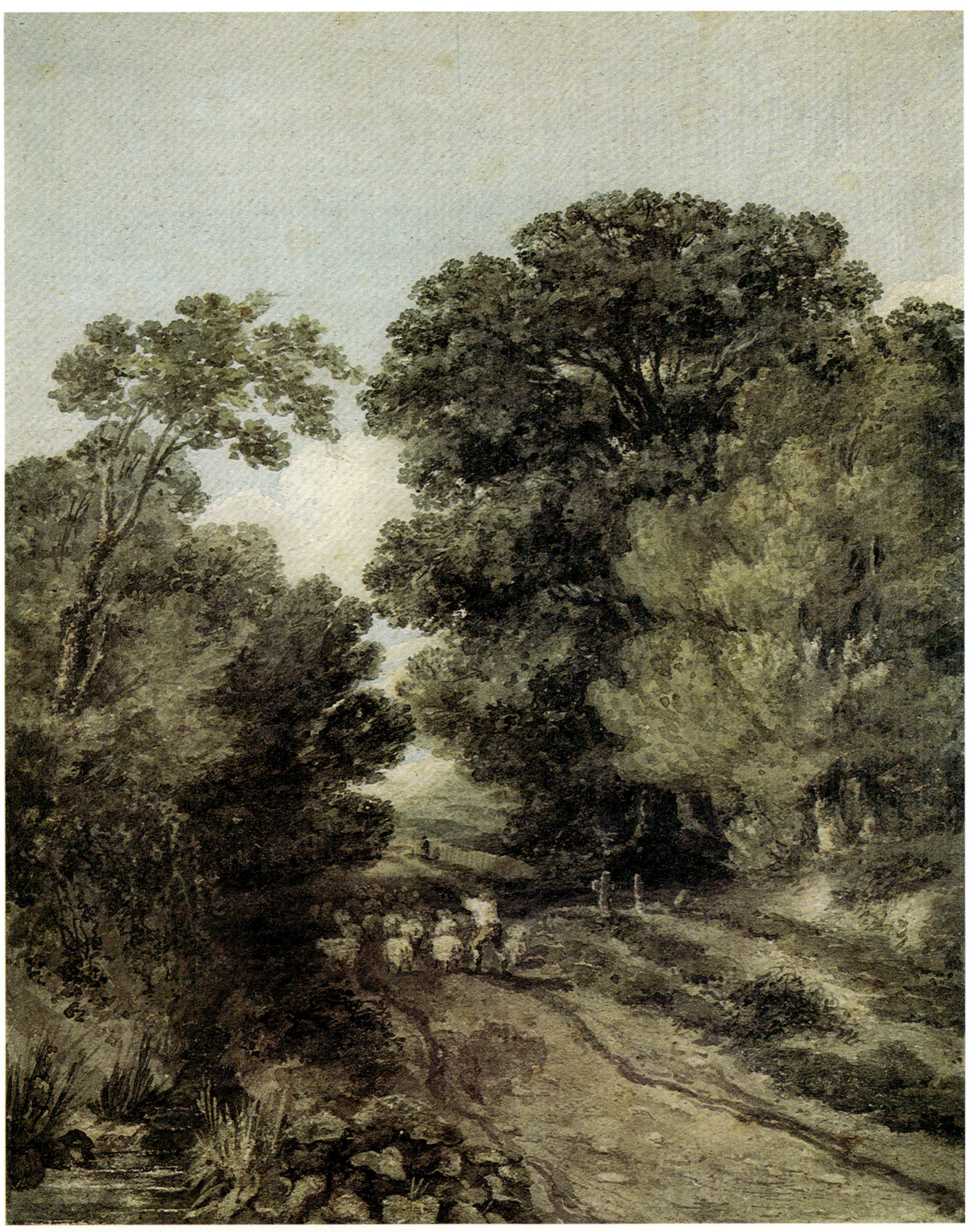

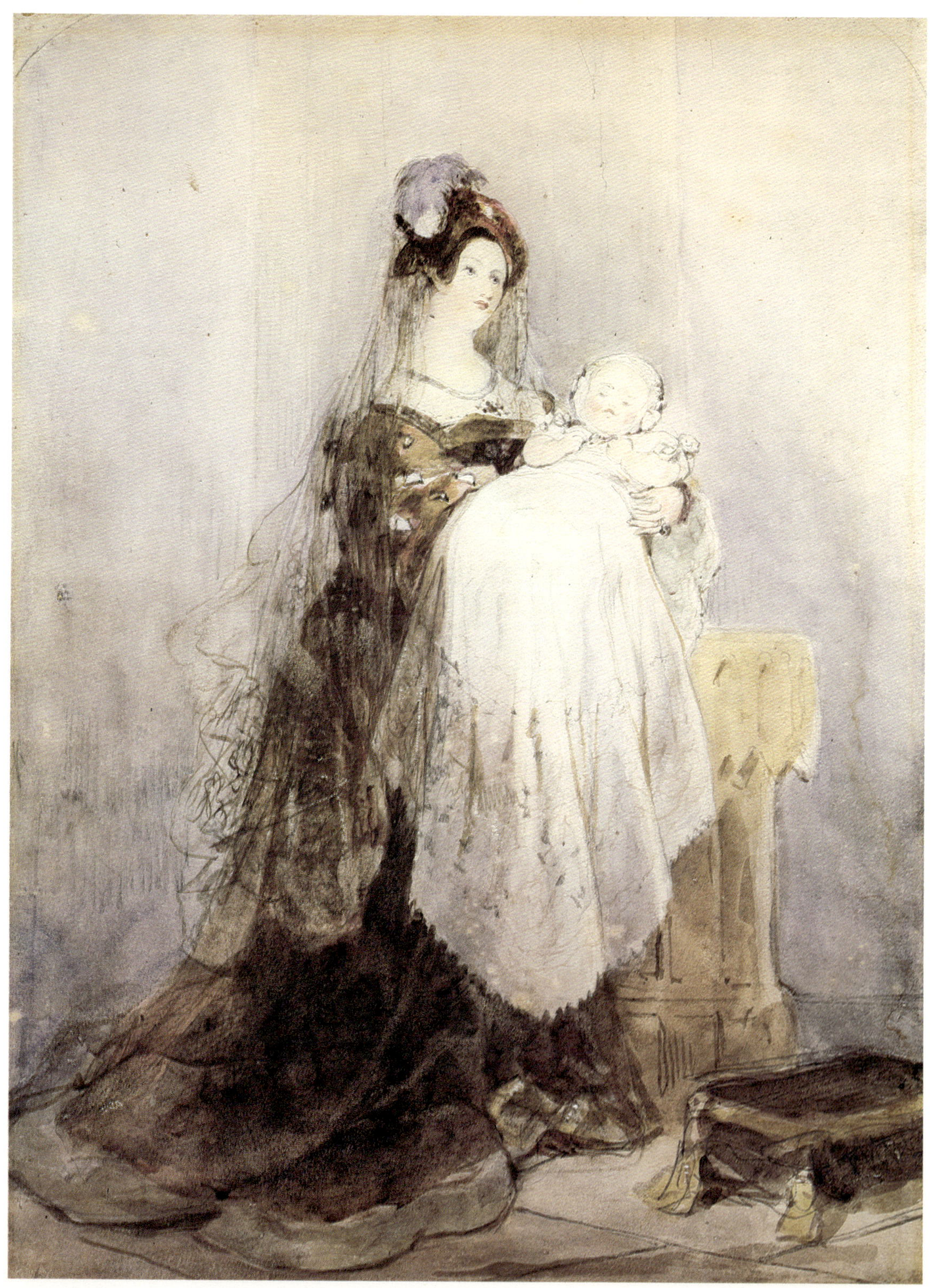

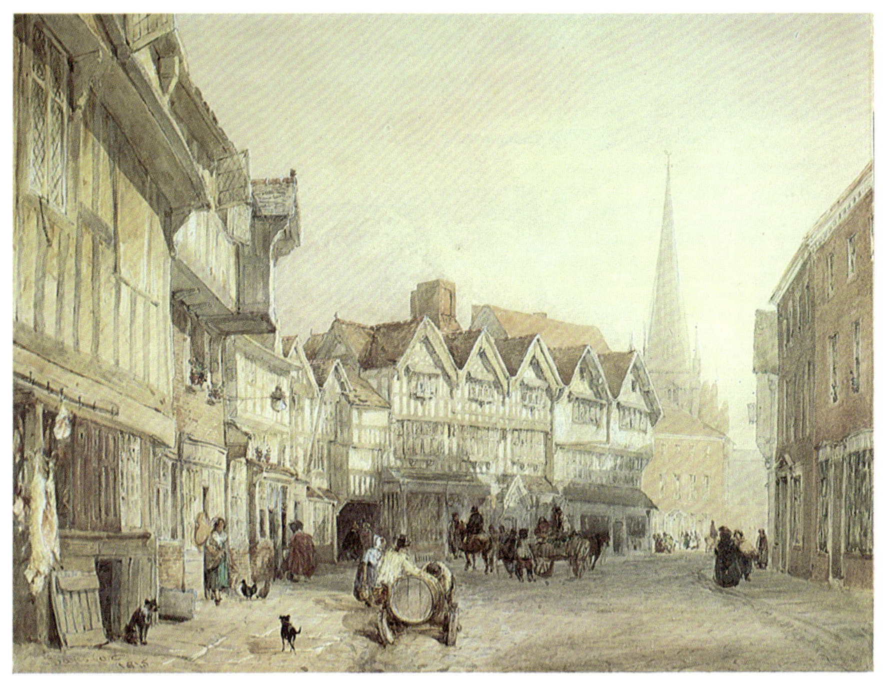

5. *Butchers' Row, Hereford* (cat. no. 27)

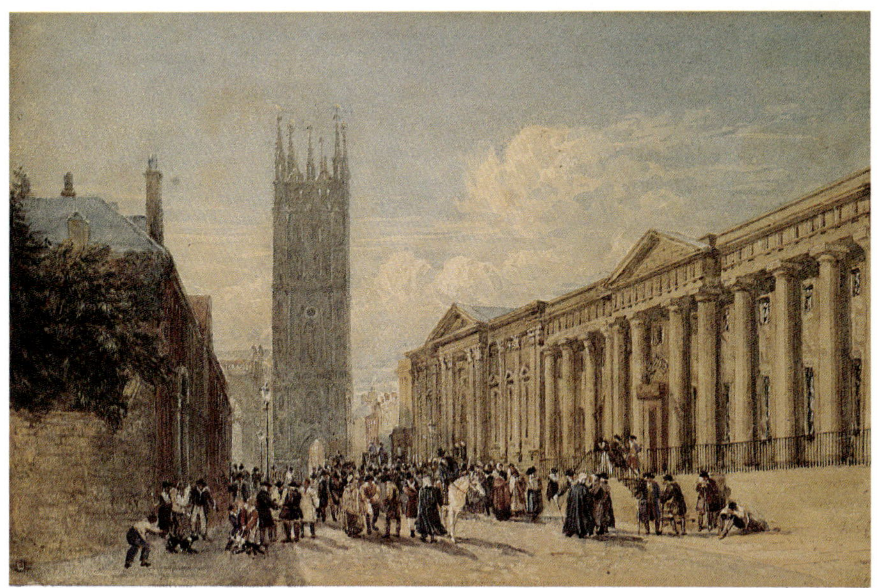

6. *Warwick: St. Mary's Church, County Hall and Gaol* (cat. no. 129)

4. *The Christening* (cat. no. 26)

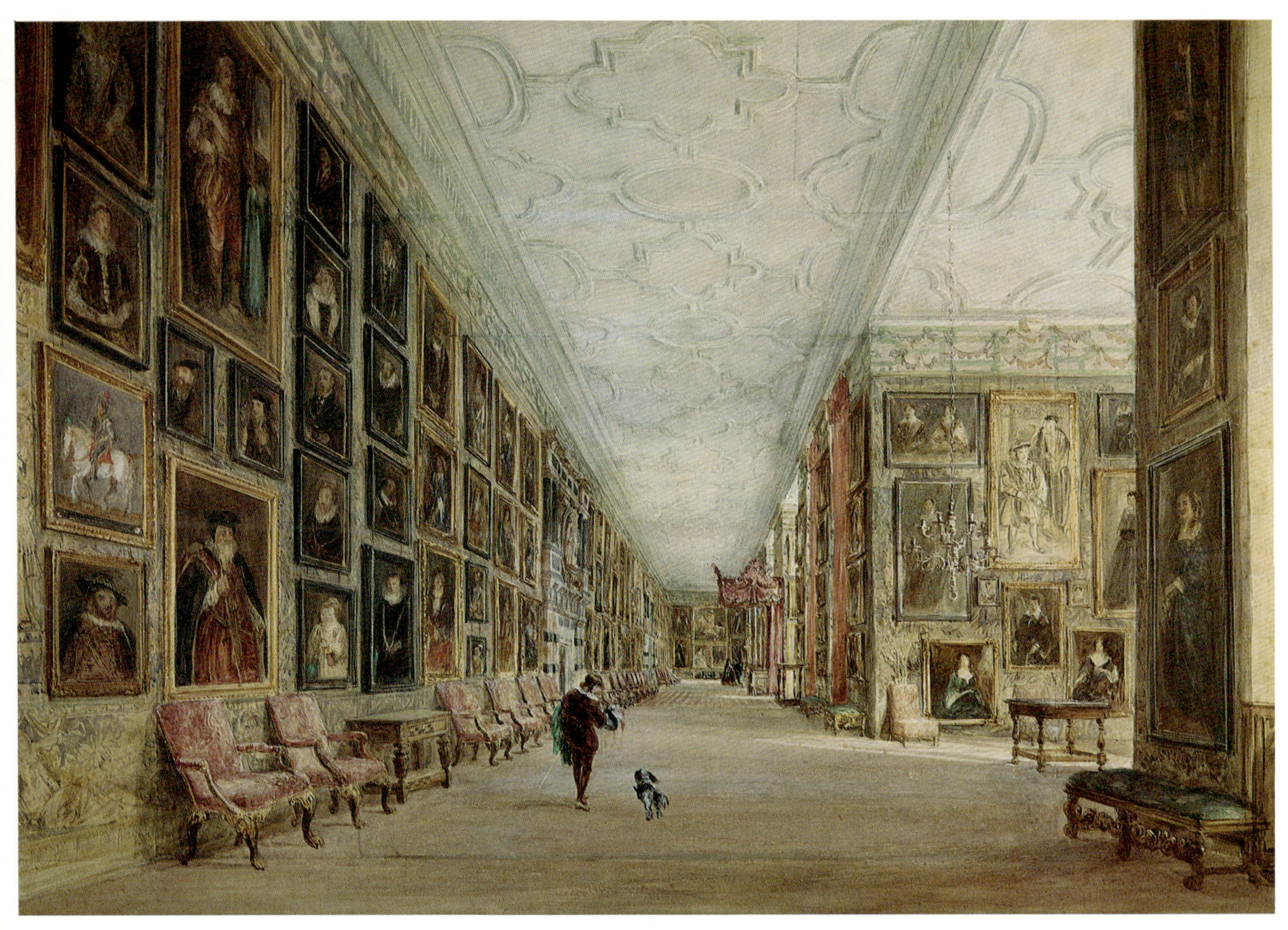

7. *The Long Gallery, Hardwick Hall* (cat. no. 47)

8. Frontispiece from *The Young Artist's Companion*, 1825

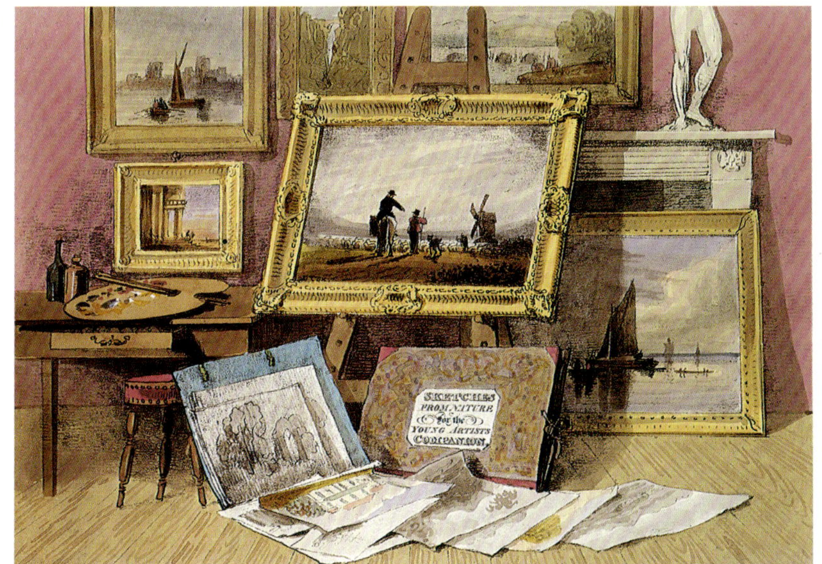

9. *Greenwich Hospital* (cat. no. 32)

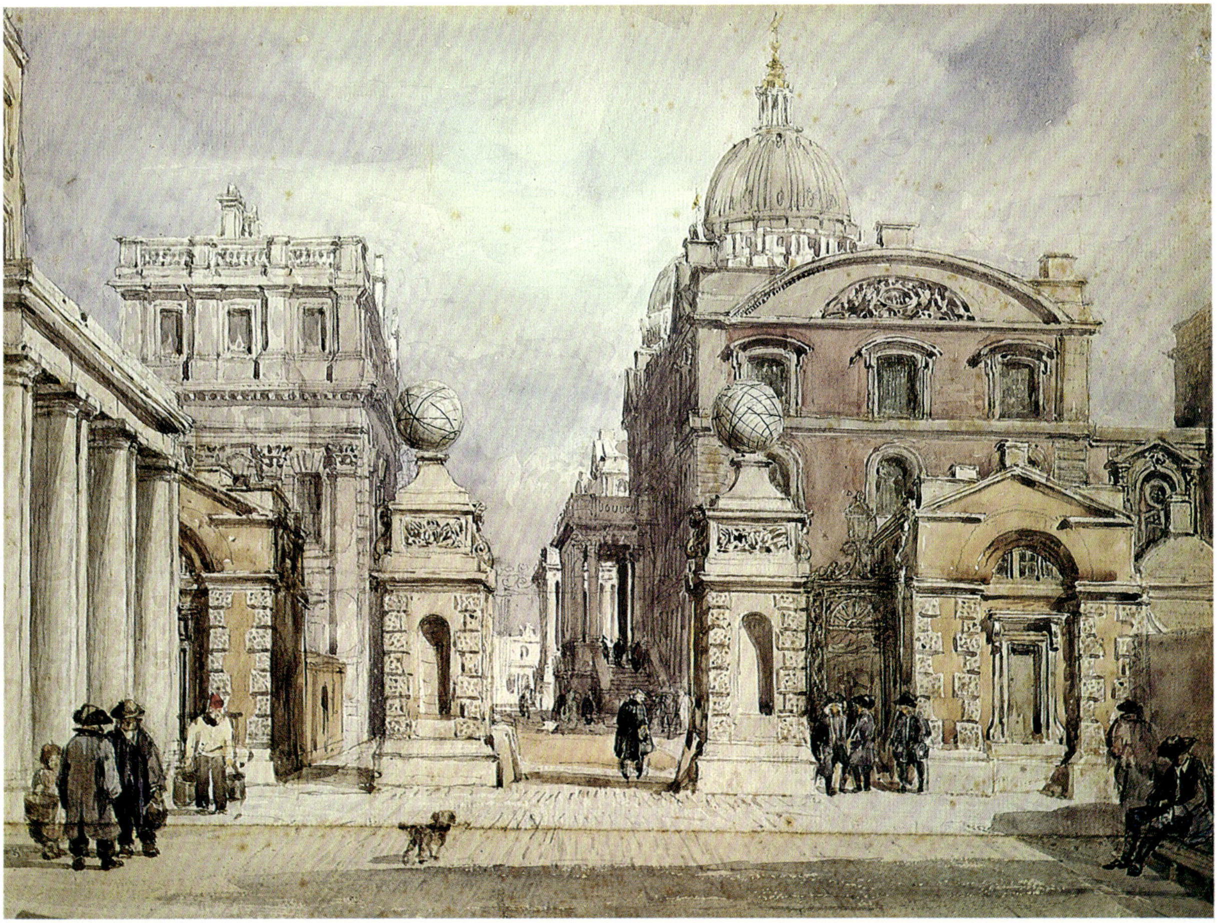

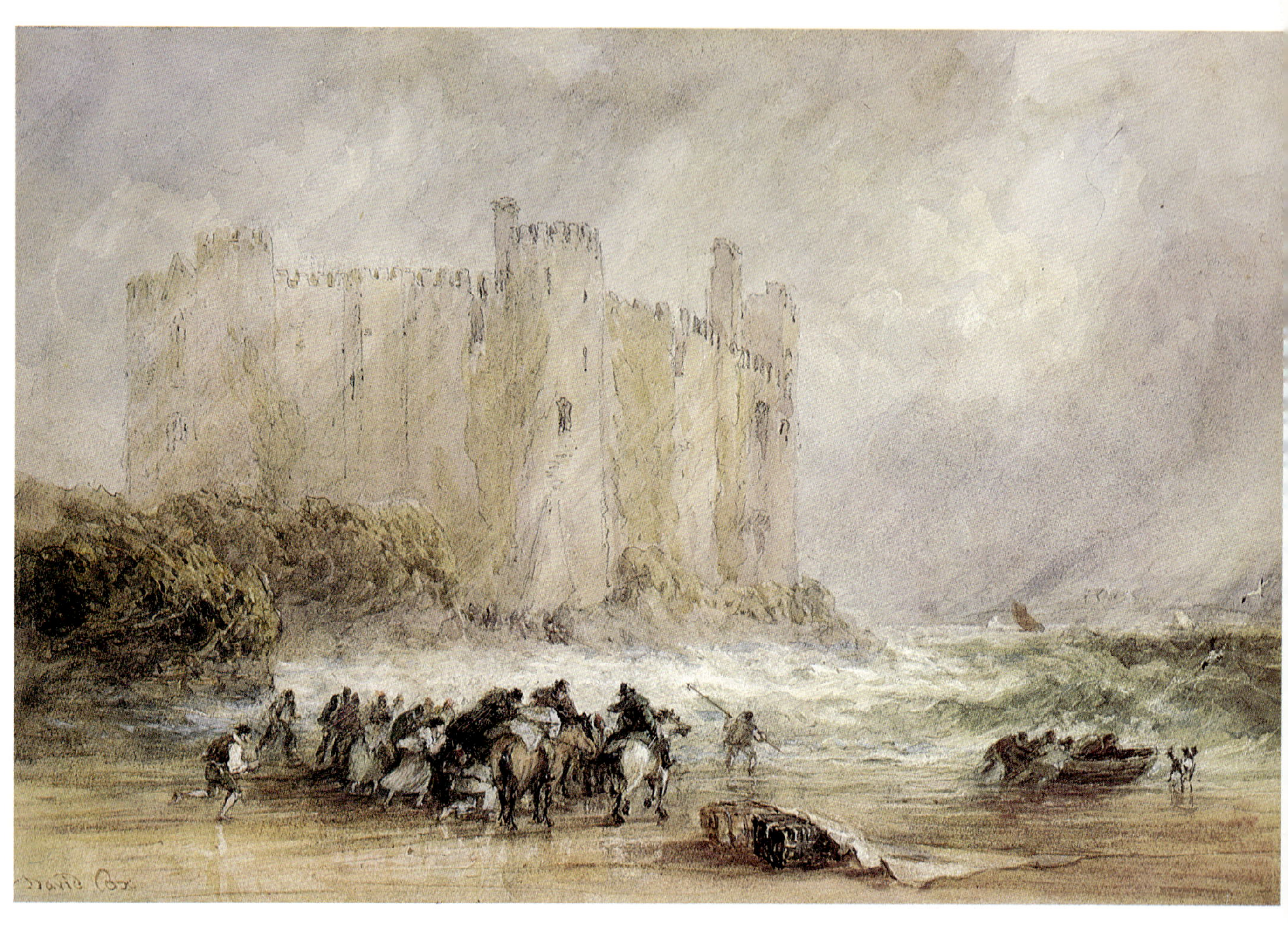

10. *Laugharne Castle, Carmarthenshire* (cat. no. 43)

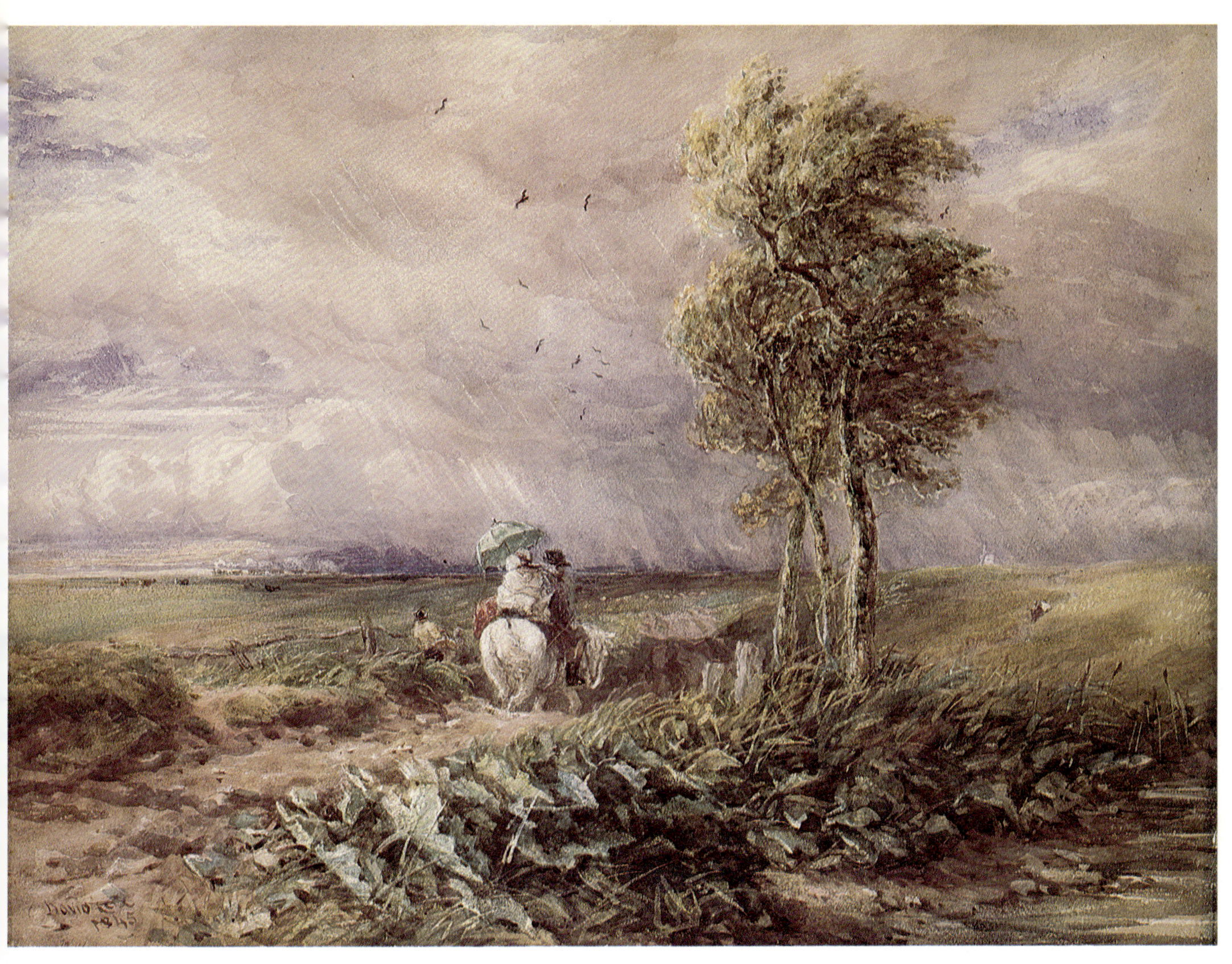

11. *Sun, Wind and Rain* (cat. no. 75)

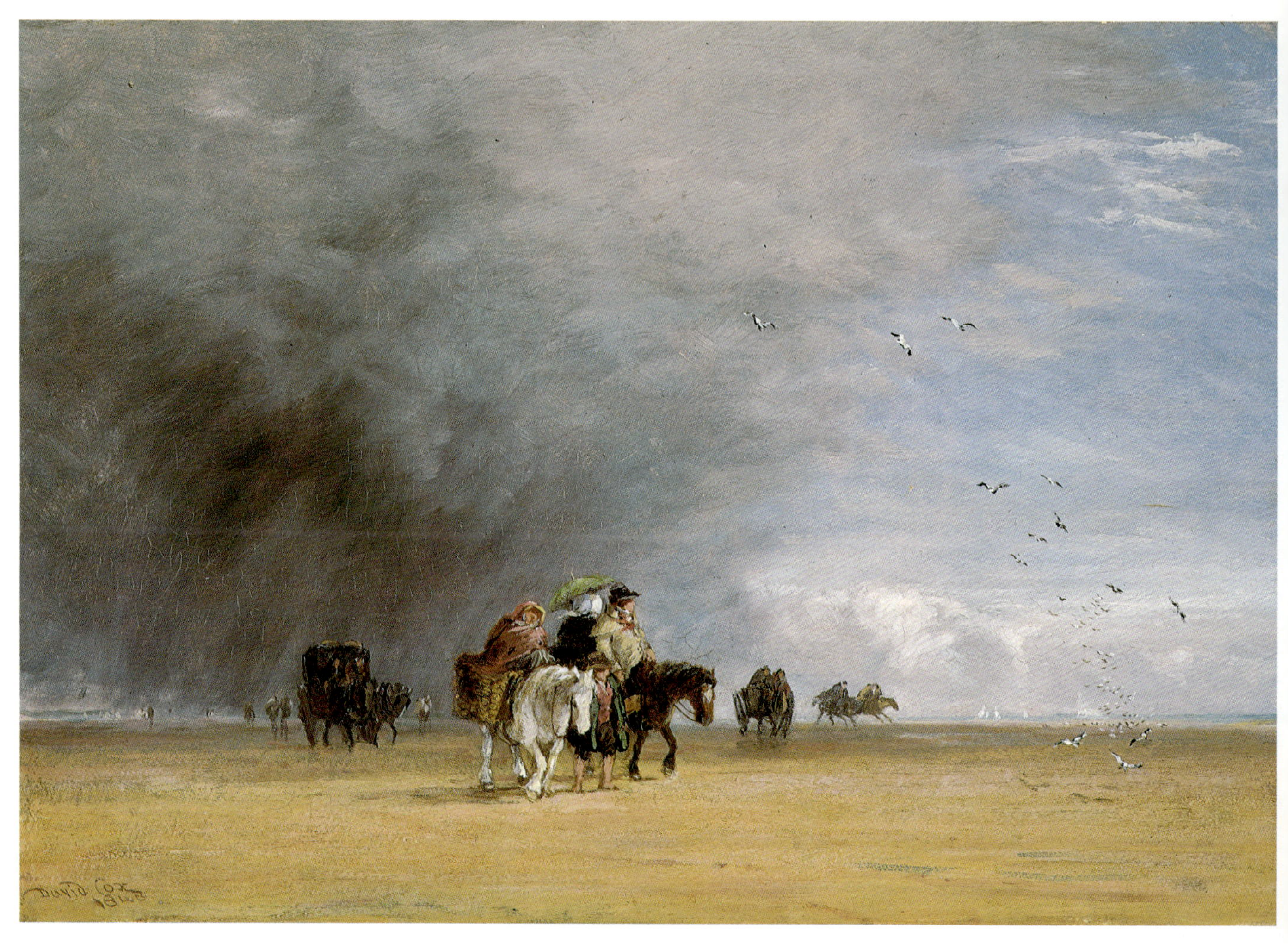

12. *Crossing the Sands* (cat. no. 87)

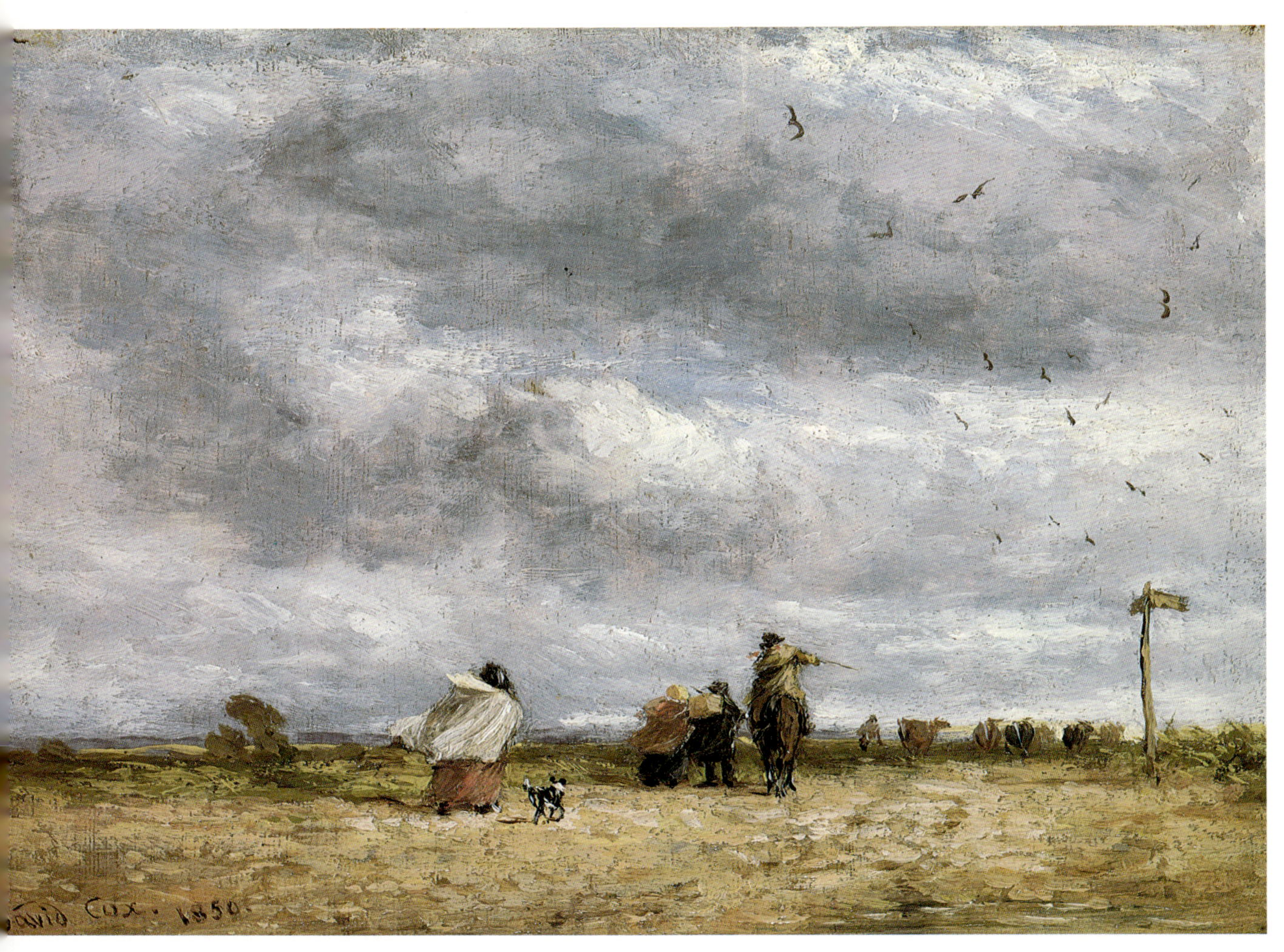

The Cross Roads (cat. no. 91)

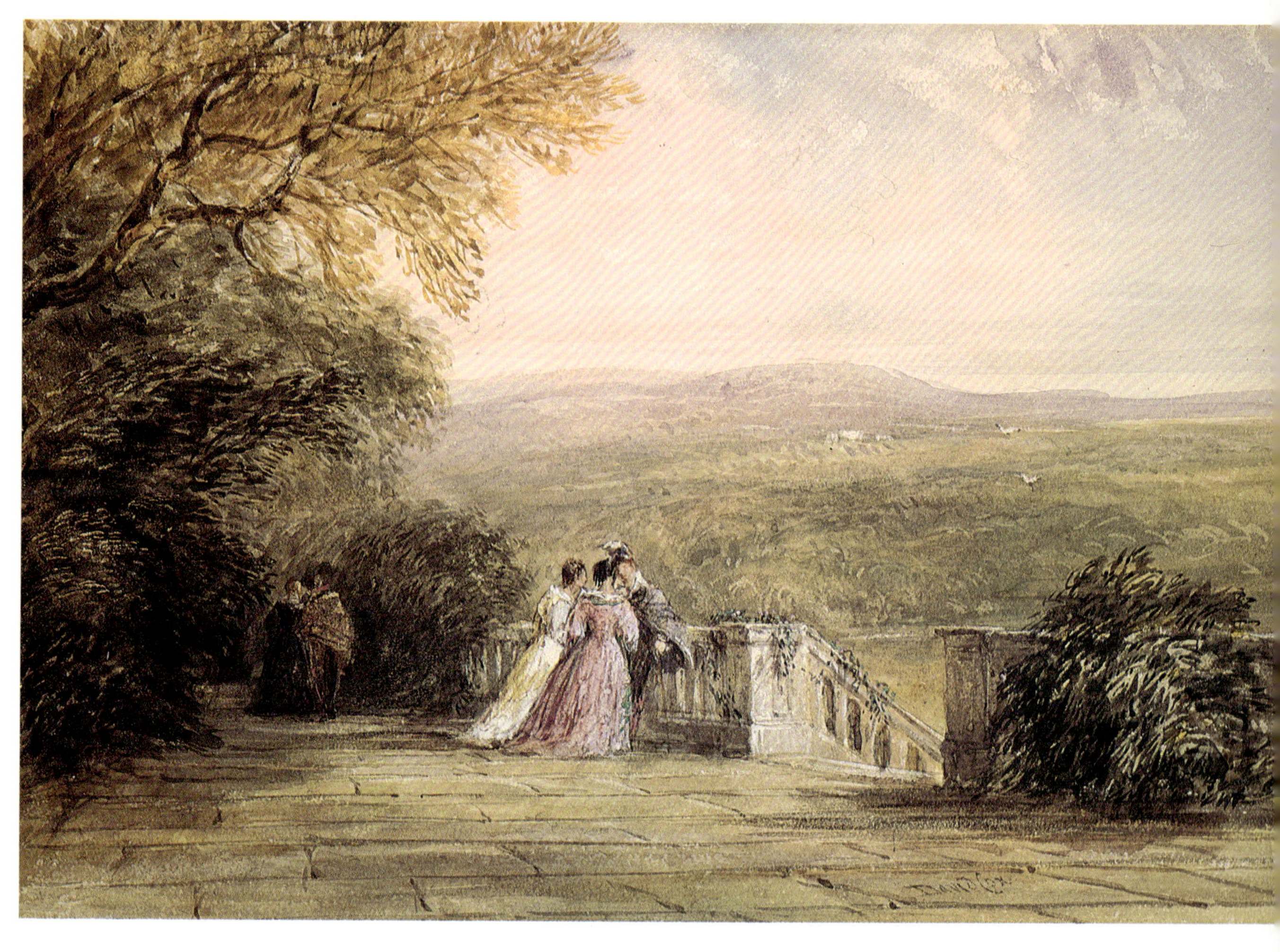

14. Haddon Hall: *The Terrace, with Figures* (cat. no. 109)

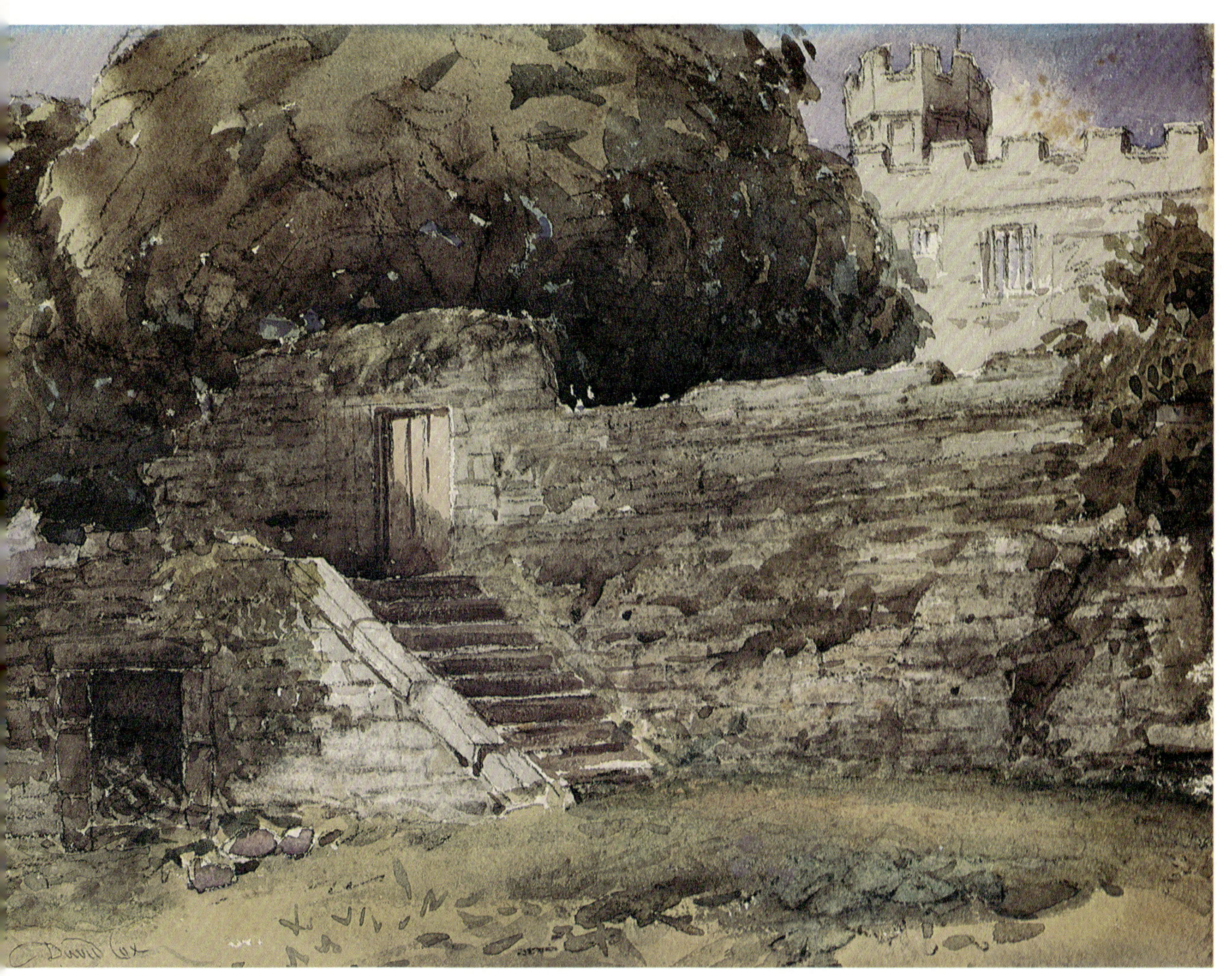

Haddon Hall: *The River Steps* (cat. no. 110)

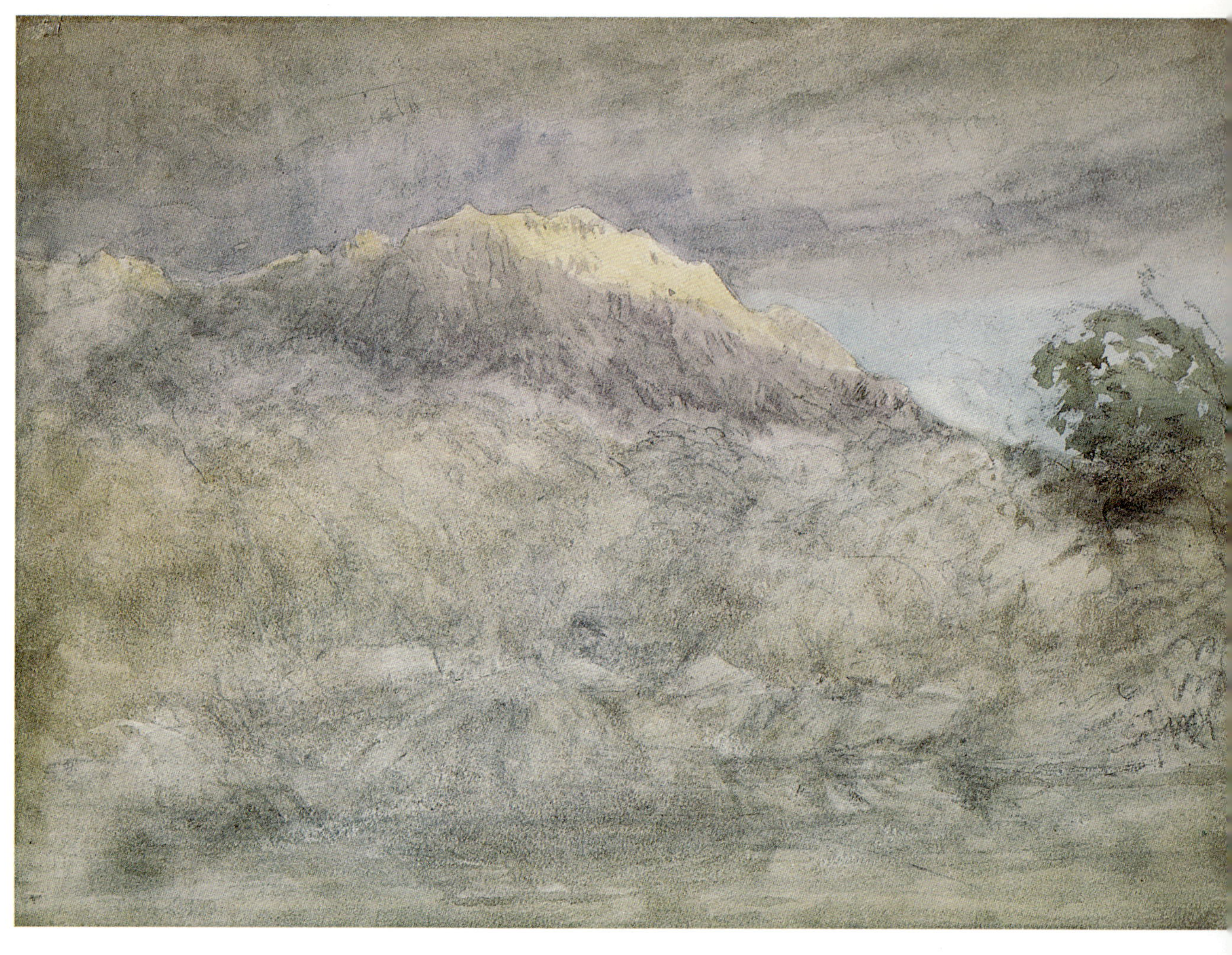

16. *An Impression: The Crest of a Mountain* (cat. no. 96)

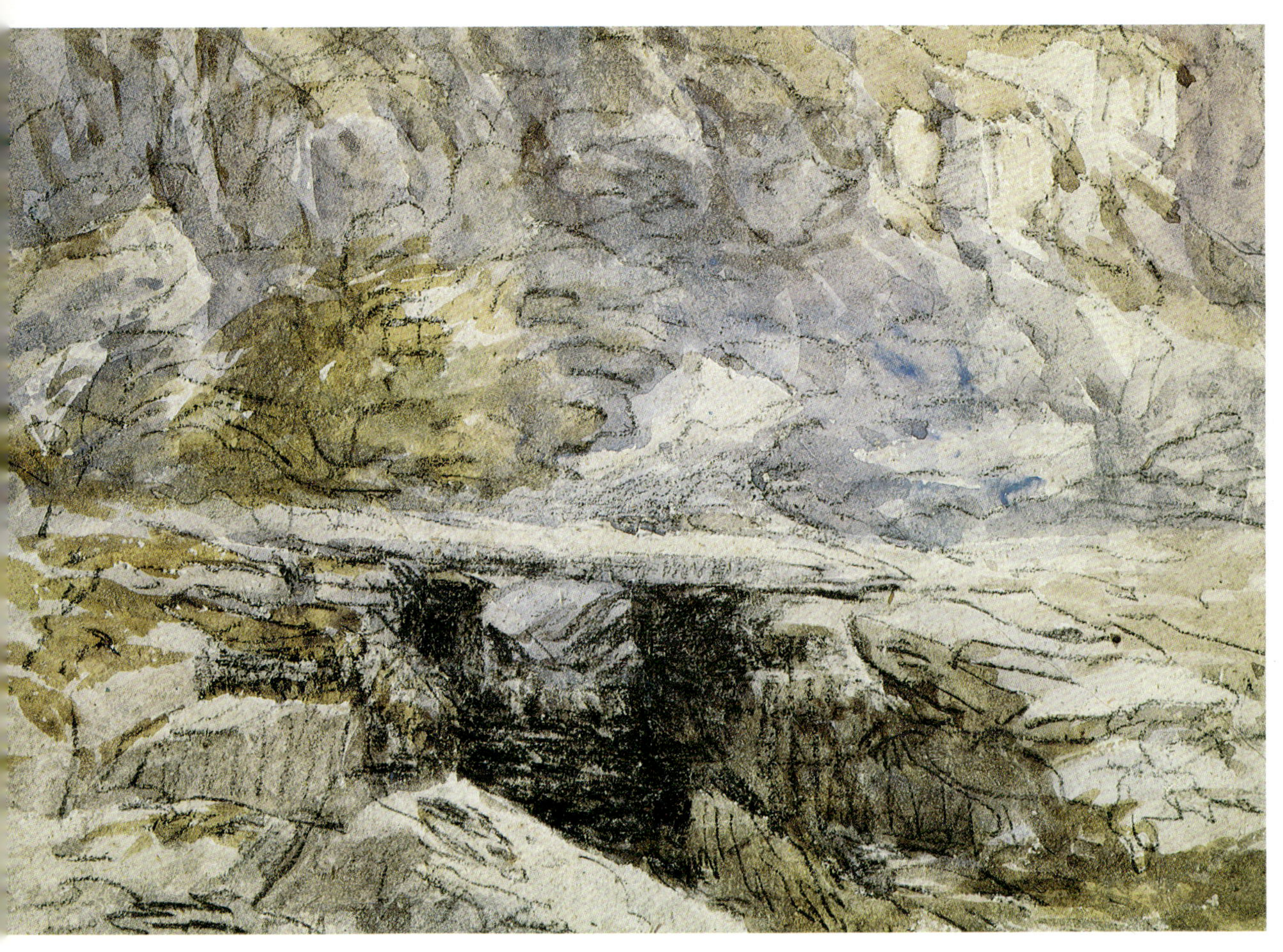

17. *Stone Bridge, Wales* (cat. no. 119)

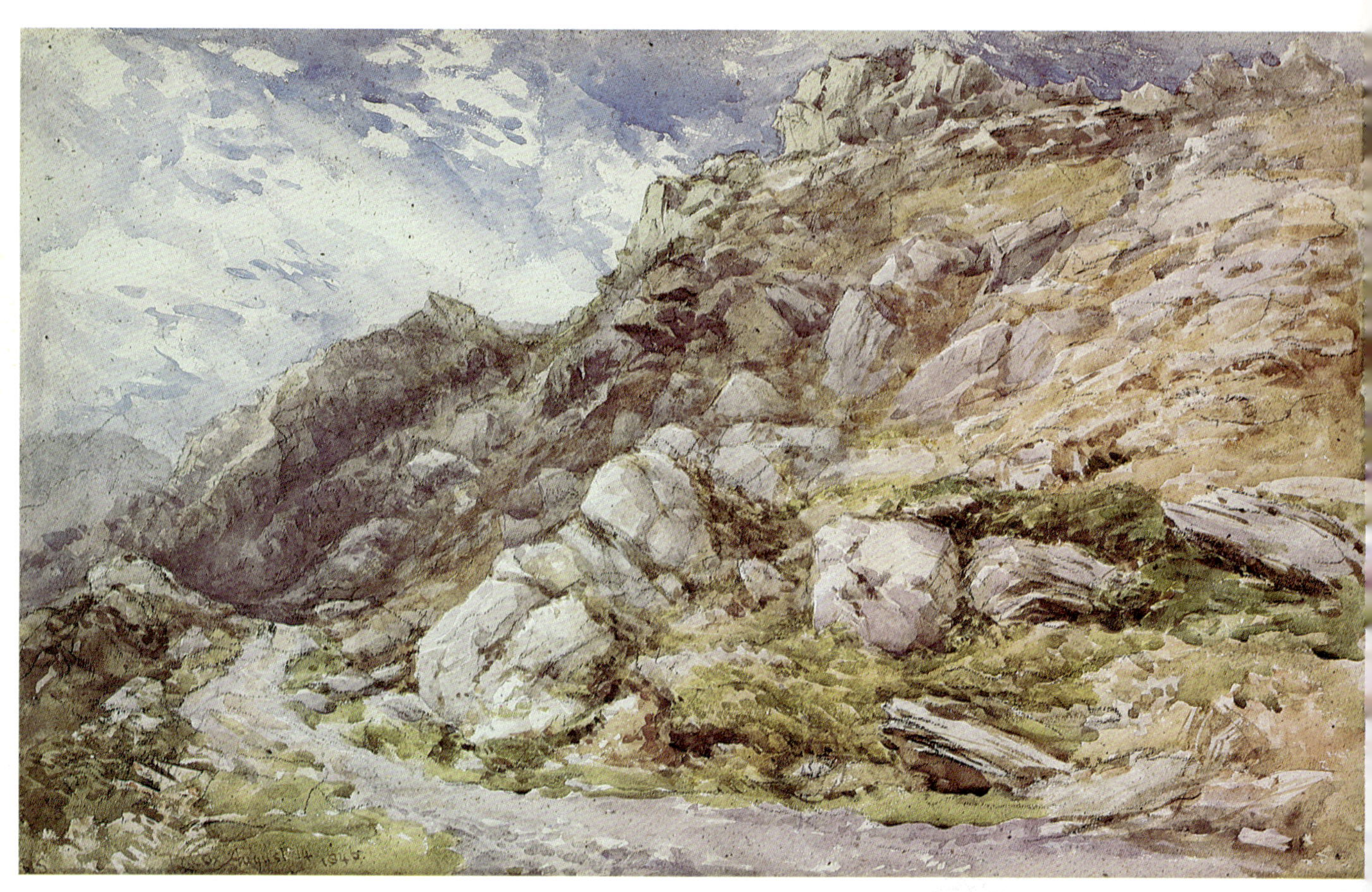

18. *View near Bettws-y-Coed* (cat. no. 123)

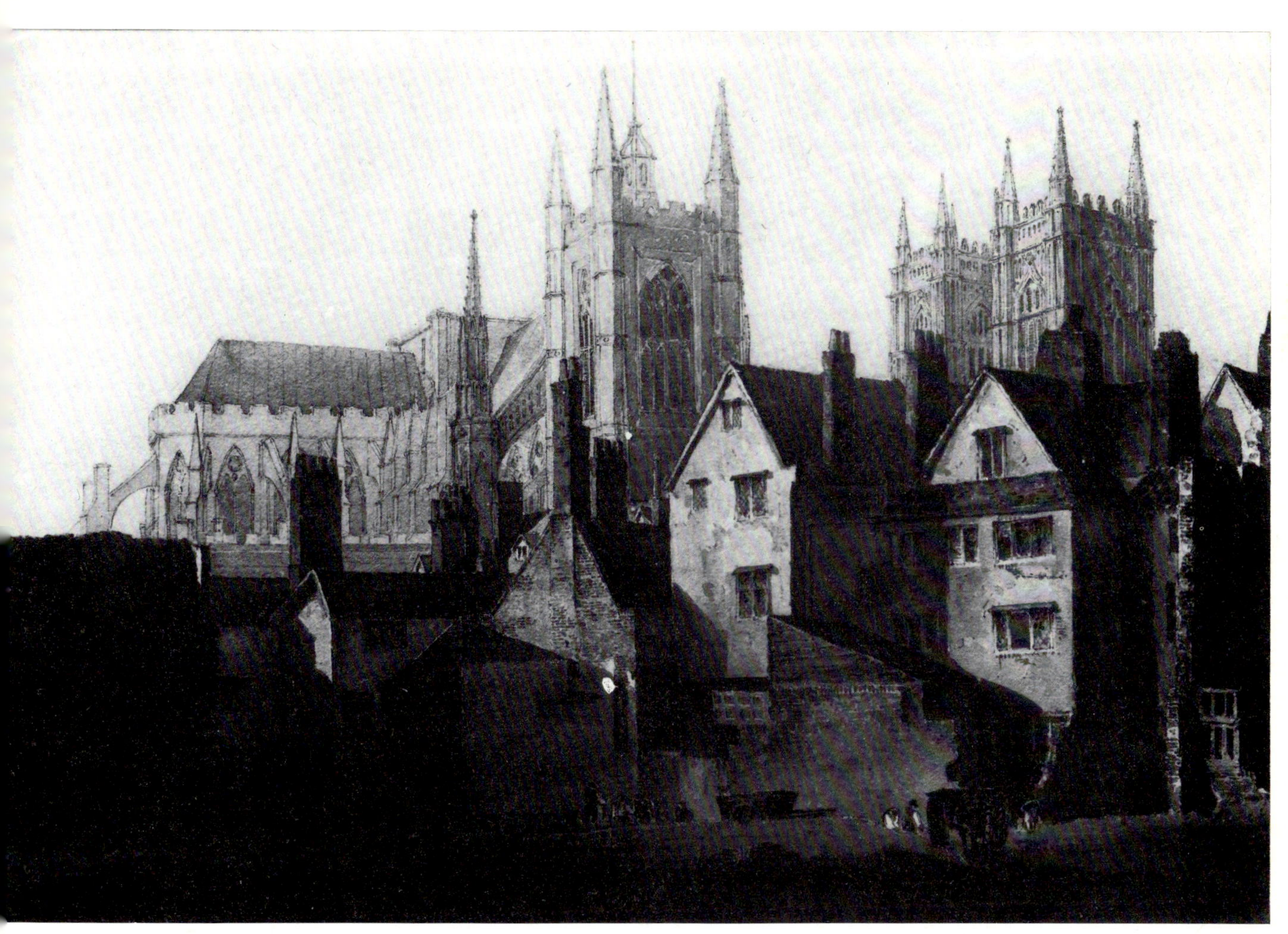

Old Westminster 1811 (cat. no. 9)

as models for copying and teaching purposes. Their apparent simplicity, appropriate to the kind of illustration Cox himself was to provide in his early drawing-books, belies a great subtlety of touch. Not surprisingly, a stylistic comparison may be made with the Thames-side subjects of the Varley circle, Havell (who published *A Series of Picturesque Views of the River Thames* in 1811) and de Wint.

9. Old Westminster 1811

see p. 49

Watercolour, with stopping-out, over pencil 33 × 45.5 (13 × 17⅞).
PROV: Palser Gallery 1929; bequeathed by John Wigham Richardson (JWR 57).
EXH: *Two Centuries of British Water Colour Painting*, Newcastle 1962 (25).
LIT: *British Water-Colours in the Laing Art Gallery*, 1976, pl. 26.
Laing Art Gallery, Newcastle-upon-Tyne

Signed and dated May 1811 on the reverse, this ambitious watercolour is an expanded version of no. 1, and has the appearance of an exhibition piece. It may conceivably have been intended as an exhibit for the Associated Artists in Water Colours, the ill-fated society of which Cox was briefly President in 1810. The V & A has an almost identical view ascribed to John Gendall, and there is yet another in private hands; neither appears to have quite the same grandeur as this work. A large watercolour of *Westminster Hall and Abbey* (RA 1818) by Gendall at Yale may indicate that this artist, who was employed as a lithographer at Ackermann's studio from 1811, chose or was commissioned to make copies of Cox's design.

10. Fishing Boats, Hastings

Oil on panel 14.6 × 22.2 (5¾ × 8¾).
PROV: David Cox junior; bequeathed by Joseph H. Nettlefold 1882 (2486'85).
EXH: BMAG 1890 (72); Swansea 1953 (82); BMAG 1959 (8).
LIT: Roe 1924, p. 93; Cox, p. 39; BMAG Oils, p. 34.
Birmingham Museums and Art Gallery

11. All Saints' Church, Hastings

Oil on panel 14.6 × 22.2 (5¾ × 8¾).
PROV: David Cox junior; bequeathed by Joseph H. Nettlefold 1882 (2509'85).
EXH: BMAG 1890 (74, incorrectly as *A Herefordshire Village Church*); BMAG 1959 (10); *Decade* 1969–70 (16, repr.); *Painting from Nature* 1981 (67).
LIT: Roe 1924, p. 93; Cox, p. 39, repr. colour pl. I; BMAG Oils, p. 35.
Birmingham Museums and Art Gallery

Solly (pp. 25–6) records that Cox took his wife and son to Hastings in the spring of 1812, where their lodgings were close to where William Havell was then staying. 'Early and late they pursued their enjoyment, and Cox used to boast that he painted a sunrise in June, and then awoke his friend by flinging pebbles at his bedroom window to show what he had done whilst the other slept.' Joseph Farington noted in 1808 that 'in consequence of Chrystall's drawings made last summer having been much admired . . . a Host of Artists are preparing to go to Hastings' (*The Farington Diary*, ed. J. Greig, Vol. V, 1925, p. 60). Joshua Cristall may not actually have 'discovered' Hastings as a sketching-ground, but was certainly soon followed by many leading artists, including J. J. Chalon, Linnell, Prout and Turner.

Cox found amongst the picturesque streets, busy fish markets and beaches ample subjects for individual works (a *Fish Market, Hastings* [OWCS 1816] was painted on commission from Lady Arden), and there are several Hastings scenes amongst the plates in the *Treatise*. One of these, a sepia study engraved in aquatint, (Studio 1922, pl. XXXVI) is clearly derived from no. 11. This little group of oil sketches from nature (a second view of All Saints is in the Birmingham collection, a monochrome beach scene at the Fitzwilliam Museum, Cambridge) is not only an extraordinary and unique experiment for Cox, but is outstanding even in the wider context of English painting of this date. In their simple but vivid depictions of the English scene, with such deftly-handled details as the passage of sunlight through a boat's sail, they rightly take a place beside Constable's sparkling oil sketches, and have been described as 'surely some of the most brilliant examples of the genre in England' (*Decade*, p. 12).

2. The Drawing Master

For a discussion of Cox and his drawing books, see Richard Lockett's essay above. In this section are some possible pointers to Cox's practical method as a teacher, a selection from the many surviving preparatory drawings for illustrations to each of the drawing-books, and some miscellaneous studies, including figure drawings, which show the very wide scope of his art.

The textual matter of the drawing-books is prosaic, to say the least, and there can be no doubt that Cox was no theorist, but a teacher by example. His difficulty with the laws of perspective is recalled by the anecdote of his flinging a copy of Euclid at and through the lath-and-plaster wall of his Dulwich cottage, whilst Hall (p. 44) reports Cox as saying that 'many a time, when he has knocked at a pupil's door, to give a lesson, he has not had the faintest conception of what he should do as an example, but that, when he had taken his seat to begin, colours, paper, and pencils before him, an idea had suddenly flashed across his mind, of some effect previously seen, which, coupled with a well-remembered subject, he dashed upon the paper, the result surprising even himself.'

This intuitive approach was amply supported by the abilities as a draughtsman demonstrated in the exhibited studies of all the various 'effects' of nature – landscape, architecture, human and animal activity, still-life. Solly rightly commented on Cox's having educated *the eye and mind of the beholder.*

12. Studies in composition method *see p. 20*

Pencil on toned paper 24.8 × 30.8 (9¾ × 12¼).
PROV: not recorded (49/1948).
Dudley Art Gallery

This sheet of studies appears to demonstrate, through thumb-nail sketches, the simple tonal structure (from D[ark] to L[ight]) and method of composing basic watercolour subjects, and may therefore be a rare survival of a drawing made for demonstration during a lesson. The little compositions may be compared with Plate 2 ('Perspective subjects') of *A Series of Progressive Lessons*. The few letters and notes on this sheet and another in the same collection (51/1948) demonstrating methods of drawing foliage could be in the hand of either Cox or his son, who assisted his father in teaching.

13. 'Left at a Girls' School'

Watercolour over pencil 21.6 × 3.5 (8½ × 12⅜).
PROV: presented by J. Arthur Kenrick 1925 (333'25).
EXH: Swansea 1953 (18, as *Farm Buildings*).
Birmingham Museums and Art Gallery

The tantalising inscription, on the reverse of a former mount, suggests that this drawing was left for a pupil to copy (the signature, if genuine, must have been added for a later owner). Cox taught at Miss Croucher's school for girls in Hereford from 1815. There are many miscellaneous watercolours ascribed to Cox and said to be 'lessons' (e.g. in Birmingham and the V & A, from the J. R. Holliday collection), but without documentation such pieces can only be taken at face value. *A Lesson to a Pupil* in Wolverhampton Art Gallery, an exercise in four basic watercolour washes, is a more plausible candidate.

14. Sketchbook for students' use

Pencil, sepia and watercolour sketches by Cox(?), Cox junior and pupils(?) pasted into oblong sketchbook 20.5 × 26.6 (8¼ × 10½).
PROV: presented by the Association of Friends of the Art Gallery 1937 (384'37).
Birmingham Museums and Art Gallery

An ink inscription on the inside cover of the book reads: 'These studies are for Students use only; and must be kept intact in this book David Cox', probably in the hand of David Cox junior. It is a good indication, therefore, of the staple diet offered by the Cox drawing school in its later years. The examples shown are two monochrome drawings showing how a composition is built up first by washes and then with touches of darker tone and white bodycolour; two pages further on, there is a larger finished version of the subject, complete with scratched-out highlights.

15. Old Houses at Kenilworth

Indian ink wash 23.8 × 27.6 (9⅜ × 10⅞).
PROV: presented by subscribers 1907 (380'07).
EXH: BMAG 1959 (13).
LIT: Cox p. 50.
Birmingham Museums and Art Gallery

A study in the massing of shapes and tones to create an architectural 'effect', of the sort demonstrated by two similar drawings reproduced in aquatint in the *Treatise* (*Old Buildings, Hastings* and *Old Buildings, Lambeth*). There is a particularly appealing landscape subject of this type, *Pont Aberglaslyn*, of which there are versions in Cambridge, Oxford and Leeds.

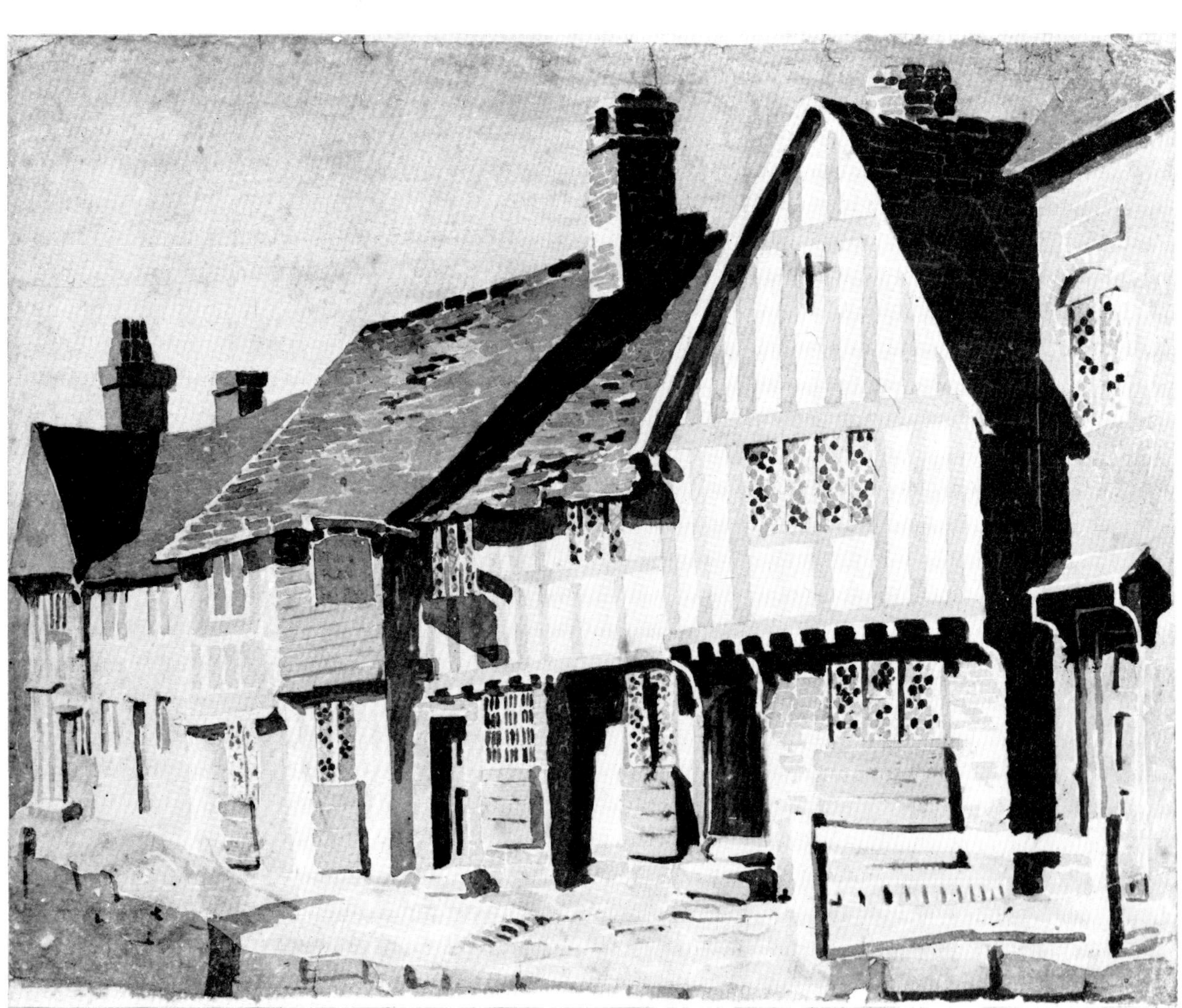

Old Houses at Kenilworth (cat. no. 15)

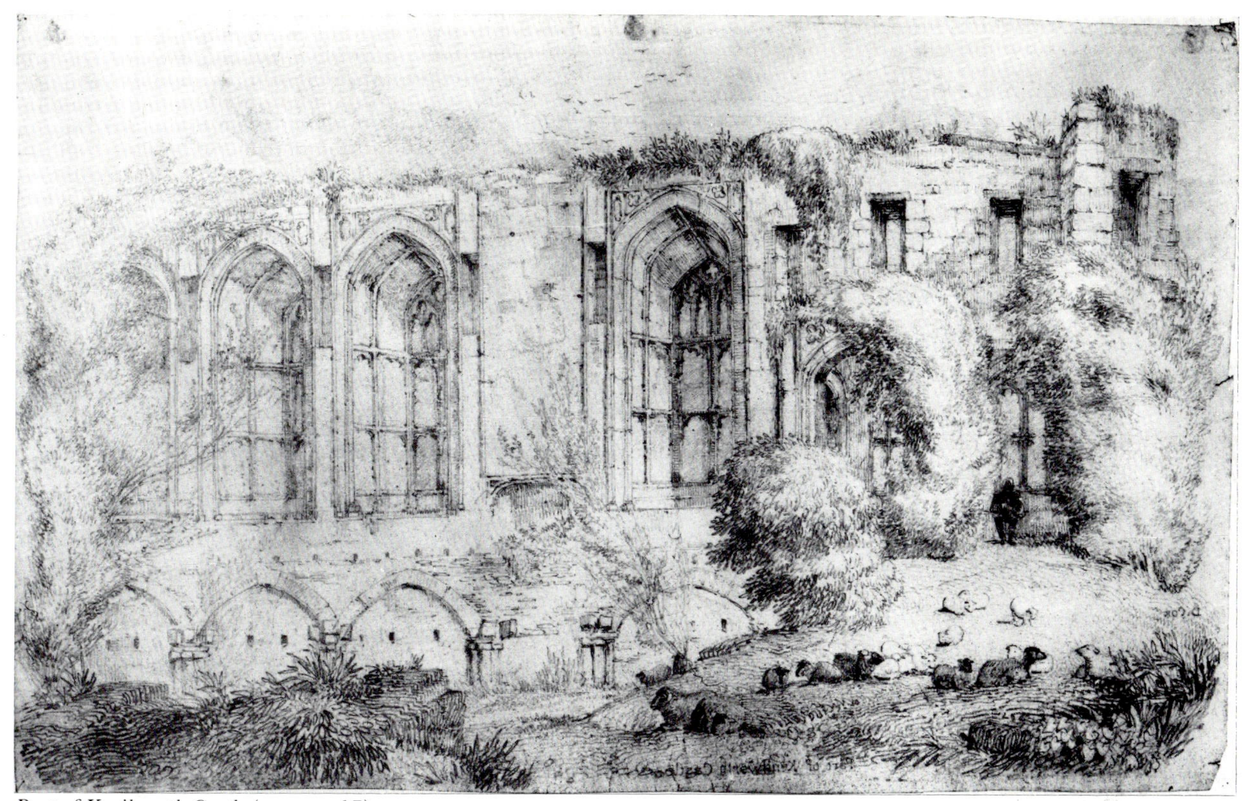

Part of Kenilworth Castle (cat. no. 17)

16. Aston Hall

Pencil and red chalk 23.8 × 39.1 (9³/₈ × 15³/₈).
PROV: bequeathed by John Henderson 1878 (1878-12-28-2).
LIT: Binyon p. 265 (no. 44).
The Trustees of the British Museum

Inscribed in reverse, for transfer to soft-ground etching, as Plate 20 of the *Treatise*; the plate is dated 1 June 1813. Aston Hall, the Holte family mansion of 1618–35, lies close to the centre of Birmingham, and has been a city museum since 1864; Cox's view shows the south-west corner, with the end window of the Long Gallery at the left.

17. Part of Kenilworth Castle

Pencil and red chalk 25.7 × 41.3 (10¹/₈ × 16¹/₄).
PROV: A Coulter; Wm. G. Shiell; presented 1954 (9/54-24).
LIT: *Dundee City Art Gallery Catalogue* 1973, p. 38.
Dundee City Art Gallery

Reproduced in soft-ground etching as Plate 22 of the *Treatise*. The romantic ruin of Kenilworth clearly held a strong attraction for Cox (see also nos. 3, 103) who made many drawings and watercolours of the medieval and Elizabethan Warwickshire stronghold. The Birmingham collection has several blue-paper drawings in the manner of no. 5, probably of 1810, which Cox may have used in preparing this plate.

18. Morning, Eton College

Brush and brown wash over pencil 22.1 × 34 (8³/₄ × 13³/₈).
PROV: bequeathed by J. R. Holliday 1927 (no. 1295).
EXH: *Paintings of the Thames Valley*, Reading Museum 1968 (47); *Beauty, Horror and Immensity*, Cambridge 1981 (166).
LIT: Bicknell (166, repr. pl. 91).
The Syndics of the Fitzwilliam Museum, Cambridge

Also known as *The Brocas, Eton*, the design appears as

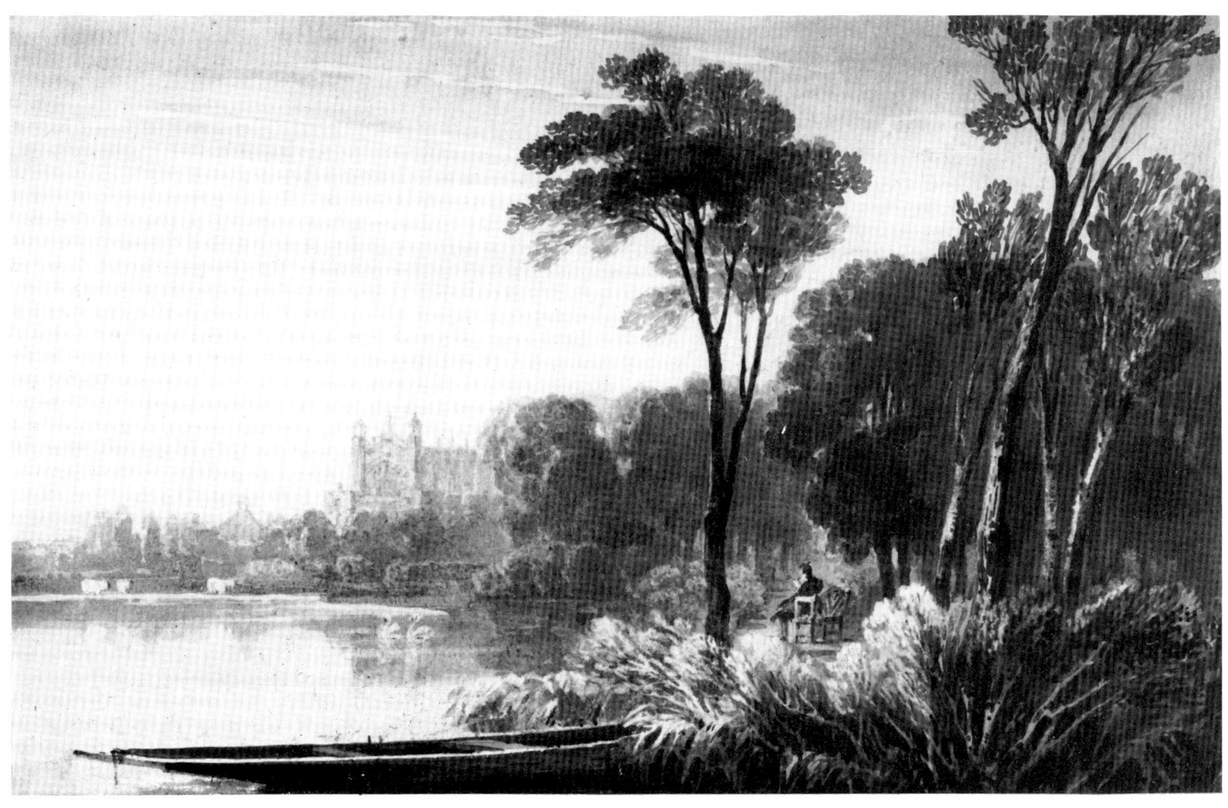

Morning, Eton College (cat. no. 18)

sepia Plate 15 of the *Treatise*, dated 1 Oct. 1813: a remarkably faithful rendering in aquatint by R. Reeve of a magically limpid drawing.

19. Birch

Pencil and red chalk 30.5 × 22.2 (12 × 8¾).
PROV and LIT: as no. 17 (9/54-3).
Dundee City Art Gallery

The design for Plate 15 of *Progressive Lessons on Landscape*, the series of twenty-four soft-ground etchings dated March 1816. As well as buildings and trees, there are several delightful animal groups in the series, reminiscent of the spirited etchings of cattle, sheep and horses published by Robert Hills in the 1800s to provide models of 'embellishment' for landscape paintings.

20. Old Windmill on Moseley Common

Pencil and red chalk 16.8 × 25.2 (6⅝ × 9⅞).
PROV: bequeathed by J. R. Holliday 1927 (686'27).
EXH: BMAG 1959 (16).
Birmingham Museums and Art Gallery

The drawing for Plate 30 of the last of Cox's drawing books, *The Young Artist's Companion*; signed and dated 1819 (in reverse). The plate is dated 1 May 1820.

21. Dot y Myllyn Fall, North Wales

Pencil and red chalk 16.2 × 25.1 (6⅜ × 9⅞).
PROV and LIT: as no. 17 (9/54-23).
Dundee City Art Gallery

Cox drew on old and new sketches for the dozens of illustrations required for his drawing books; in this case, trips to Wales in 1818 and 1819 probably provided the source material. This design, which shows preparatory pencil strokes in the bottom right-hand corner, is for Plate 36 of *The Young Artist's Companion*, dated 1 July 1820. It bears the semi-monogram with linked initials that Cox only used at this date.

22. Basket and Foxgloves

see p. 56

Watercolour 16.5 × 24.8 (6½ × 9¾).
PROV: bequeathed by J. R. Holliday 1927 (36′31).
EXH: BMAG 1959 (17).
LIT: Cox p. 51; Alice Coats, 'Burdocks boiled or in paint', *Country Life*, 29 October 1964, fig. 1.
Birmingham Museums and Art Gallery

Reproduced as one of the twelve hand-coloured aquatints in *The Young Artist's Companion* (entitled *Harvest Scene*; plate dated June 1823), but without the signature, 'D. Cox/Hereford' charmingly placed on the cider barrel.

23. Two plant studies

see p. 56

Watercolour (a) 19 × 14.5 (7½ × 5¾); (b) 14 × 16.9 (5½ × 6⅝).
PROV: bequeathed by J. R. Holliday 1927 (681-682'27).
EXH: BMAG 1959 (11).
Birmingham Museums and Art Gallery

Plant and foliage studies are found amongst the work of most landscape painters of a keen and inquiring mind, and in the work of English artists from Van Dyck onwards. They are naturally not uncommon with drawing-masters, including Varley and de Wint; two other good studies by Cox are in the Courtauld Institute Galleries. Cox liked flowers, and kept hollyhocks and roses, of which he was particularly fond, in his garden both in Hereford and Harborne.

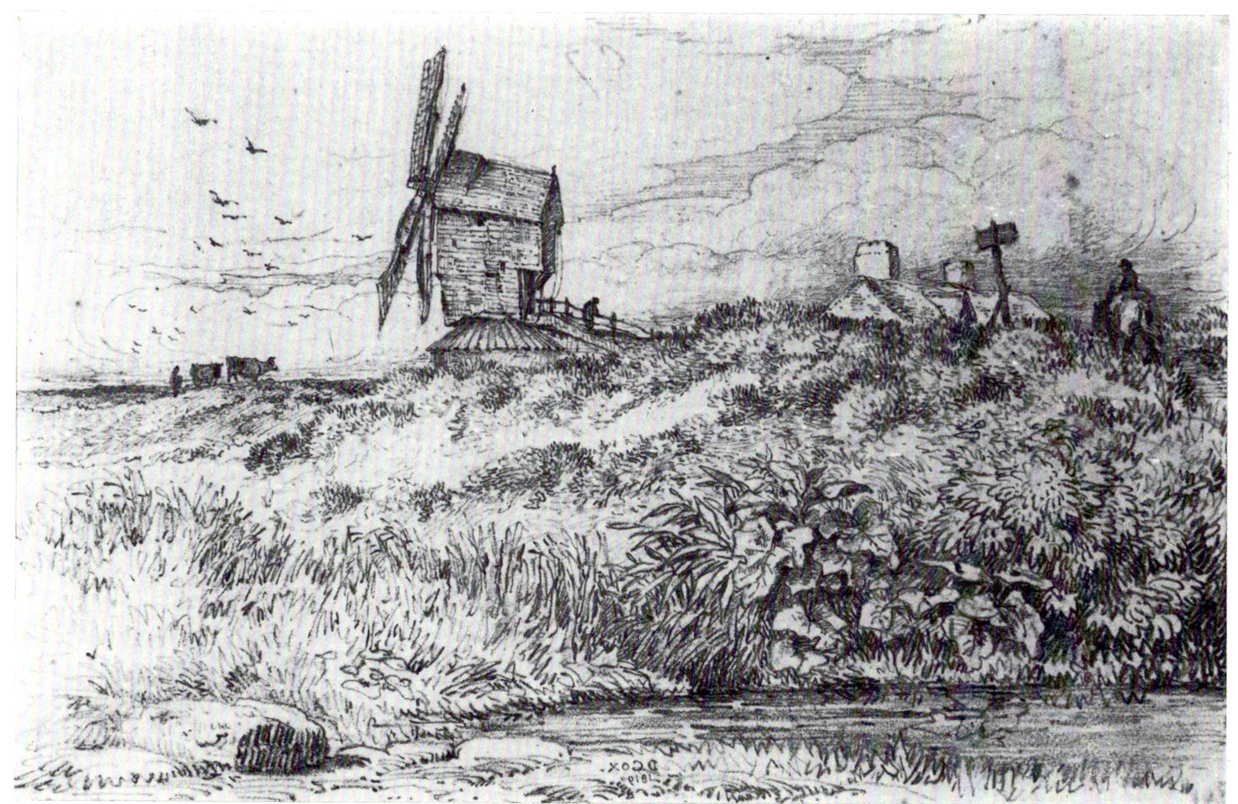

Old Windmill on Moseley Common (cat. no. 20)

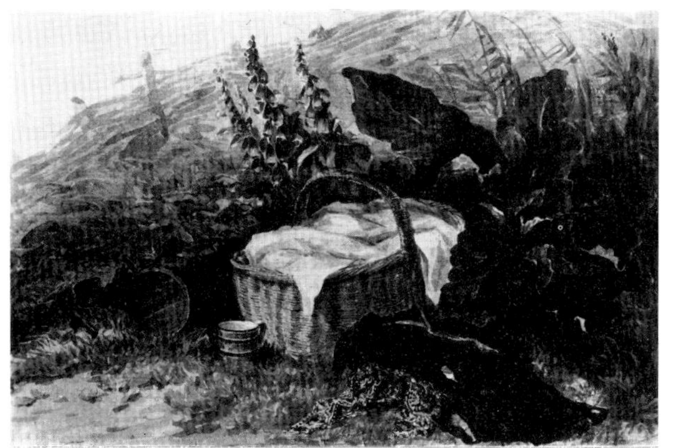

Basket and Foxgloves (cat. no. 22)

24. Still Life

Watercolour over black chalk 17.2 × 22.2 (6¾ × 8¾).
PROV: bequeathed by J. R. Holliday 1927 (4307).
The Trustees of the Tate Gallery

A similar still life, also of bottles and jugs on a shelf, appears as Plate 53 – another of the hand-coloured aquatints – in *The Young Artist's Companion* (plate dated 1 March 1821). Another, slighter, sketch was with Colnaghi's in 1972. For a clearly comparable still life by de Wint, see Scrase, no. 35 (collection Mr and Mrs Cyril Fry).

25. Study of a woman in a yellow skirt

Watercolour over pencil 23 × 12 (9 × 4¾).
PROV: found in collection, source unknown (P5′59).
Birmingham Museums and Art Gallery

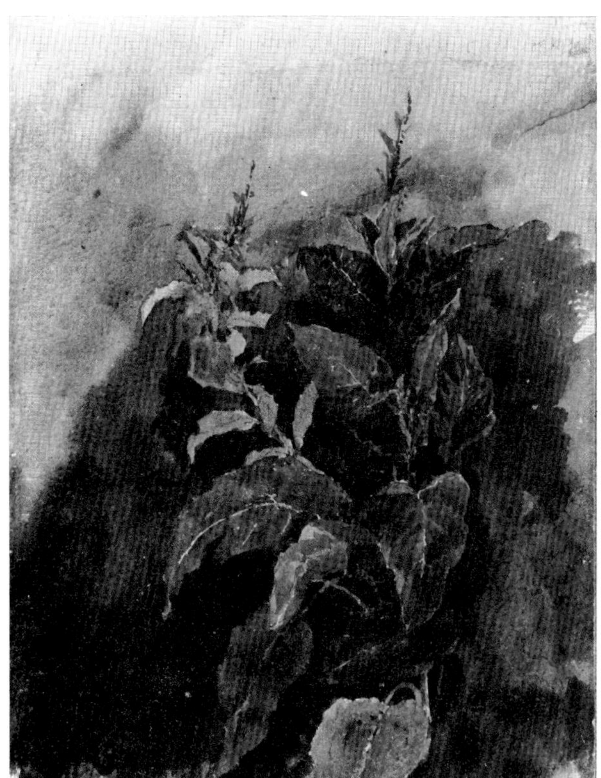

Plant study (cat. no. 23a)

26. The Christening

Pencil and watercolour 34 × 24.5 (13⅜ × 9⅝).
PROV: presented by Mr M. Brown (P55′70).
EXH: Bourges 1970 (15).
LIT: Cox, pl. 12.
Birmingham Museums and Art Gallery

Figure drawing, which Cox himself had never been taught, would probably not have been included in Cox's lessons, but these two drawings are included here to show the wide variety of the artist's work. Whilst there are many surviving small sketchbook figure and costume studies, larger drawings are very scarce; Cox was evidently not confident in this sphere, and yet, as these two works show, he could achieve charming and elegant results when he chose.

The identity of the mother and child in *The Christening* is not known, but it might well be the *Mrs Roberts and Child* of a watercolour in Manchester City Art Gallery (their 1982 catalogue, no. 44). *A lady seated on a sofa* (Ashmolean Museum, Oxford), in a full black dress and ringlets, may also be the same model.

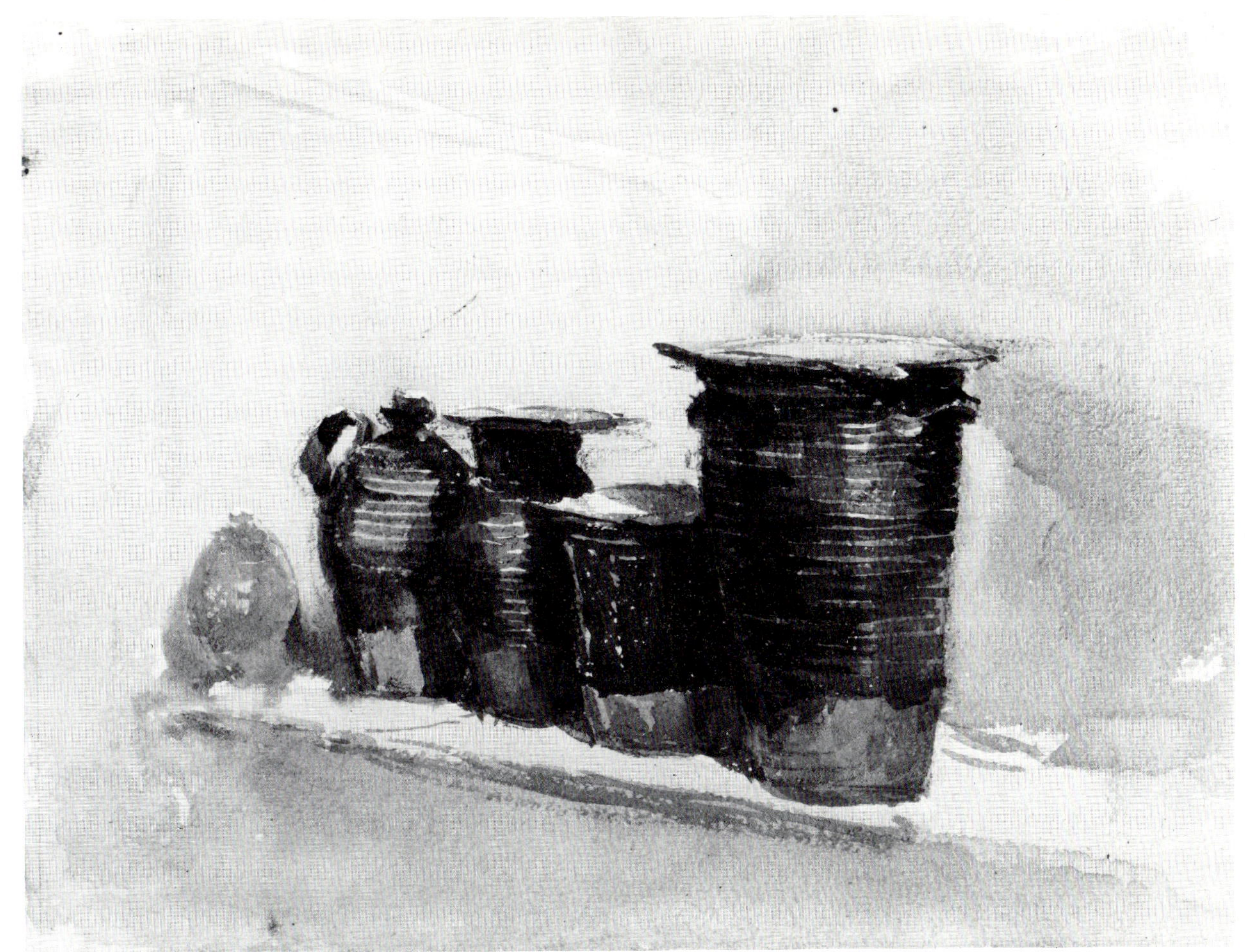

Still Life (cat. no. 24)

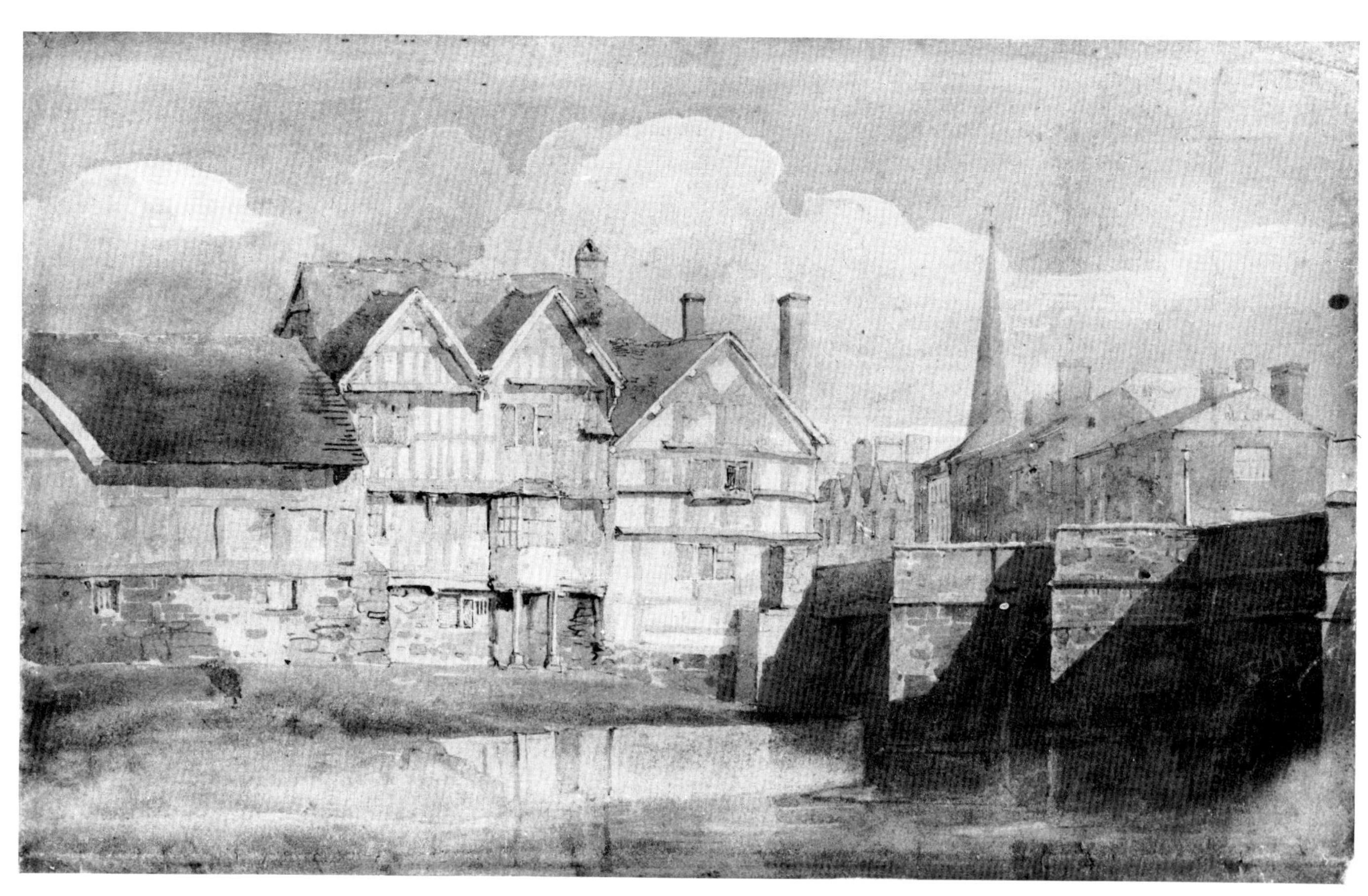

Old Houses, Hereford (cat. no. 28)

3. Hereford and London 1815–40

Cox's apparently sudden removal to Hereford in 1815, whilst it might also have been a means of resolving the unsettling drawing-mastership at Farnham Staff College, is not as strange as it might seem. The art market in London was in something of a depression; Cox must have felt the need for a change of surroundings after a decade in the capital, and the teaching position he saw advertised in The Times *and secured would have provided him with security, a quiet, pleasant new home town, and the opportunity to travel to the north and west of the country more easily.*

Watercolours of Hereford itself (nos. 27, 28) show his immediate attachment to the city, but others here of London (nos. 29–32) are reminders that it was easy enough for Cox to return to London periodically – to exhibit at the OWCS and see other shows and friends. The maturity of his style happily coincided with commissions for illustrative work, both before and after his eventual return to London in 1827. The market for art in London had picked up, and Cox was able to look to more ambitious work (nos. 47, 49), even if the bulk of his now very substantial output lay in quantities of small, readily saleable watercolours such as no. 48.

*His exhibits at the OWCS in 1837 are typical – only one sizeable work (*Infantry on the March*) unsold at thirty-five guineas, and a number of minor drawings at four or five guineas disposed of. One of these was to the critic John Ruskin, who therefore knew what he was talking about when he pinpointed the watercolourist's dilemma at about this time. 'Such pictures as artists themselves would wish to paint could not be executed under very high prices; and it must always be easier, in the present state of society, to find ten purchasers for ten-guinea sketches, than one purchaser for a hundred-guinea picture.' (Preface to the second edition of* Modern Painters; Works of John Ruskin, *ed. Cook and Wedderburn, III, 46 note).*

27. Butchers' Row, Hereford 1815 (col. pl. 5)

Watercolour and bodycolour over pencil 41.5 × 54 (16⅜ × 21¼).
PROV: bought from the artist by Charles Spozzi, Hereford; sold to Dr Cam, Hereford, 1865 (£57); Charles Anthony; W. J. Davies; Mr and Mrs S. H. Phillips; presented by Allan H. Bright, JP (2746).
EXH: Hereford 1926 (51); Hereford 1928 (13).
LIT: Adrian Bury, *The Hereford Art Gallery*, OWCS Club Vol. XXXIV, 1959, p. 16 and pl. IV.
Hereford City Museum and Art Gallery

This is quite the best of Cox's early topographical works, and a remarkably ambitious piece to have undertaken in his first year of residence in Hereford. Varley, who seems always to have gone before, drew two major Hereford views in 1802 (*St Peter's from Butchers' Row*) and 1803 (*High Town, from the East*), but Cox's deserves to be remembered as a quintessential evocation of the late Georgian country town. Careful examination will reveal painstaking details of technique – dabs of red over green for the flower pots, the very sparing use of bodycolour on the highlights (the barrel, the ladies' bonnets, the side of beef), a little scratching-out to bring up the ham on its hook at the extreme left – which combine to invest the whole scene with a lively atmosphere.

28. Old Houses, Hereford

Watercolour over pencil 29.2 × 45.5 (11½ × 17⅞).
PROV: presented by subscribers 1907 (331'07).
EXH: Swansea 1953 (14); BMAG 1959 (14).
LIT: Solly, p. 35; Roe 1924, pp. 72–3; Long pl. II; Cox p. 50, pl. 4.
Birmingham Museums and Art Gallery

Solly describes the typical early Hereford watercolours as being 'low in tone, but pleasing in composition and in the arrangement of light and shade.' Interestingly, the 1907 gift to Birmingham also includes *High Street, Hereford*, a pencil drawing on blue paper from the 1810 sketchbook (391'07).

29. George IV embarking for Scotland from Greenwich

Watercolour 69 × 107 (27⅛ × 42⅛).
PROV: J. A. Hunt; John Allnutt; sold Christie's 19 June 1863 (325), bt. Agnew (£210); Lord Brassey; sold Sotheby's 24 November 1948 (62), bt. Fine Art Society (£75); H. Rupert Turner.
EXH: OWCS 1823 (234); German Gallery 1859 (4); Laing Art Gallery, Newcastle-upon-Tyne, *Inaugural Exhibition* 1904 (350); *London and the Greater Painters*, Guildhall Art Gallery 1971 (46).
LIT: *Ackermann's Repository*, June 1823, p. 362; *Athenaeum*, 2 April 1859; *Art Journal*, May 1859, p. 145; Walker Art Gallery, *Early English Drawings and Watercolours* 1978 (24, pl. 21).
Walker Art Gallery, Liverpool

A remarkable work in any context, the *Art Journal* rightly described this watercolour as 'a kind of subject very rare from the hand of this artist: it is an elaborate composition, gorgeous in colour, and picturesquely treated'. *Ackermann's Repository*, in a rare contemporary review of Cox's work, further declared it to be 'pre-eminently good'. What prompted Cox to paint this subject is not known; perhaps his being in London on 10 August 1822, to see the historic beginnings of the first visit to Scotland by a Hanoverian monarch, stirred dormant theatrical memories. He may simply have recognised a good subject for next year's OWCS exhibition. George IV's expedition is best remembered for another artistic enterprise, Turner's series of watercolours of the visit (see Gerald Finley, *Turner and George the Fourth in Edinburgh, 1822*, 1982).

Cox must have made a number of preparatory sketches on the spot (one was shown at the Manning Gallery, 1963), as he did several years later to depict another Thames pageant, the opening of the new London Bridge on 1 August 1831 (studies in Yale and Fitzwilliam Museum, Cambridge). Solly (p. 67) describes how, on that occasion, a small boy who had watched the artist at work, asked to be given the drawing: 'Oh! my lad,' replied Cox, 'do you know it is worth five pounds?' By coincidence, the *George IV* was shown in the same summer season that saw Constable's *Opening of Waterloo Bridge* hung at the RA.

30. Buckingham House from the Green Park 1825

see p. 8

Watercolour with scratching-out 22.4 × 44 (8¾ × 17¼).
PROV: presented by J. Palmer Phillips 1911 (68'11).
EXH: Swansea 1953 (19); BMAG 1959 (19); Bourges 1970 (6); *London and the Greater Painters*, Guildhall Art Gallery 1971 (45).
LIT: Roe 1924, pp. 73–4; Roe 1946, pl. 17; Cox p. 50, colour pl. II.
Birmingham Museums and Art Gallery

In contrast to the preceding flamboyant exhibition watercolour, a neat, delicate little study of George III's Buckingham Palace when it was still largely the red-brick house built for the Duke of Buckingham in 1702–5 (with additions of the 1760s); the grandiose enlargements of Nash and then Blore commenced in the very year this view was taken.

31. Old Whitehall 1831

Watercolour over pencil 19.5 × 30.2 (7⅝ × 11⅞).
PROV: bequeathed by Richard Newsham 1883.
EXH: *Old London*, Whitechapel Art Gallery 1911; *Early British Watercolours*, Empire Loan Society, Guildhall Art Gallery 1950 (89); *Early British Watercolours*, Guildhall Art Gallery 1958 (89).
LIT: Hibbert, no. 103; *Illustrated London News*, 20 March 1948 (repr.).
Harris Museum and Art Gallery, Preston

Cox's love of street life and architecture has been overshadowed by his work in landscape, but some London scenes, such as this and the next, are extremely appealing. Bustling figures, here including Horse Guards against the setting of the Banqueting House, appear also in the illustrations to Radclyffe's *Warwickshire*, of much the same date (nos. 128–9).

32. Greenwich Hospital

Watercolour over pencil; small strip of paper added at bottom 29 × 38 (11⅜ × 15).
PROV: presented by J. Arthur Kenrick 1925 (299'25).
Birmingham Museums and Art Gallery

Views of Greenwich Hospital, which Cox may first have visited when watching George IV depart in 1822 (see no. 28), are amongst the largest in scale of the artist's architecturally-inclined compositions. He exhibited several at the OWCS between 1823 and 1831, and this example may perhaps be identified with *Part of Greenwich Hospital*, shown in 1831. Cox

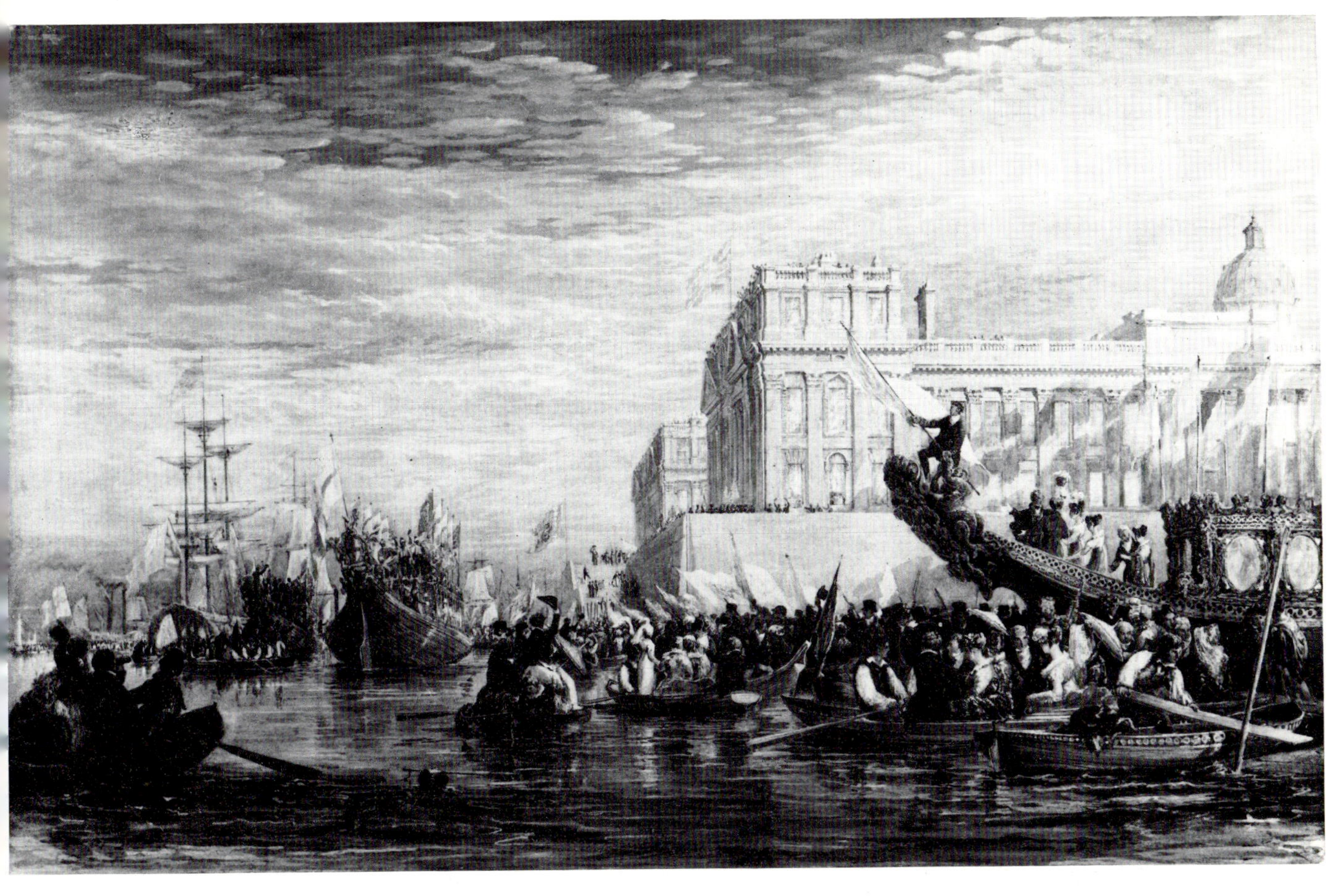

George IV embarking for Scotland from Greenwich (cat. no. 29)

chose quite dramatic viewpoints – the massive gateway here, the open colonnade in a watercolour at the Metropolitan Museum of Art, New York (exhibited in *Romantic Art in Britain*, Detroit and Philadelphia 1968, 135, repr.) – but still manages to humanise the scale with groups of indolent pensioners and the ever-present inquisitive mongrel dog.

33. The Old Exchange and Market Street, Manchester

Pencil and watercolour on three joined pieces of paper 18.3 × 43.7 (7¼ × 17⅛).
PROV: purchased 1905 (D.7.1905).
EXH: Swansea 1953 (30); BMAG 1959 (35).
LIT: Cox, p. 82 and pl. 18.
Whitworth Art Gallery, University of Manchester

Several cityscapes of both Liverpool and Manchester accrued from visits made by Cox to friends and relatives; his sister Mary Ann was the wife of a teacher of music in Manchester, living at 55 Spring Gardens in the 1830s, but moving out to Sale by 1840. The vigorous, impressionistic treatment of the crowded market stalls, and the carefully recorded inscriptions and colour notes may also be found in Cox's continental street scenes (nos. 58–9).

34. Handsworth Old Church 1828

Watercolour 43.8 × 63.5 (17⅝ × 25).
PROV: Mrs Rhodes; bequeathed by S. C. Turner 1948 (P. 23-1948).
EXH: Liverpool 1875 (91); BMAG 1959 (27).
LIT: Hardie 1967, pl. 185; Lambourne, p. 88.
Victoria and Albert Museum

Cox made small and large studies of several Birmingham churches, including St Martin's and St Philip's, and even one small oil of St Peter, Harborne (National Gallery of Ireland, Dublin).

35. Porch of St Philip's Church, Birmingham

Watercolour over traces of soft pencil; small strip of paper added at right side 28.5 × 23.7 (11¼ × 9⅜).
PROV: Sir John Jaffray; presented by John Feeney 1904 (557'04).
EXH: BMAG 1890 (198); BMAG 1959 (55); Lyon 1966 (28).
LIT: Solly, pp. 83–4, 279; Roe 1946, pl. 23; Cox, p. 84.
Birmingham Museums and Art Gallery

36. Porch of St Philip's Church, Birmingham

Watercolour 31.1 × 24.3 (12¼ × 9½).
PROV: Mrs S. A. Cope; bequeathed by Miss Florence Cope 1922 (168'22).
EXH: BMAG 1890 (239); BMAG 1959 (50).
Birmingham Museums and Art Gallery

Shown together here are two versions of the same subject: one a quick on-the-spot sketch, the other the sort of finished and peopled watercolour that might be worked up from such a study. Solly relates a story that in 1836, Cox and his friend Charles Birch were setting off from the Birmingham Society of Artists' rooms in Temple Street for some sketching in Dudley, when the artist 'saw before him such beautiful colour on the porch of St Philip's Church, that he stopped and said that he hoped his friend would excuse him, but that he really must make a study of it.' This is the sketch shown here, but its companion is stylistically somewhat earlier in date than 1836.

37. Interior of Norton Canes Church, Staffordshire

see p. 65

Watercolour 33.7 × 27 (13¼ × 10⅝).
PROV: bequeathed by J. R. Holliday 1927 (41'31).
EXH: BMAG 1959 (36).
Birmingham Museums and Art Gallery

Unusually, the drawing bears an inscription and precise date: March 15th 1831. To this pleasing exercise in a genre made almost his own by Cotman, may be added two similar church interiors – *Beckenham* (Tate Gallery) and *Maentwrog* (Hereford City Museum and Art Gallery). An interesting parallel work by Cox's long-standing contemporary Charles Barber is illustrated in Williams, pl. 270.

38. A Welsh Village 1828

see p. 64

Watercolour with stopping-out 15.2 × 21.9 (6 × 8⅝).
PROV: Presented by Mrs Duncan Best (RWS-C-69).
LIT: Solly, p. 96.
The Trustees of the Royal Society of Painters in Water-Colours

Signed and dated 1828, this scene is vividly described by Solly as a perfect example of how Cox 'introduced his incidents and figures, so naturally, and so appropriate to the place . . . Thus in a sketch of a village in North Wales, which I have lately seen, an

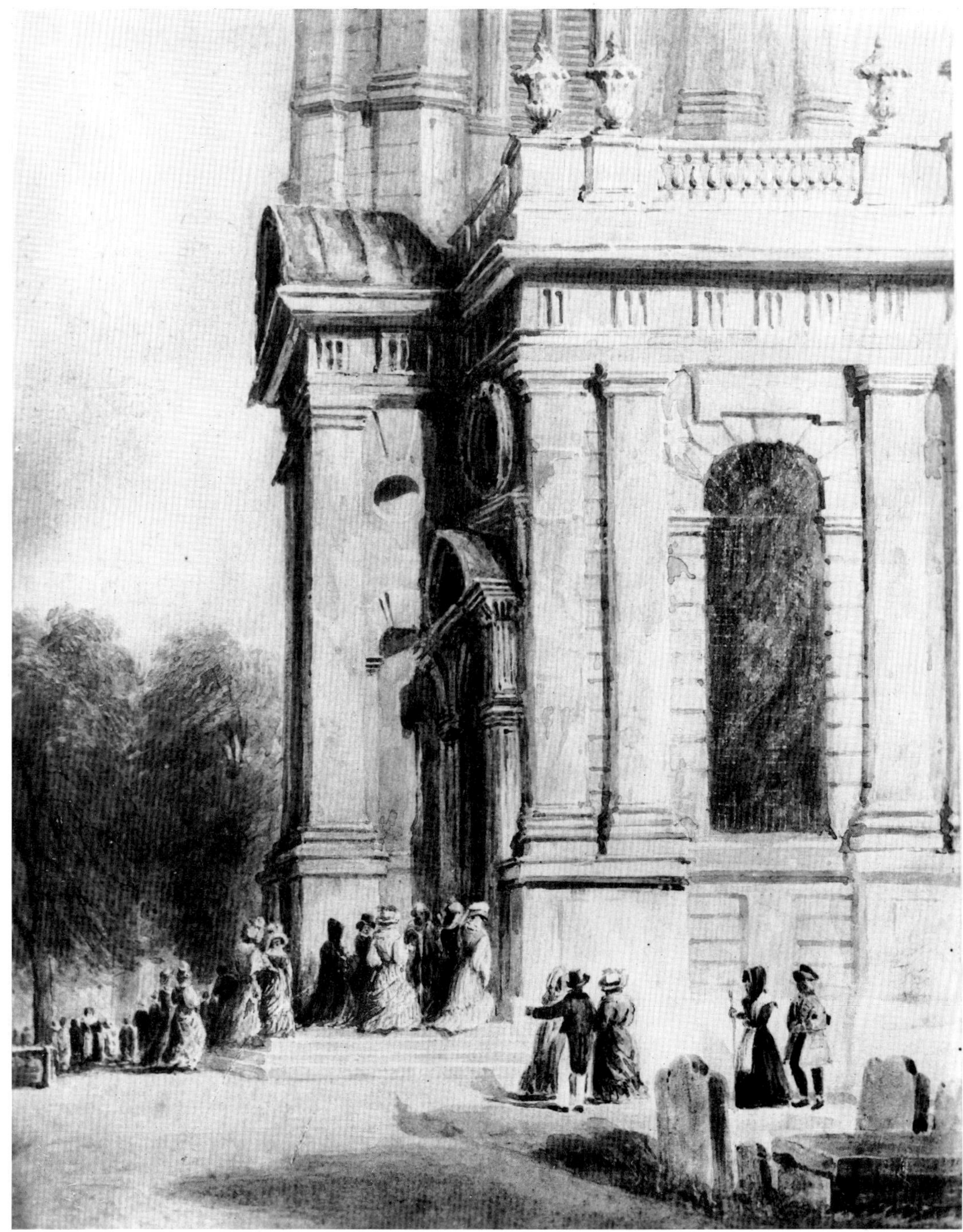

Porch of St. Philip's Church, Birmingham (cat. no. 36)

Italian organ-grinder is leading a bear, which is being saluted by the village curs, and gazed at by the wondering natives; the bear is true to Bruin's nature, and the whole is very natural and easy. It impresses you, too, as being a real scene.'

39. Valle Crucis Abbey, Llangollen *see p. 66*

Sepia wash over pencil, with scratching-out 25.7 × 34.8 (10⅛ × 13⅝).
PROV: bequeathed by J. R. Holliday 1927 (40'31).
EXH: Swansea 1953 (64).
Birmingham Museums and Art Gallery

A real tour de force in this most difficult of media. The translation of a favourite subject (one version being used as Plate XI of Roscoe's *North Wales*) into sepia allows a perfect view of the accumulation of small dabs, smudges and scratches on top of a gentle gradation of tonal washes, that all go to make up the finished Cox watercolour.

40. Rhaiadr Cwm, North Wales

Watercolour over pencil with scratching-out 70.4 × 28.5 (8 × 11½).
PROV: bequeathed by John Henderson, 1878 (1878-12-28-60).
EXH: Liverpool 1875 (271); BMAG 1959 (52).
LIT: Binyon, p. 262; Roe 1924, pp. 76–7; Cox, p. 71.
The Trustees of the British Museum

Engraved as Plate XLVIII of Roscoe's *North Wales*, 1836. The jewel-like watercolours for Roscoe's books and their translation by William Radclyffe mark the pinnacle of design and reproductive engraving in England, alongside the illustrative work of Turner and his engravers. Other artists, including

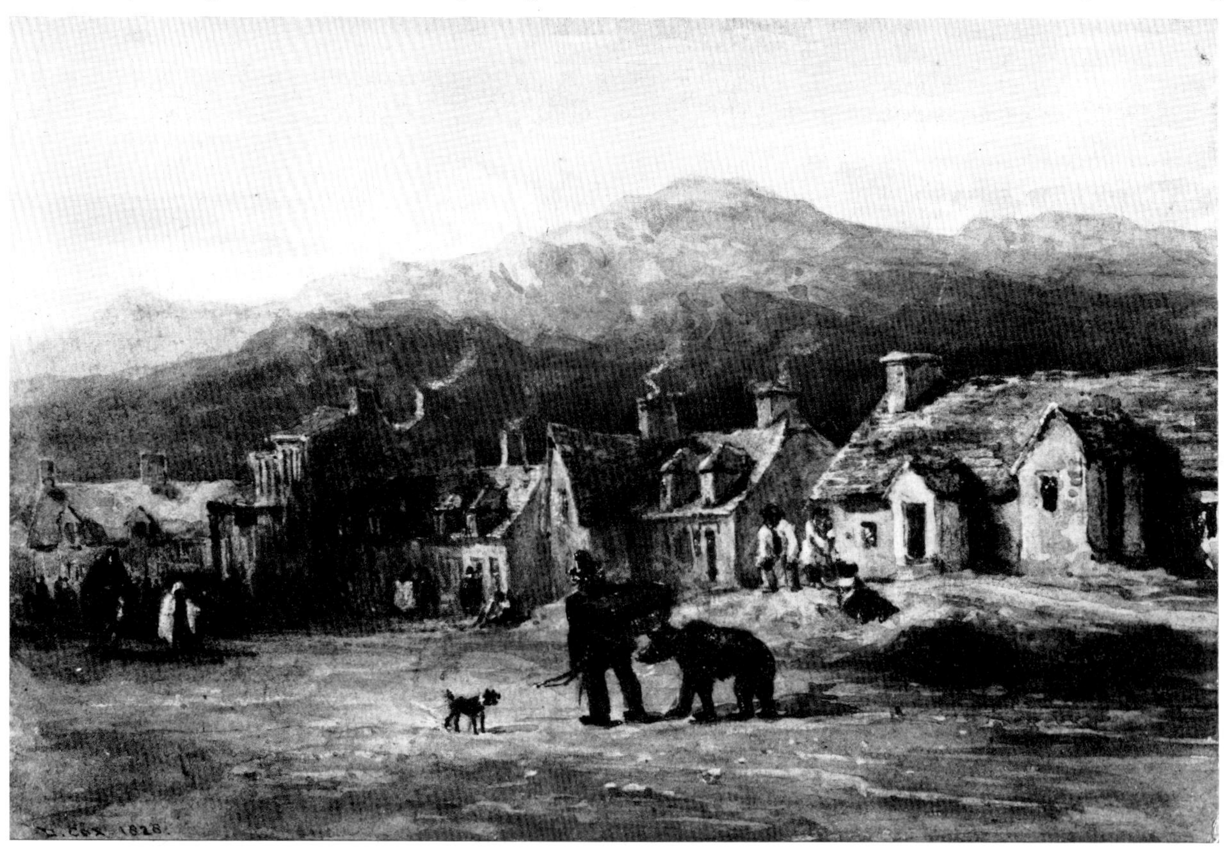

A Welsh Village (cat. no. 38)

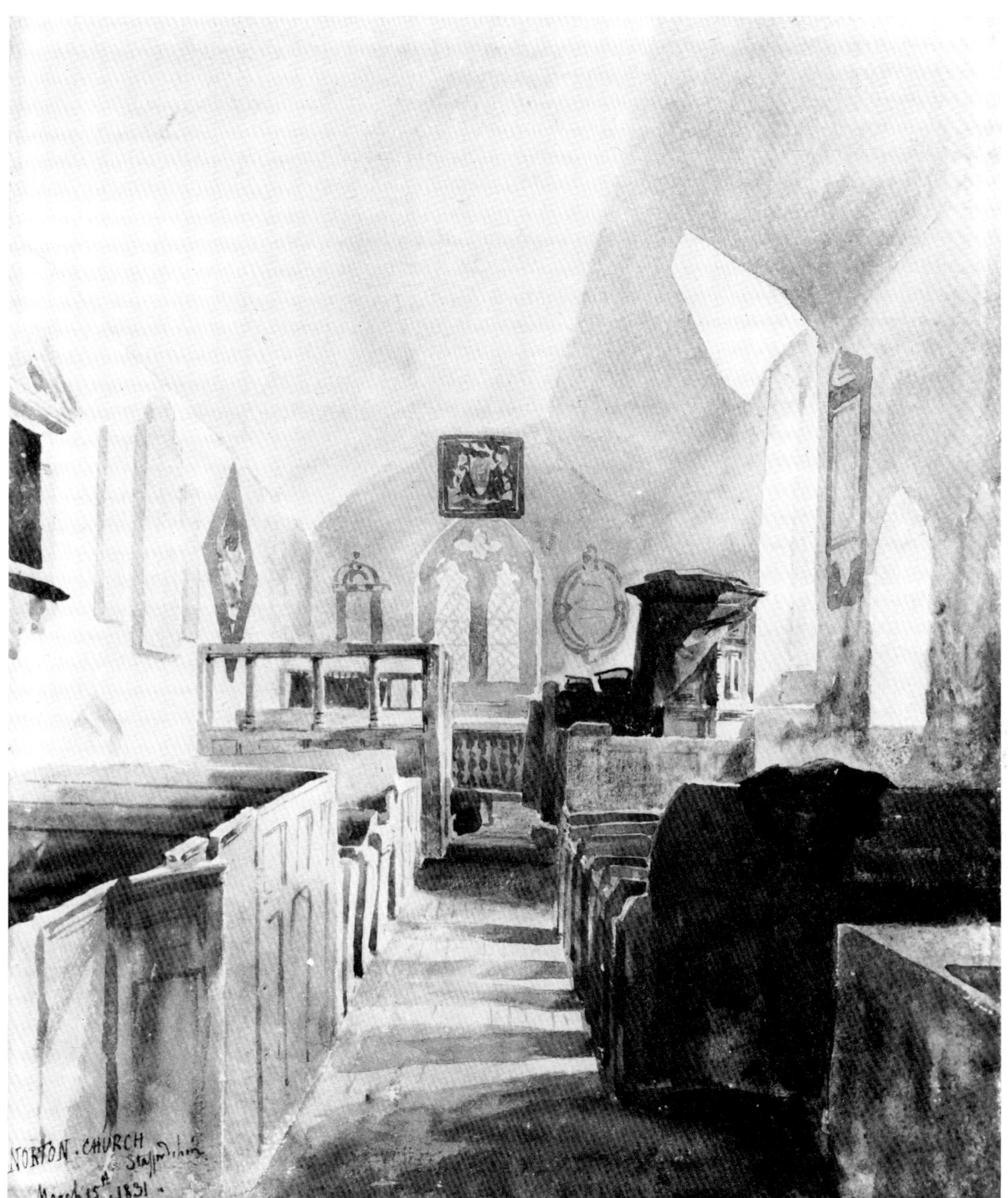

Interior of Norton Canes Church, Staffordshire (cat. no. 37)

Cattermole, Creswick and Copley Fielding, collaborated in the venture, but Cox supplied fully half the illustrations, at the very modest rate of four or five guineas each; he did, of course, visit Wales again in 1836 for the purpose of getting up new subjects.

The success of the work, however, was undeniable, and in the second of the volumes (*South Wales*, 1837) the publishers, Wrightson and Webb of Birmingham, paid their overdue tribute to the artist: 'It may not be amiss here to mention the obligations which the proprietors of this work are under to that highly-esteemed artist and faithful delineator of scenery, Mr David Cox, whose pencil has enriched and enhanced the value not only of this volume, but also of that recently published on the Northern part of the Principality.'

41. Vale of Festiniog, Merionethshire

Watercolour over pencil, with scratching-out 20.4 × 27.9 (8 × 10⅞).

PROV: bequeathed by Mrs Martha Combe (a former pupil of Cox) 1894.

The Visitors of the Ashmolean Museum, Oxford

Plate XLVII of *North Wales*. An even more Turneresque subject, the watercolour for the *Pass of*

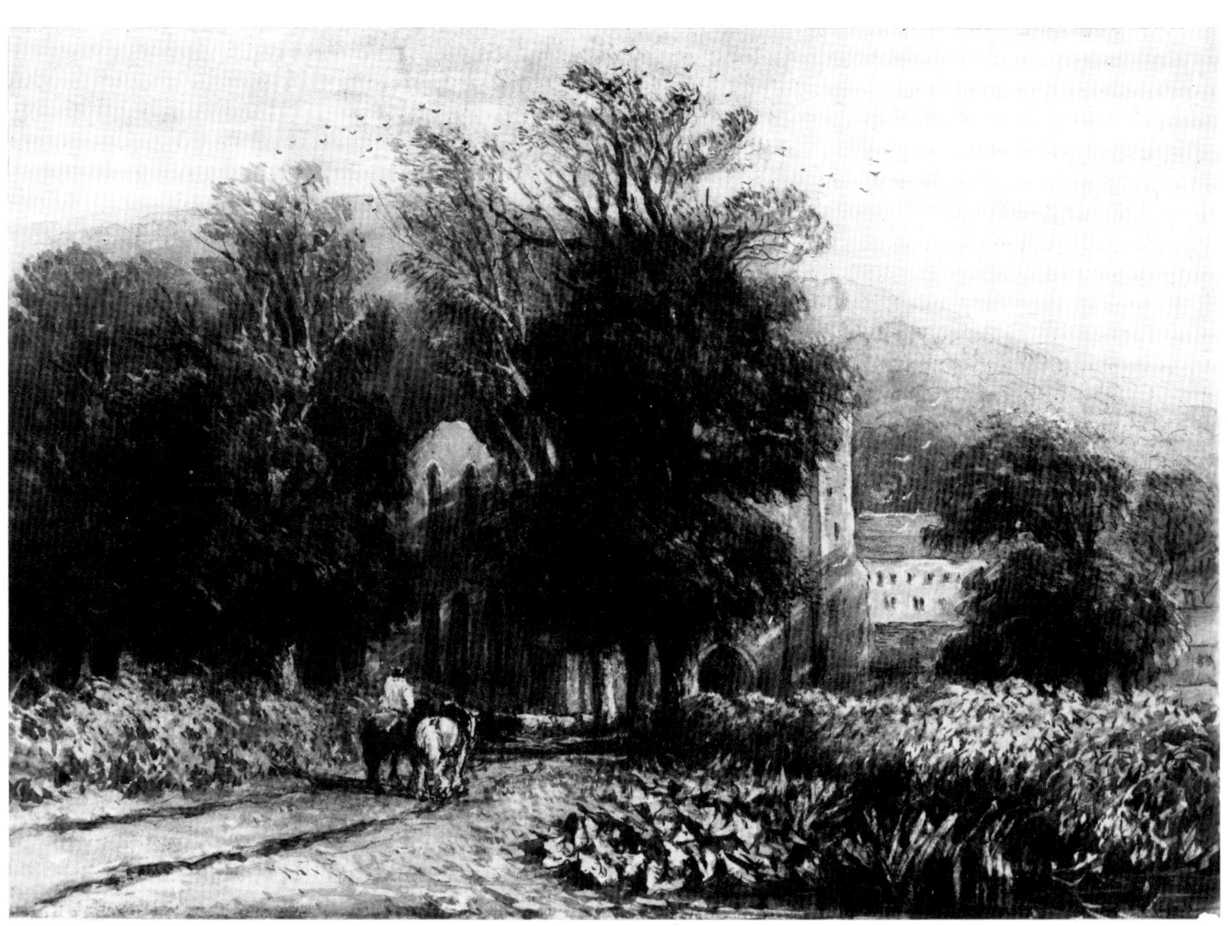

Valle Crucis Abbey (cat. no. 39)

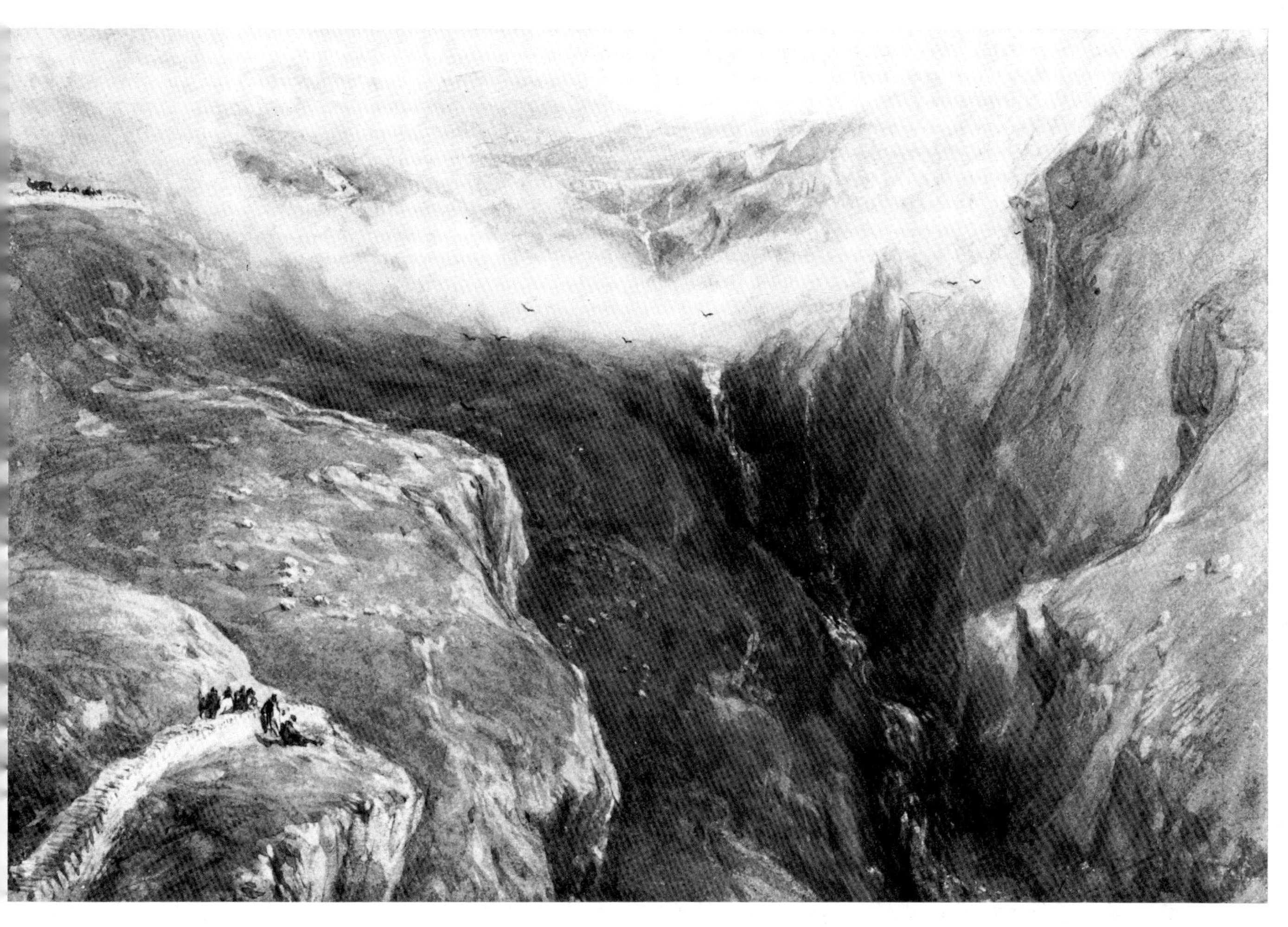

Rhaiadr Cwm, North Wales (cat. no. 40)

Llanberis frontispiece, is in the Whitworth Art Gallery, University of Manchester.

42. Hay on Wye

Watercolour, with scratching-out 21.2 × 31.3 (8⅜ × 12¼).
PROV: bequeathed by J. R. Holliday 1927 (678′27).
Birmingham Museums and Art Gallery

Similar to Plate XI of Roscoe's *South Wales*, 1837; the British Museum has a slightly larger version of this watercolour, a little broader in treatment (Sale bequest, 1915-3-13-6).

43. Laugharne Castle, Carmarthenshire

Watercolour and bodycolour over pencil, with scratching-out 20.9 × 30.5 (8⅛ × 12).
PROV: bequeathed by J. R. Holliday 1927 (39′31).
EXH: Swansea 1953 (26); *La Peinture Romantique Anglaise*, Paris 1972 (78, repr.).
Birmingham Museums and Art Gallery

Previously known only as *A Welsh Castle in a Storm*, this superb watercolour may now be identified, chiefly through its remarkable similarity to Turner's watercolour of the same subject (Andrew Wilton, *The Life and Work of J. M. W. Turner*, 1979, no. 848, repr.; Columbus Gallery of Fine Arts, Columbus, Ohio). In size, style and subject, the Cox fits into the group of Roscoe illustrations, but was not engraved. Turner's view was, however, engraved by J. Horsburgh for the *England and Wales* series in 1833, and the watercolour itself exhibited at the London galleries of Moon, Boys and Graves in the same year. Cox was on friendly terms with his great contemporary (even though Turner annoyingly used to address him as 'Daniel' when Cox called on him), and, according to Roget, made at least one copy after Turner early in his career. It is quite likely, therefore, that Cox would have known the drawing.

On the other hand, the view drawn by both artists is virtually the only prospect of the castle, and although Cox also depicts a storm and shipwreck, his foreground is quite different, populated by his usual throng of stocky, bustling figures, thrown into a greater degree of activity than usual. Perhaps a sheer coincidence of subject-matter may stand as an example of two voracious landscape painters' paths crossing.

44. Sketchbook from a tour of the North of England

Pencil, oblong quarto with morocco spine; 31ff. on Whatman paper with 1836 watermark.
PROV: bequeathed by J. R. Holliday 1927 (E.2959-1927).
Victoria and Albert Museum

This sketchbook may be dated from a curious inscription on a drawing of Boro' Bridge on the fourth page: 'This great work commenced and finished before 8 o c[loc]k in the morning of August the 7th AD 1837 & God save the Great Duke of Wellington.' Because of the great demand for Cox's works after his death, few sketchbooks can have survived intact, and this one indeed seems to be a unique survival. It gives a clear picture of daily work on a slow progress through North Yorkshire (Middleton – Brough – Barnard Castle – Greta Bridge), and the sketches are in various degrees of finish, some with elaborate colour notes. The Birmingham collection has two pencil drawings of Middleton-in-Teesdale (24′19, 71′19) which must relate to this tour.

45. Bolsover Castle, Derbyshire

Pencil on three joined sheets of toned paper 20.7 × 55.2 (8⅛ × 21¾).
PROV: bequeathed by J. R. Holliday 1927.
Laing Art Gallery, Newcastle-upon-Tyne

This panoramic drawing, heavily annotated with colour notes ('dark shadow', 'whitish cloud', etc) adds yet another dimension to Cox's repertoire of styles. From an early period (see no. 2) he could employ a very fine pencil to make not sketches, but meticulous landscape studies – landscape portraits, it might almost be said – from which he could later extract a subject for a watercolour composition, with as much information to hand as if he were on the spot.

46. Bolsover Castle, Derbyshire

Pencil and watercolour 36.5 × 50.6 (14⅜ × 19⅞).
PROV: presented by subscribers 1907 (334′07).
EXH: *Three Centuries of British Water-Colours*, Arts Council 1951 (40); Swansea 1953 (29); Bourges 1970 (22).
LIT: Cox, p. 81 and pl. 17B.
Birmingham Museums and Art Gallery

Here, a similar pencil outline, with stronger strokes for the landscape, forms the basis of a composition

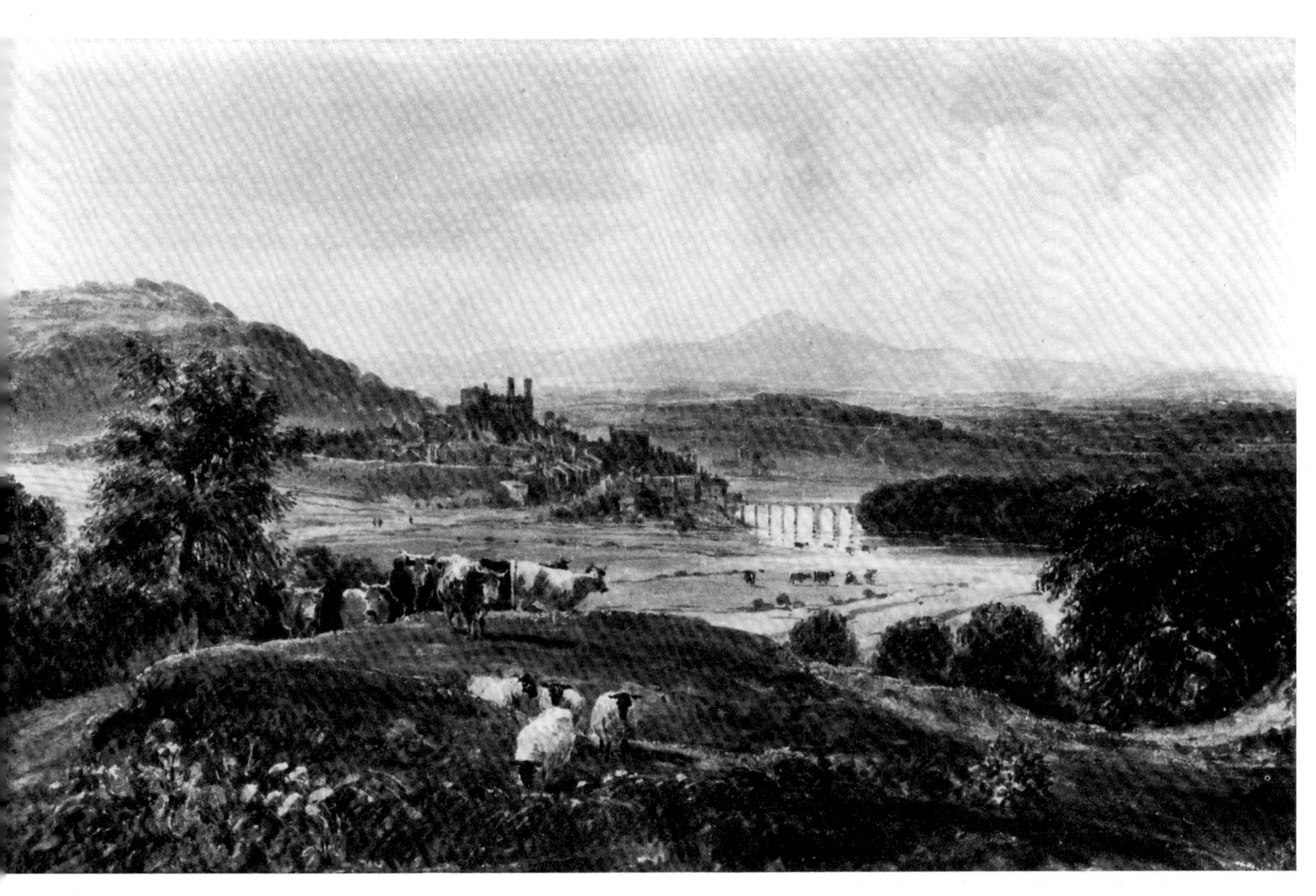

Hay on Wye (cat. no. 42)

over which Cox has put in a lowering sky in washes of cobalt (mixed with a little vermilion, perhaps, for the darker tones) and the earth colours, gamboge, indigo and ochre, for the middle ground. The work is left unfinished (several works would be in progress at any one time), without the 'mosaic' of small patches of local colour detailing foliage, especially in what would be a bright foreground to offset the dark sky. But as it stands, the work demonstrates the first stage in the method of indoor working which Cox recommended to his son in a letter of 18 November 1842: 'Try by lamplight a subject in charcoal, and don't be afraid of darks . . . When you have done all this, have your colours quite soft, and colour upon the charcoal. Get all the depth of the charcoal, and be not afraid of the colour.' (Solly p. 119).

47. The Long Gallery, Hardwick Hall

Watercolour and bodycolour over traces of pencil, on five joined sheets of paper 77 × 107.5 (30¼ × 42¼).
PROV: ?6th Duke of Devonshire (1790–1858); thence by descent.
EXH: ?OWCS 1840 (89); *Treasures from Chatsworth: The Devonshire Inheritance*, International Exhibitions Foundation 1979–80 (128) (USA and London).
LIT: Solly, p. 257.
The Trustees of the Chatsworth Settlement

Slightly larger than *George IV* (no. 28) and the Ashmolean's version of *The Challenge*, this work is rivalled in size amongst Cox's watercolours only by *Cader Idris: Evening* of 1850 (Christie's, 4 June 1974); because of the splendour of its subject, it is the most spectacular of his large works.

The Elizabethan Hardwick Hall completes the trilogy of Cox's beloved Derbyshire houses, after Haddon and Bolsover (he did also draw at Chatsworth, but mostly on a small scale). Cox wrote to William Roberts on 5 September 1835: 'It stands equally as fine as Bolsover, but there is no good inn near. However, we must continue to see it. The interior is fine, and there are some good pictures' (Solly, p. 79). Solly records further visits in 1837 and 1838, 'when he made the celebrated drawings of the interior of the picture gallery' (p. 86), but gives 1839 as the date elsewhere; one would expect this work to be the *Portrait Gallery, Hardwick Hall* exhibited at the OWCS in 1840, but there is a smaller watercolour of the Gallery, also with costumed figures but a view from the opposite end of the room, at Birmingham (672'27).

48. 'The Little Hayfield' 1839

see p. 72

Watercolour over soft pencil, with scratching-out 18.7 × 27.6 (7⅜ × 10⅞).
PROV: bequeathed by John Henderson 1878 (1878-12-28-58).
EXH: Burlington 1873 (28).
LIT: Binyon, p. 262.
The Trustees of the British Museum

The title simply differentiates this work from a slightly larger (and coarser) version of the same subject, dated 1838, also in John Henderson's bequest. The balance of colour, fresh figure group and lively, rather broken handling of foreground foliage make this an archetypal small landscape of Cox's maturity, of a kind which he produced in considerable quantity, with ranging degrees of success.

49. Ulverston Sands

Watercolour, with touches of bodycolour and gum, with scratching-out 60.5 × 85.5 (23¾ × 33⅝).
PROV: Albert Levy; Lord Armstrong by 1910; Ernest Ruffer; bequeathed by Arthur C. Kenrick 1956 (P13'56).
EXH: OWCS 1835 (6); BMAG 1890 (45, date wrongly given as 1846); Laing Art Gallery, *Inaugural Exhibition* 1904; RBSA 1968 (48); Bourges 1970 (19).
LIT: Solly, pp. 261–62 (as *Lancaster Sands*); Roget, II, p. 153 (as *Crossing the Sands*).
Birmingham Museums and Art Gallery

'A highly finished drawing, on smooth paper, and one of the most perfect of this delightful subject, full of atmosphere and movement . . . full of life, action, and gesticulation. On the right some horsemen are hurrying across the sands, whilst in the distance a heavy shower is seen approaching, and a flight of sea-gulls adds to the feeling of the unsettled and treacherous state of the weather . . . The colour throughout is clear and beautiful.' (Solly)

Cox first visited Lancaster and the Sands in July 1834, returning the following year, and again in 1840. From 1835 to 1847 he produced a great many drawings (and several small oils) on the theme of travellers crossing, or preparing to cross, the wide and treacherous sands. Grundy (Nettlefold Collection Catalogue) writes: 'The sands stretch across the head of Morecambe Bay and are separated into two

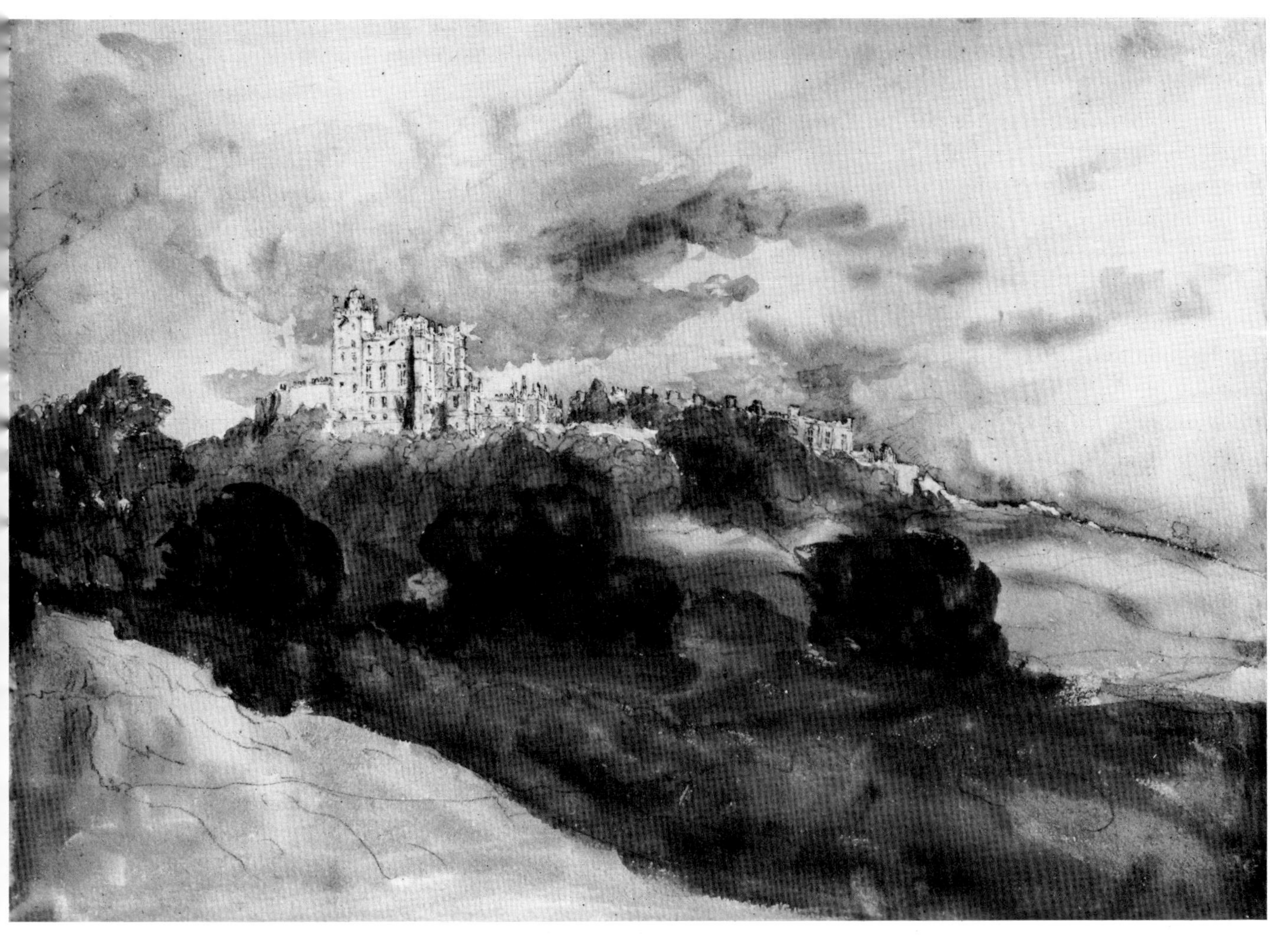

Bolsover Castle, Derbyshire (cat. no. 46)

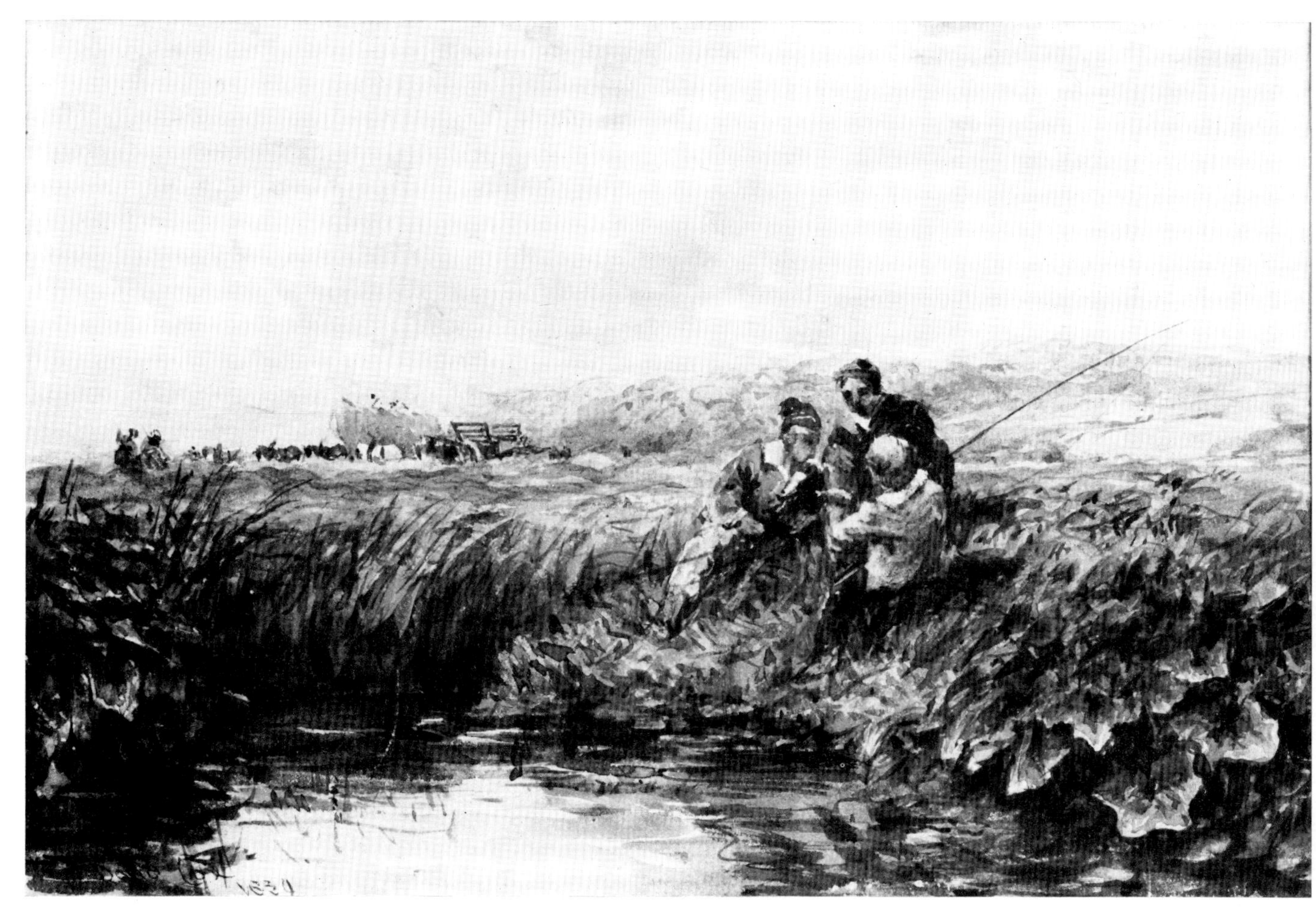

'The Little Hayfield' (cat. no. 48)

portions by the little peninsula of Cartmel. It might be supposed that the west portion only would be called Ulverston Sands, as being nearest that town, while the eastern portion would be called Lancaster Sands, but both names seem to have been applied indiscriminately to the whole expanse of sand, probably according to the direction in which the spectator is looking.' (Vol. 1, p. 154)

50. Blackpool Beach 1840

see p. 74

Watercolour and bodycolour over pencil 24.4 × 36.6 (9⅝ × 14⅜).
PROV: ?William Roberts; presented by J. Arthur Kenrick 1925 (274'25).
EXH: Swansea 1953 (43); *British Watercolours 1760–1930 from Birmingham*, Arts Council 1980–81 (42, repr.).
LIT: Solly, p. 97–98; Cox, p. 87.
Birmingham Museums and Art Gallery

Cox joined his friend William Roberts in Blackpool in August 1840, but found little there worth painting, arguing that the scenery in the neighbourhood of Manchester was far prettier! Solly records, however, that he made two sketches of the sea-front (including their lodgings) which he presented to Mrs Roberts. Apart from being a bright and attractive work in its own right, this little sketch may have sowed the seed that was to grow into the composition of *Rhyl Sands* (no. 93).

51. Lancaster Sands 1844

Watercolour with bodycolour over pencil 33.3 × 48.8 (13⅛ × 19¼).
PROV: John Hollingsworth; Richard Newsham; his bequest 1883.
EXH: *Festival of Britain*, Lancaster 1951.
LIT: Hall, pp. 53–4; Hibbert, no. 99; *Magazine of Art*, December

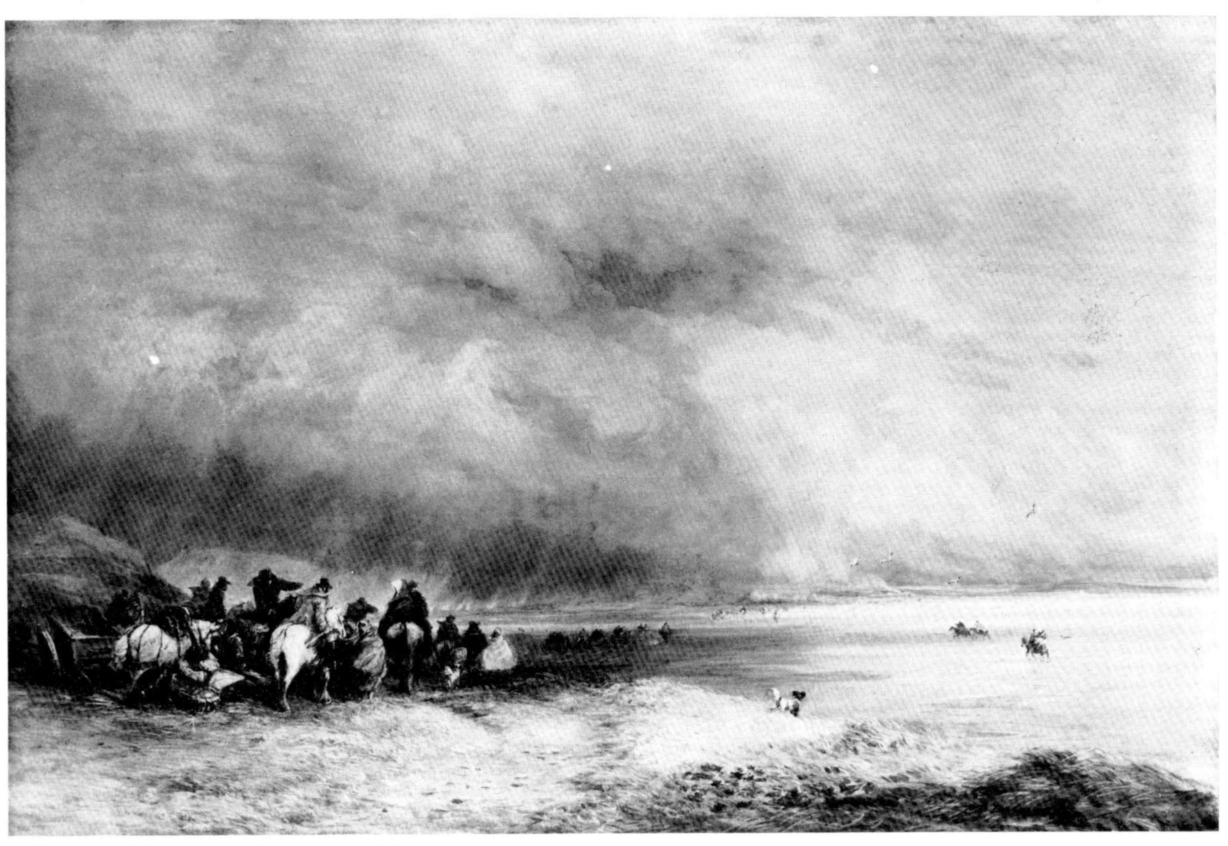

Ulverston Sands (cat. no. 49)

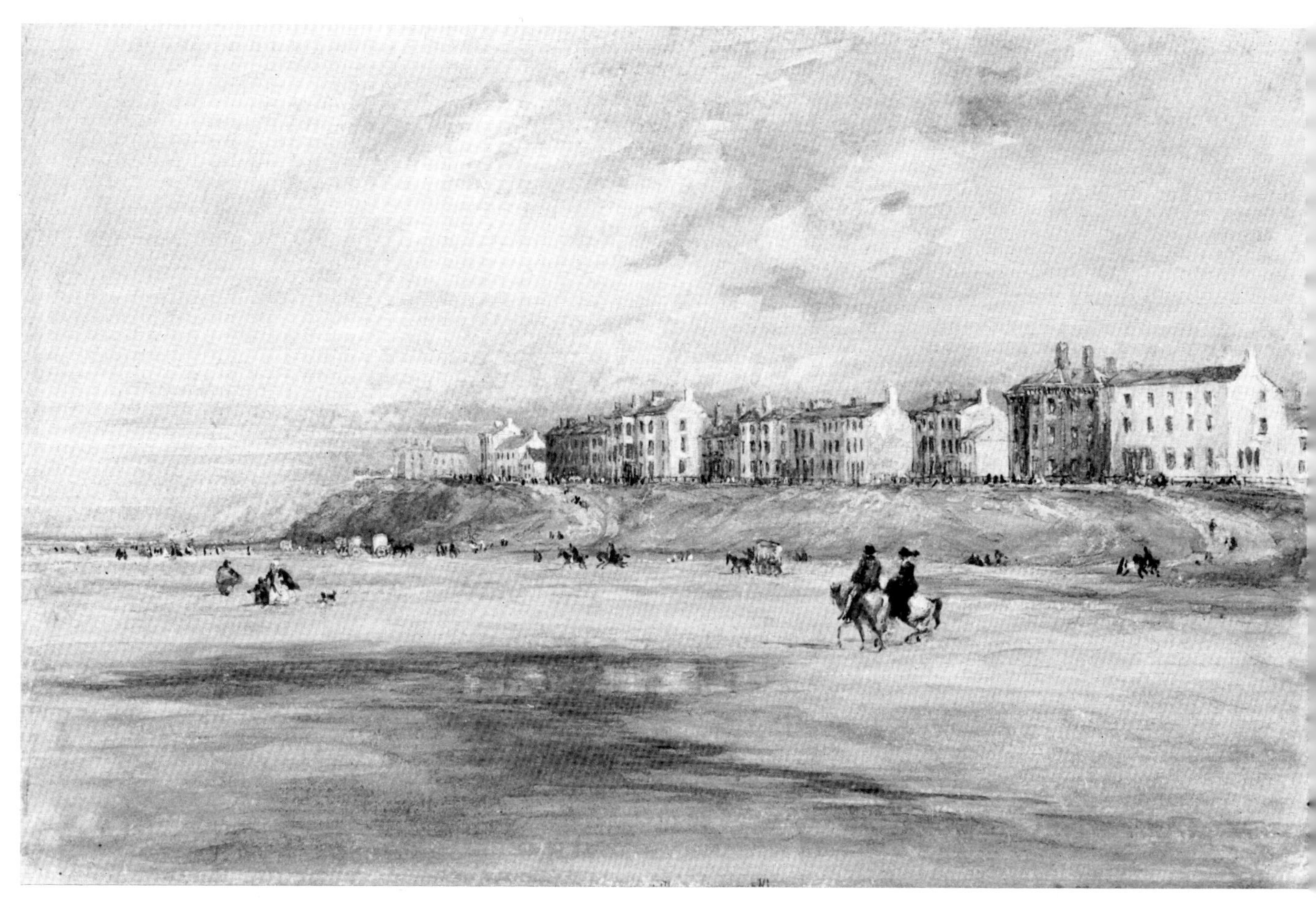

Blackpool Beach 1840 (cat. no. 50)

1900, p. 52; *Windsor Magazine*, March 1912, p. 454.
Harris Museum and Art Gallery, Preston

The inscription emblazoned by Cox on the bottom of this work ('I sold this drawing to (J.) Hollingsworth Esq.') is explained by Hall. 'The writer calls to mind a most lovely drawing of Lancaster Sands, of small dimensions, but full of light, splendour, and most beautiful colour . . . Cox himself prized this drawing highly. In his portfolio it was protected with tissue paper; and not wishing to part with it, he put upon it a price which he thought would prevent anyone purchasing it. In fact he asked as much as £18 for the drawing – a sum about £8 in advance of his usual charge for works of this size. Strange to say the extra price had the desired prohibitory effect, until a short time before the artist's death, when a purchaser was found who was too happy to be permitted to take it at what the artist though the exorbitant price of £18!'

Hibbert gives as subtitle to the work 'The Guide blowing his horn for the Travellers to draw together in order to cross the Channel in a party.' Hall thought the watercolour 'luminous as any Turner' and the comparison is appropriate in view of Turner's famous *Lancaster Sands* watercolour of *c.*1814–15 (Birmingham Museums and Art Gallery, P406'53).

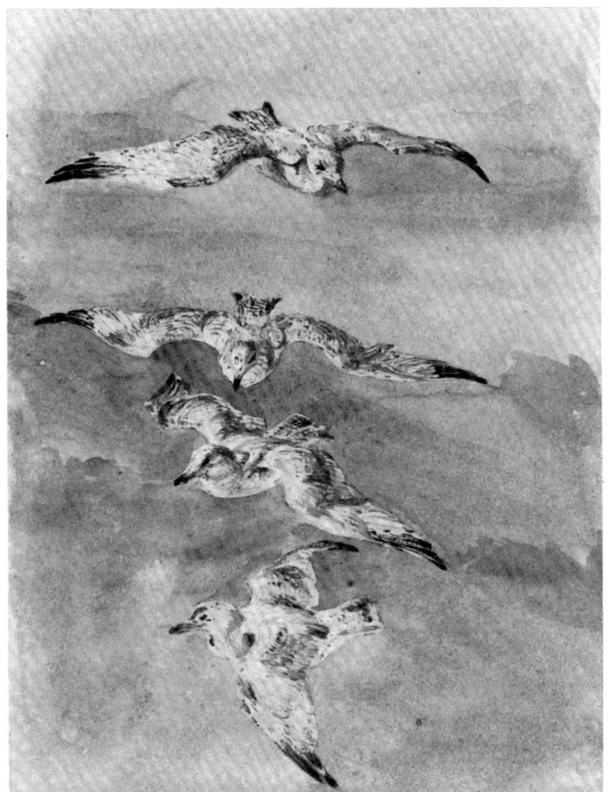

Seagulls (cat. no. 52)

52. Seagulls

Pencil, watercolour and bodycolour 18.6 × 14 (7¼ × 5½).
PROV: bequeathed by J. R. Holliday 1927 (38'31).
EXH: BMAG 1959 (145); *British Watercolours 1760–1930 from Birmingham*, Arts Council 1980–81, 41 (repr.).
Birmingham Museums and Art Gallery

Studies of animals and birds form an unfamiliar, but not uncommon, aspect of Cox's work. These splendid seagulls must be the product of a spare moment on Rhyl or Lancaster Sands!

53. Hares

Watercolour over pencil 22 × 34.4 (8⅝ × 13½).
PROV: presented by subscribers 1907 (332'07).
LIT: Cox, p. 81.
Birmingham Museums and Art Gallery

Occasionally, Cox would develop a small study; related to this work is another watercolour in the Birmingham collection (*The Rabbit Warren*, 290'25), of which there is an oil study on board (BMAG 1959, 107; Phillips, 13 November 1982, lot 78, repr.).

54. Scotch Firs

Watercolour
PROV: Mrs Anderson Weston; Sotheby's 16 February 1922 (lot 99), purchased (PD-1922).
EXH: *British Watercolours 1750–1850 from the Victoria and Albert Museum*, International Exhibitions Foundation 1966–67 (20, repr.).
LIT: Lambourne, p. 87 (repr.).
Victoria and Albert Museum

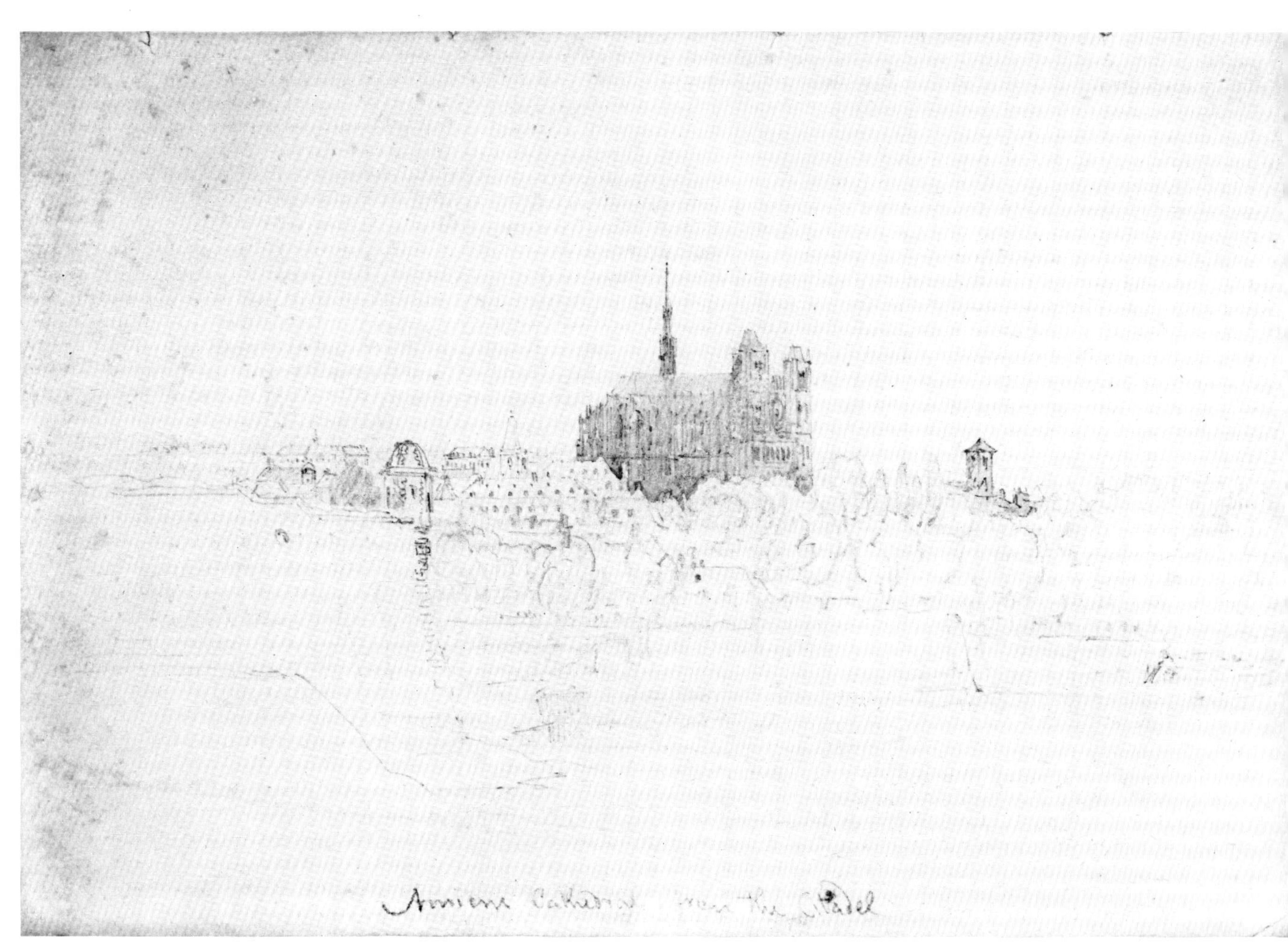

Amiens Cathedral, from the Citadel (cat. no. 57)

4. The Continent 1826: 1829: 1832

The three trips paid to the continent of Europe by Cox between 1826 and 1832 were each in their way unusual and more accidental than systematic, in character more like carefree summer holidays in good company than planned painting tours by an artist eager for the sights of a minor Grand Tour. Rightly described by Sir Trenchard Cox as 'incredibly insular', Cox undoubtedly enjoyed seeing the coasts, rivers and towns of France and Flanders, but unlike contemporaries such as Turner and Bonington, found there no great new inspiration for his art. Also unlike those artists, and many others, he felt no urge or need to travel further afield than he did – for instance, to Italy or the Alps. Solly (p. 72) records Cox's remark to a much-travelled gentleman trying to persuade the artist's son to visit Switzerland: 'Don't try to induce David to go on the Continent in search of scenery. Wales, Yorkshire, and Derbyshire have been good enough for me, and I quite believe they may yet do for him.'

The tour of Belgium and Flanders in the summer of 1826 was instigated by Cox's brother-in-law, named Gardner, who had been commissioned by his map-seller employer to go and see a map of the world recently published in Brussels. Young David also joined the trip, but returned home before his father, who was invited to join the party of the Rev. Mr Hopton of Canon Frome, whose daughter had been a pupil of Hereford days. This piece of serendipity extended Cox's tour into Holland, it would seem chiefly by canal, through Dort, Rotterdam, Delft, Amsterdam and Haarlem.

Cox's first French visit, in 1829, was more purposeful – an intended six-week tour of Northern France. In Calais he visited F. L. Francia, pupil of Girtin and teacher of Bonington, and a watercolourist close in spirit and style to Cox himself. Here he spent a week working at the first of many subjects depicting Calais pier and sands. Visiting Amiens, Beauvais and Rouen en route, Cox reached Paris, where he suffered an enforced but not unhappy stay as the result of a minor accident.

The number of subjects accruing from this albeit truncated tour may have decided Cox on a third and final crossing of the Channel in 1832, when he concentrated on visiting and painting the northern ports – Calais, Dieppe and Boulogne (where he witnessed a review in honour of Louis-Philippe) – offering the kind of picturesque coastal scenes already dear to his heart and guaranteed to succeed on the walls of the Old Water Colour Society.

Forty-three continental subjects duly appeared amongst Cox's exhibits at the OWCS between 1829 and 1838, demonstrating what good use the artist made of quick sketches produced in a very limited time.

55. View in Ghent

Watercolour over chalk, inscribed with colour notes 24 × 47.2 (9½ × 18½).
PROV: Hannah Cox; ?Walker's Galleries; Sir Thomas Barlow; bequeathed by Helen Barlow.
LIT: *Catalogue of the Helen Barlow Bequest*, National Gallery of Scotland 1979 (no. 9 repr.).
The Trustees of the National Gallery of Scotland

Surviving town and landscape scenes from the Belgian part of Cox's 1826 tour are rare. This Ghent view shows the tower of St Nicholas's Church on the right, and the Dominican Convent (demolished in 1863) on the left. Another, in the Whitworth Art Gallery, University of Manchester, shows the church of St Michel in the background (Cox, pl. 8B); the Fitzwilliam Museum, Cambridge, has a small version of this. All must be amongst the finest of the 'very clever views' mentioned by Solly (p. 49).

56. Sketchbook from the 1829 tour in France

Pencil and watercolour, small oblong quarto.
Bears label 'Werner / M^{d} Papetier / Rue Vivienne No 2 bis / Paris' and inscription 'David Cox Foxley Road London 1829'.
Private Collection

A small but vivid souvenir of the 1829 tour undertaken, according to inscriptions in this sketchbook,

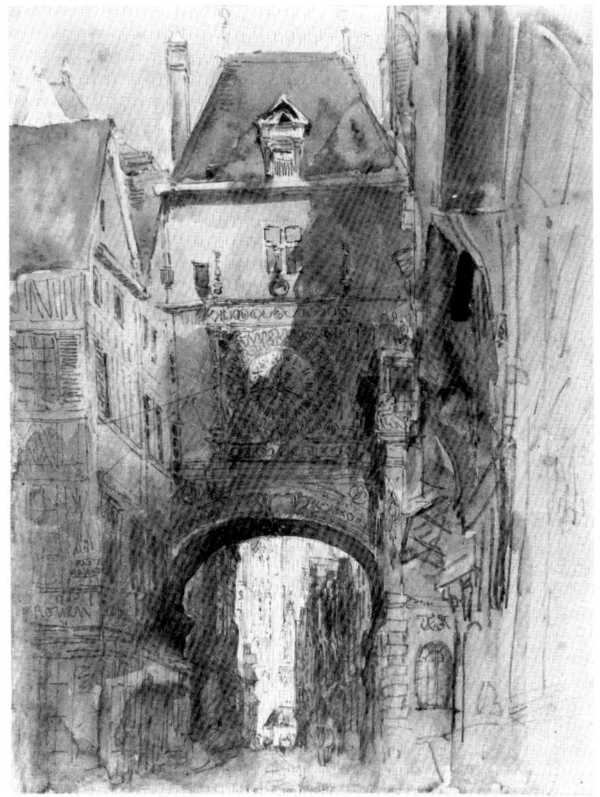

Tour d'Horloge, Rouen (cat. no. 58)

in the company of Frederick Birch. The drawings here are of Dieppe and St Omer as well as Paris, and the sketchbook may therefore have been used on the second French tour in 1832, when Cox is known to have visited Dieppe.

57. Amiens Cathedral, from the Citadel

Pencil and watercolour 26.7 × 38.4 (10½ × 15⅛).
PROV: presented by Augustus Walker 1909 (no. 3322).
LIT: Solly, p. 64.
The Syndics of the Fitzwilliam Museum, Cambridge

The use of a single watercolour wash for the cathedral adds a delicate touch to a very strong pencil drawing. Cox may just have been experimenting with a rose madder lake colour, the madder plant then being grown largely in France and Holland.

Solly records that Cox and his son, having spent the first week of their 1829 tour in Calais, took the diligence to Amiens, and 'remained there two days, sketched the cathedral from the citadel, the Rue de Condé, and other subjects'. From Amiens they walked to Beauvais, and only took the diligence from there to Paris on account of the very hot weather.

58. Tour d'Horloge, Rouen

Pencil and watercolour 33.6 × 25.7 (13½ × 10⅛).
PROV: presented by the NACF 1967 (Herbert Powell Bequest) (T.977).
EXH: *Zwei Jahrhunderte Englische Malerei*, Munich 1979–80 (186, repr.).
LIT: *Catalogue of the Herbert Powell Collection of Water-Colours* 1931 (no. 31, repr.); Hardie 1967, pl. 187.
The Trustees of the Tate Gallery

Perhaps the outstanding image of Cox's continental work – a bravura drawing in which every stroke of the pencil and each touch of the brush is a telling one. The contrast between the shadow over the arch and the sunlight seen beyond is brilliantly achieved, and there is just the right balance of watercolour and pencil (the stylised rendering of the clock-face should be noted).

Rouen was popular with British artists; a view of the Rue du Gros Horloge is perhaps the best-known plate of Bonington's 1825 *Voyages Pittoresques et Romantiques dans l'Ancienne France*, whilst Thomas Shotter Boys produced a chromolithograph view for his *Picturesque Architecture in Paris, Ghent, Antwerp, Rouen* (1839). Cotman came to Rouen in 1828, a year before Cox's visit.

59. Near the Pont d'Arcole, Paris

Pencil and watercolour 24.5 × 37 (9⅝ × 14½).
PROV: bequeathed by J. R. Holliday 1927 (4302).
The Trustees of the Tate Gallery

One of the most spirited of the Paris street scenes of 1829, complete with colour notes, shop lettering and details of street furniture. Other fine Parisian subjects are to be found in Worcester and in the Institut Néerlandais, Paris (*Rue Vivienne*, exhibited in Munich, 1979–80 [200, repr.]). The Pont d'Arcole joins the Île de la Cité with the right bank near the Hotel de Ville.

An unfortunate sprained ankle confined Cox to

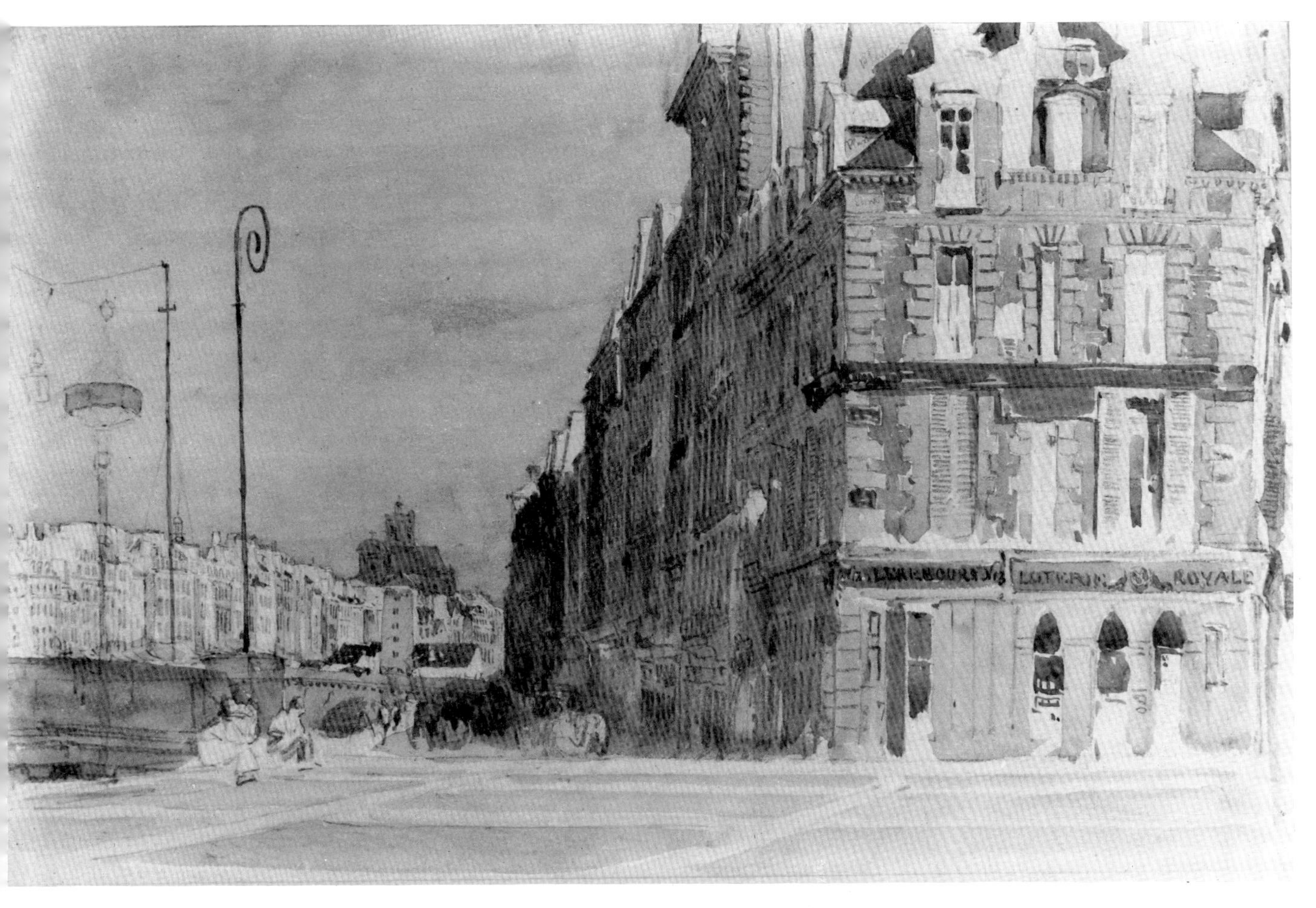

Near the Pont d'Arcole, Paris (cat. no. 59)

Paris for most of his six-week tour, but he was not to be deterred. 'He was not to be baffled in his intention of sketching the monuments of Paris; so, with his usual spirit, especially when the pursuit of art was in question, he used to drive out in a fiacre, or cab, every day, and making it stop when he came to an interesting subject that took his fancy, he painted away indefatigably for many weeks, seated in the cab, or occasionally in a chair near the Seine or in some other not overcrowded spot. In this way he secured views of the Tuileries, Palais de Justice, Chambre de Deputies, Rue St Honore, Montmartre, the bridges over the Seine, and many others.' (Solly, p. 64)

60. The Pont des Arts and the Louvre from the Quai Conti

Watercolour and bodycolour, with scratching-out 40.6 × 67.3 (16 × 26½).
PROV: Sir John Holder, Bt.; presented by F. J. Nettlefold 1948 (P.13-1948).
EXH: ?OWCS 1838 (78); RA Winter 1892 (91).
LIT: *Catalogue of Pictures and Statuary*, Pitmaston 1911 (126, repr.); Grundy, I, 152 (repr. colour); Lambourne, p. 88 (repr.).
Victoria and Albert Museum

61. The Pont des Arts and the Louvre from the Quai Conti

Soft pencil on toned paper 27.7 × 38.5 (10⅞ × 15⅛).
PROV: Hannah Cox; Walker's Galleries (E.4900-1960).
Victoria and Albert Museum

This is the most ambitious surviving watercolour resulting from any of Cox's continental tours, and its preparatory drawing equally the most carefully observed. It may perhaps be identified as *The Louvre and Tuilleries, from Pont Neuf* (OWCS 1838), a title with distinct echoes of Girtin's panoramic drawing *The Louvre and Tuileries*, published as a soft-ground etching in 1803. Cox also painted a vertical watercolour of *The Tuileries at the end of the Pont Royal (Pavilion de Flore)* (Leeds City Art Galleries), and the Fitzwilliam Museum, Cambridge has a small sketchbook study of the *Quays by the Tuileries*.

62. Passengers going on board an East Indiaman

Watercolour over pencil 21.5 × 27 (8¼ × 10½).
PROV: Sotheby's 11 November 1982 (lot 183, repr., as *An Indiaman taking passengers on board at Gravesend*).
LIT: Solly, p. 48.
Private Collection

This can safely be identified with one of the seven drawings listed by Solly as having been sent (presumably sold) to the publisher Clay in London, in February 1825. Although not strictly related to Cox's own journeys, this watercolour has been inserted here to represent the substantial number of marine, harbour and estuary views made by Cox, especially in the 1820s and 1830s. It must be admitted that many of these scenes are awkwardly handled in comparison with the landscapes, but on occasion Cox could bring off delicate, tranquil marine effects; he does so here, in combination with work on a very fine scale in the figures and rigging.

63. Calais (?)

Watercolour and black chalk 20.6 × 30.3 (8⅛ × 11⅞).
PROV: bequeathed by Walter Turner 1948 (P29'48).
Birmingham Museums and Art Gallery

A sketch remarkable for its freshness, not only of handling but also in the preservation of the colours, especially the blue of the sky. Cox has captured the spirit of a lively quayside (probably Calais in 1829) in the age of sail.

64. Fort Rouge, Calais, with Shrimpers 1833

Watercolour 19.4 × 27.9 (7⅝ × 11).
PROV: presented by Miss Mary Paton 1936 (P.33-1936).
EXH: *British Watercolours 1750–1850 from the V & A*, International Exhibitions Foundation 1966–67 (22, repr.).
LIT: Lambourne, p. 88 (repr.).
Victoria and Albert Museum

The French visit of 1832, taking in Boulogne, Calais and Dieppe, spawned almost as many *Sands* pictures as Lancaster. The first of these was *On the Sands, Calais* (OWCS 1833, 100). 'The forts and sands of Calais were also a favourite subject with J. M. W. Turner. Both these great artists have produced some of their finest effects of sea and sky, full of light and

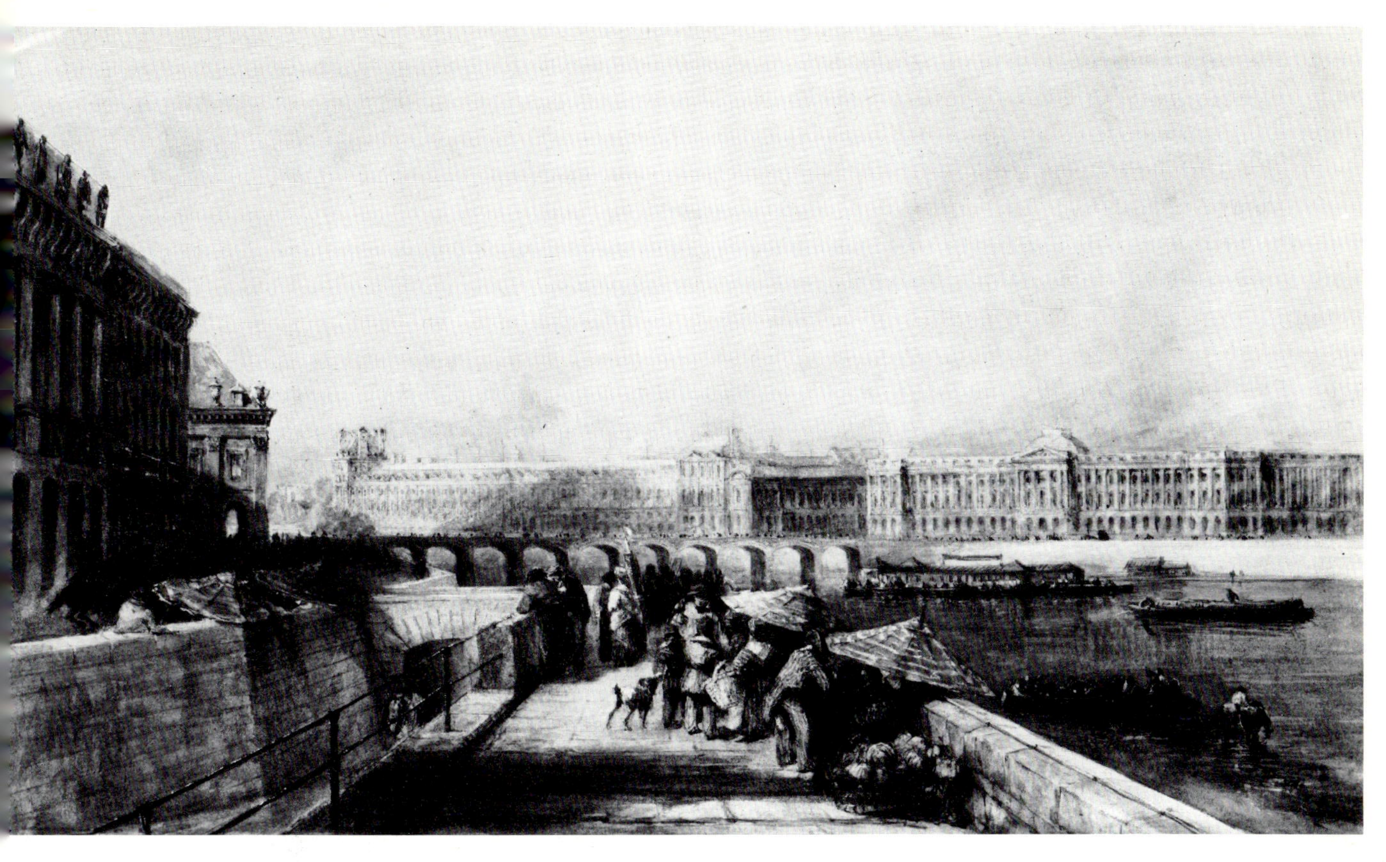

The Pont des Arts and the Louvre from the Quai Conti (cat. no. 60)

movement, on this part of the coast of France.' (Solly, p. 73). Cox must have seen Turner's great oil, *Calais Sands*, at the RA in 1830 (now in Bury Art Gallery) and would also have been familiar with Bonington's wide, wet shrimping subjects; he added to the genre a characteristic watercolour palette of blues, yellows and browns. Fort Rouge, a 17th-century construction, was demolished in 1864; the Royal Society of Painters in Water-Colours has a very similar watercolour.

65. Calais Pier 1844–5

Oil on canvas 45.2 × 73.3 (17 13/16 × 28 7/8).
PROV: David Cox junior; Christie's 3/5/1873; ?Murrieta sale Christie's 30/4/1892, bt. Agnew; George Holt (£500); Emma Holt Bequest, Sudley 1944 (203).
EXH: ?Liverpool Academy 1845 (218); Whitechapel Art Gallery 1920 (172).
LIT: Solly, p. 209 (but gives date incorrectly as 1846); *The Emma Holt Bequest, Sudley: Illustrated Catalogue*, pp. 21–2 and pl. 34.
Walker Art Gallery, Liverpool

This appears to be the only oil painting to be derived from a continental subject. Of Cox's many *Calais Pier* watercolours, those in Birmingham, the British Museum and the Whitworth Art Gallery, University of Manchester, are the closest 'models' for the oil. As Mary Bennett points out in the Holt Bequest Catalogue, the popularity of the subject can be traced directly to Turner's 1803 oil, and she rightly presumes that Cox is likely to have sought that work out. Mrs Cox wrote to her son on 9 October 1844 that '[Cox] is finishing the Calais Pier and wants to see the sea' (Solly, p. 131); naturally, he would have wanted fresh direct inspiration for the creamy impasto of *Calais Pier*'s rolling waves, and to capture the salt-laden wind gusting over the long, crowded pier. Solly further records that the finished work 'was a great favourite with Cox and used to hang in his parlour at Greenfield House.'

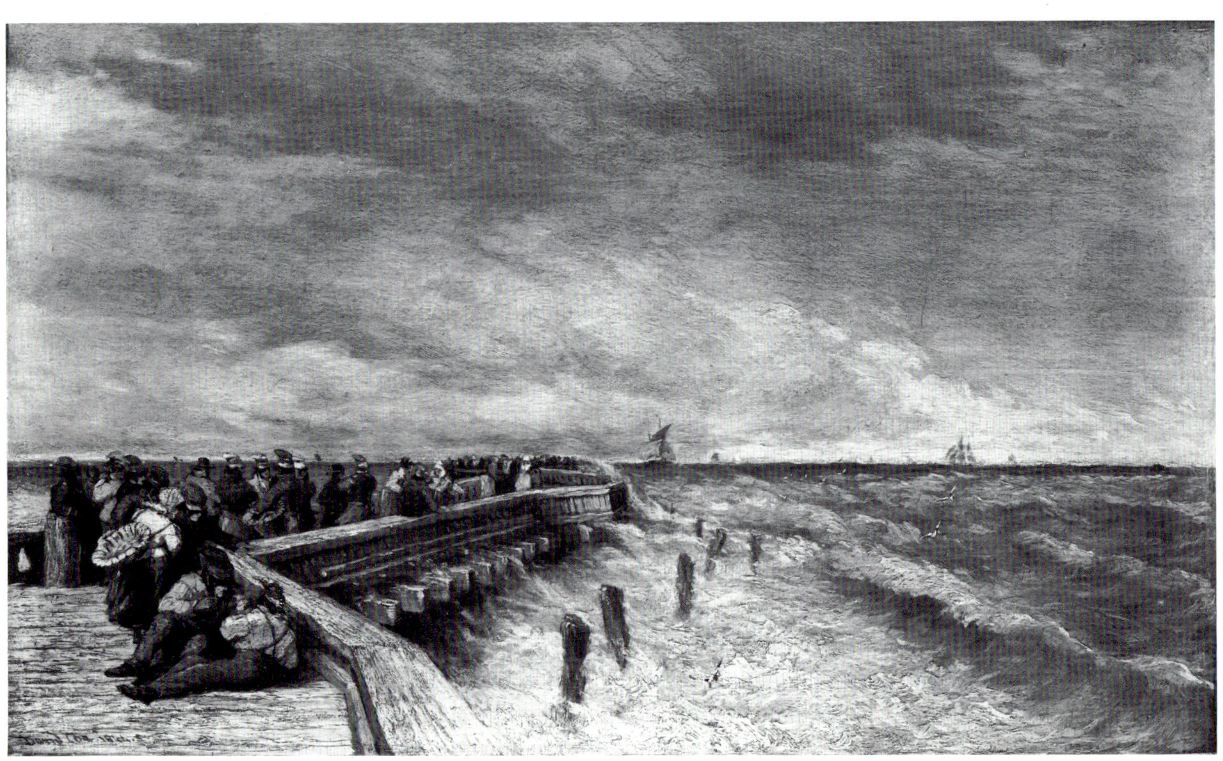

Calais Pier 1844–5 (cat. no. 65)

5. Return to Birmingham 1841–49

The 1840s was unquestionably the most important decade in Cox's career. Having established a style, a market, a circle of admiring friends and patrons, as well as a family, Cox was in a position to draw a bow at almost any venture he pleased. By the time of Ruskin's criticism, in the 1843 edition of Modern Painters, *of Cox's lack of imagination and ambition, the artist had not only uprooted himself again from London – this time to return for good to his roots on the rural edge of Birmingham – but had also taken up the challenge of oil painting.*

The works exhibited here show firstly the expansion of subject matter, sketching ground and style that grew out of the welcome removal from London. Bolton Abbey and Knaresborough proved fertile ground for a series of dramatic compositions (nos. 68–72), whilst in the tactile qualities of the Scotch paper Cox had discovered in 1836 lay a whole series of landscape effects in microcosm (nos. 76, 81). More 'subject' pictures came to fruition, too, in this period, and when confined to simple compositions could command great intensity and power (nos. 77, 79).

But it was in finding a latent touch in oil painting that gave Cox new inspiration in the 1840s. After only perfunctory tuition from W. J. Müller – but probably more advice and influence than has hitherto been supposed – Cox simply relied on determination and endless practice ('I will succeed', *he wrote to his friend William Roberts in 1841) to achieve the result he knew he could reach. By 1843 he was truly in his element, and in a bubbling letter to his son, telling him to go out to paint in oils from nature, he confessed: 'Give me oil. I only wish I had begun earlier in life; the pleasure of painting in oil is so very satisfactory.' His progress as a painter in only nine years, from first tentative experiments to glorious set-pieces such as* The Skylark *and* The Vale of Clwyd, *is one of the greatest, but least recognised, achievements of any British painter.*

66. Snowdon

see p. 85

Watercolour on Scotch paper, with scratching-out 26.4 × 36.8 ($10^{3}/_{8}$ × $14^{1}/_{2}$).
PROV: bequeathed by John Henderson 1878 (1878-12-28-64).
LIT: Binyon, p. 261.
The Trustees of the British Museum

A prime example of the sort of small-scale watercolour that could well have been completed on the spot, exploiting the irregularities and absorbency of Scotch paper. Impure flecks in the paper are incorporated into the rich watercolour to give the landscape a texture of rocks or branches. Cox contrasts the deep blue of Snowdon's mass with the wet greens of the valley and the sombre hues of the slopes, contoured with judiciously scratched-out highlights. This perfect evocation of 'Wild Wales' is the outcome of Cox's belief, as expressed in a letter to his wife of 19 June 1842: 'It is the pleasantest country to go to for quiet and grand scenery . . . it is in the truly rural simple state of nature.' (Solly, p. 116)

67. A Risky Position 1843

see p. 84

Watercolour over pencil, with scratching-out 47.5 × 31 ($18^{3}/_{4}$ × $12^{1}/_{4}$).
PROV: presented by J. Arthur Kenrick 1925 (331'25).
Birmingham Museums and Art Gallery

Vertical compositions, it will have been noticed, appear but seldom in Cox's work. His passion for the open sky and the wide hills demand a wide rather than a tall canvas. The upright composition of a river flanked by trees is one that may derive from oils by W. J. Müller, such as the *Gillingham* subjects. Cox's *On the Lledr*, 1852 (Wolverhampton Art Gallery) is one of only a few vertical oils, and, like *A Risky Position*, features anglers prominently.

68. Bolton Woods Sept 4 1844

Charcoal 26.6 × 18.2 (10½ × 7¼).
PROV: John Hollingsworth; sold to Thomas Wrigley 1873; presented by his children 1897 (Wrigley 36).
LIT: Bury 1901, p. 30.
Bury Art Gallery

69. Barden Tower 8 Sept 1844

Charcoal 27 × 18 (10⅝ × 7⅛).
PROV: as no. 68 (Wrigley 48).
LIT: Bury 1901, p. 30.
Bury Art Gallery

For the purposes of this exhibition, these two works have to represent not only a type of drawing often employed by Cox, but also two subjects that recur almost as frequently. The instant sketch of a view glimpsed from a hill or through trees whilst travelling was always an irresistible attraction to Cox, but on sketching tours in Yorkshire in the 1840s he seems to have combed the countryside for serendipitous vantage points. Exceptionally in his work, the groups of drawings in black chalk or charcoal (Cox used the latter term to cover most graphic media) done around Bolton Abbey in September 1841, August 1843 and September 1844, are precisely dated – no fewer than fourteen from the last group (31 August to 10 September 1844) are known to the compiler. The largest number of this purposefully impressionistic series is the eight at Bury, initially from the collection of John Hollingsworth of Birmingham (see no. 51) by way of 'the artist's own hands'.

As to the subjects here depicted, both were famous beauty spots, Bolton Abbey to the point of being hackneyed by the 1840s (an *Art Journal* critic of 1847 remarked that 'we are heartily weary of Bolton Abbey'). Cox's views of it are pleasant but uninspired (the small oil at Birmingham, P32′48, is perhaps the best), those of Barden more ambitious, but still rather dull – and sombre in mood. Of the large 1849 watercolour (Whitworth Art Gallery), the *Art Journal* commented that 'few will seek their amusement in those passages of landscape, how romantic soever, if they would escape a wetting.' (June 1849, p. 177)

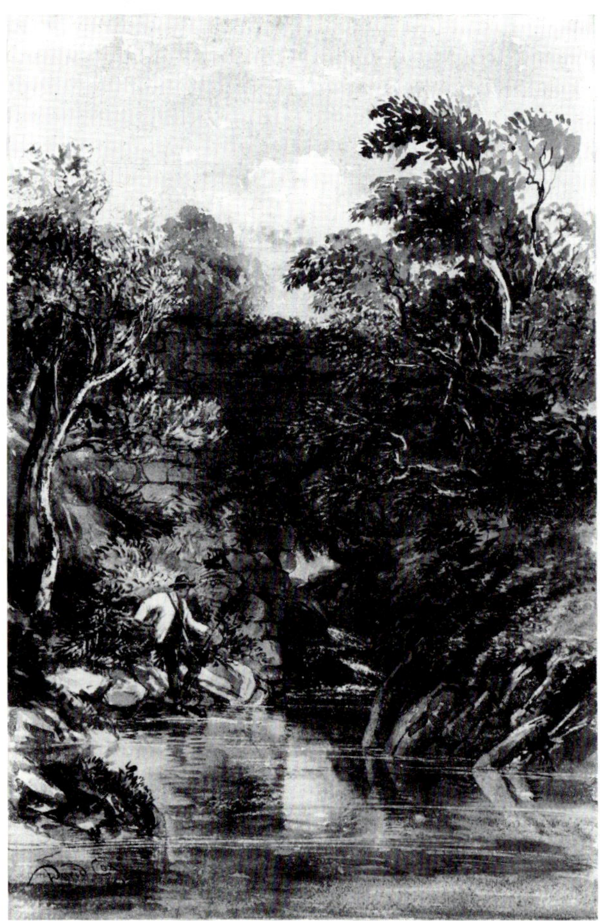

A Risky Position 1843 (cat. no. 67)

70. Knaresborough Castle Sept 7 1844

Charcoal 47 × 55.5 (18½ × 21⅞) (irregular; max. dimensions).
PROV: bequeathed by J. R. Holliday 1927 (698′27).
Birmingham Museums and Art Gallery

71. Knaresborough Castle

Watercolour and bodycolour, with scratching-out 60.4 × 85.1 (23¾ × 33½).
PROV: bequeathed by Richard Newsham 1883.
EXH: OWCS 1845 (101).
LIT: Solly, pp. 130–33; Hibbert, no. 100.
Harris Museum and Art Gallery, Preston

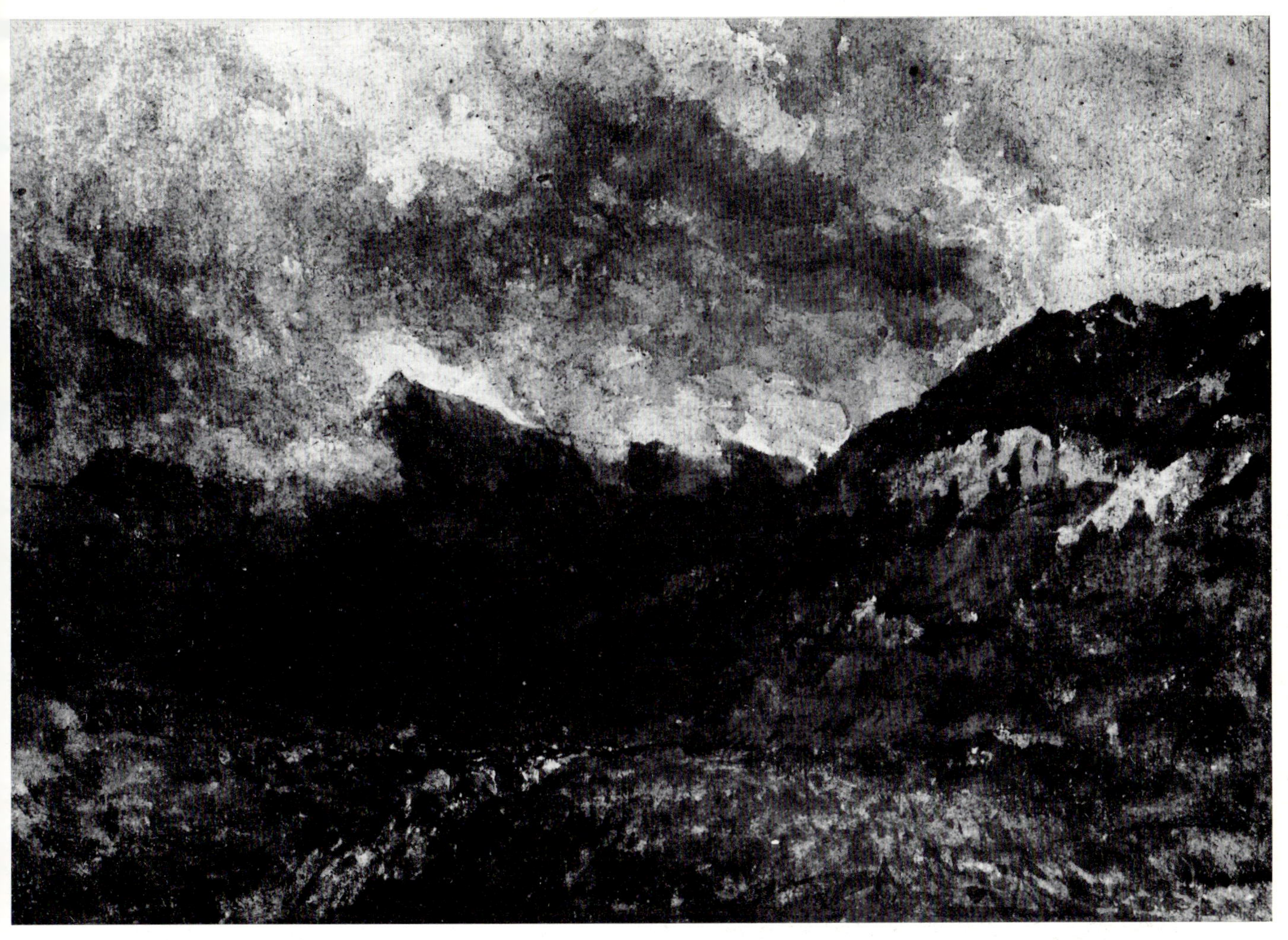

Snowdon (cat. no. 66)

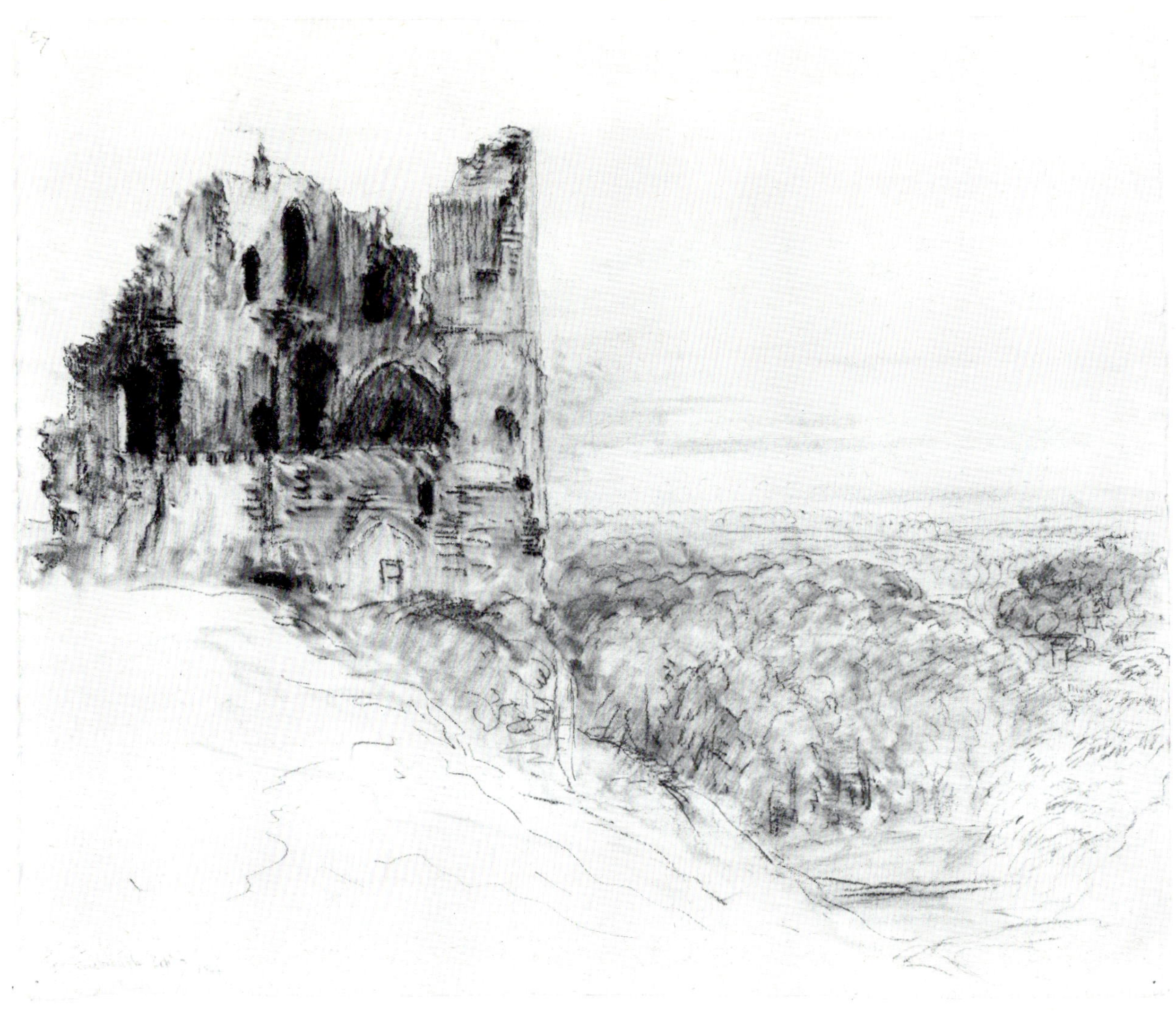

Knaresborough Castle Sept 7 1844 (cat. no. 70)

72. View at Knaresborough

Watercolour over black chalk on Scotch paper 36 × 75.7 (14¼ × 29¾).

PROV: Merrick Bequest and Friends of the Art Gallery 1945 (4757).

Hereford City Museum and Art Gallery

These three rather over-size views of the dramatic hilly Knaresborough site are symptomatic of a loss of direction in Cox's watercolour art around 1845. Some exhibition pieces, such as *Sun, Wind and Rain* (no. 75) were immediately effective, albeit they represented enlargements of essentially small-scale work; others like *Knaresborough Castle*, impressive as it may be in sheer scale, were unsatisfactory to artist and public alike. 'I finished my drawings last evening, and am quite dissatisfied with them. They are too slight, and I hope and wish I may never make another large drawing; I cannot finish to please the public' (letter to Roberts, 23 April 1845: Solly, p. 133). Relief came in oil painting, an immediate pleasure and necessarily on a small scale to begin with, and in the discovery of Bettws-y-Coed, a haven far from the art market. Something of the burgeoning of his style, especially in drawing and texture, that developed in Wales from 1844 onwards is detectable in the more informal *View at Knaresborough* – an orchestration of small, disparate effects far more satisfying than the rhetoric of an exhibition piece.

73. (a) Crossing the Sands

Brown chalk and stump on buff paper 17.6 × 28.8 (6⅞ × 11⅜).
PROV: presented by Dyson Perrins 1919.

(b) Asking the Way

Black chalk and stump on buff paper 17.4 × 28.7 (6⅞ × 11⅜).
PROV: presented by Dyson Perrins 1919.
The Visitors of the Ashmolean Museum, Oxford

A noticeably freer drawing style begins to develop in the late 1840s; Cox conjures up familiar images with very simple means by reducing gesture and detail to a minimum and concentrating on linear movement and effect.

74. 'Windsor – The Queen!'

Black chalk 27.6 × 37.8 (10⅞ × 14⅞).
PROV: Walker Galleries 1904; bequeathed by Sir Robert Witt 1952 (1432).
EXH: *Meisterwerke englischer Malerei aus drei Jahrhunderten*, Vienna Secession 1927 (277); *Three Centuries of British Water-Colours*, Arts Council 1951 (44) BMAG 1959 (109).

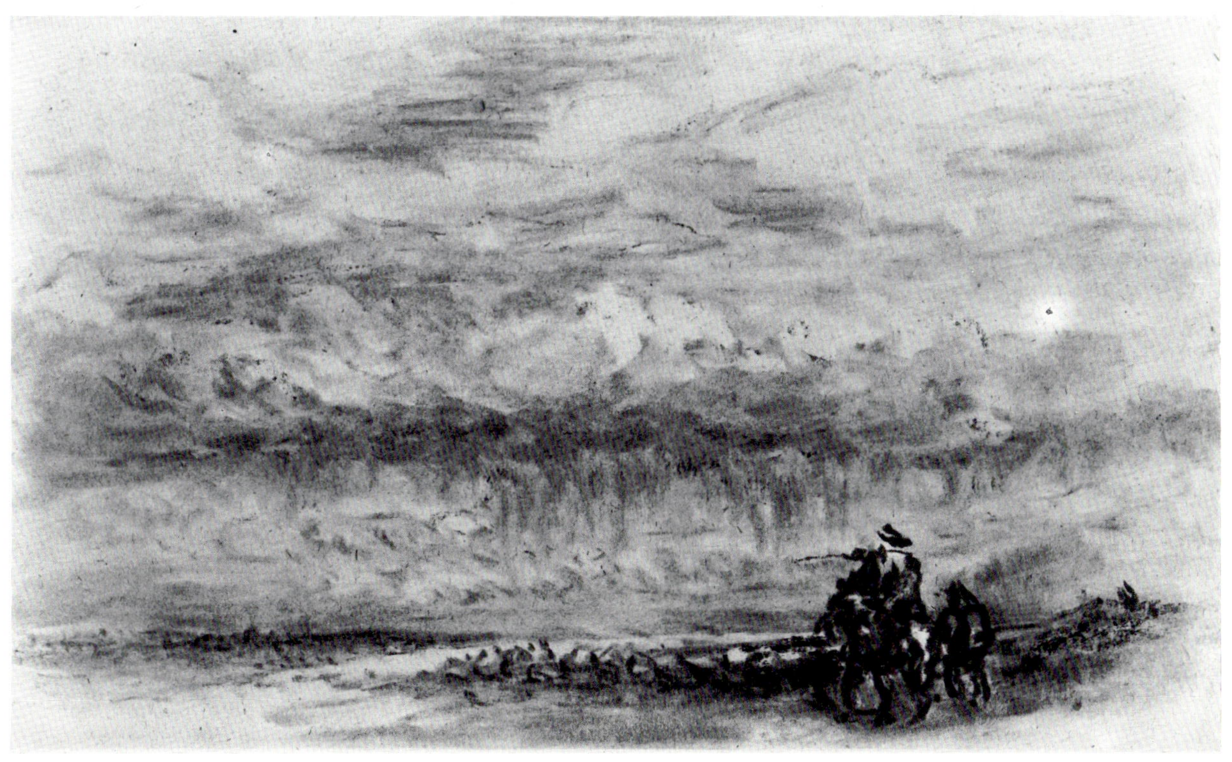

Asking the Way (cat. no. 73b)

LIT: Roger Fry, *Reflections on British Painting* 1934, pl. XIX; Cox p. 117, repr. pl. 31.
Courtauld Institute Galleries (Witt Collection)

A delightfully free study of equal size with the spirited watercolour (repr. Oppé, pl. XXI). There is a later large-scale watercolour of 1853 (*Windsor Castle: The Queen is coming*; Solly p. 253) which probably lacks the power to focus attention on the tiny figures of the Queen and her consort around which this composition revolves.

75. Sun, Wind and Rain 1845

Watercolour and bodycolour, with scratching-out, on Scotch paper 46.5 × 60.5 (18¼ × 23¾).
PROV: presented by J. Arthur Kenrick 1925 (269'25).
EXH: BMAG 1959 (85); Bourges 1970 (31; repr. colour).
LIT: Roe 1946, pl. 25; Cox, pp. 82–3, 90, repr. colour pl. III.
Birmingham Museums and Art Gallery

One of Cox's best-known works, and one which seems to encapsulate all the essential ingredients of his art: the feel of unpredictable weather, the stoical plod of the farmer and his wife, the earthy greens and browns of English landscape, the almost concealed detail of the train steaming along the

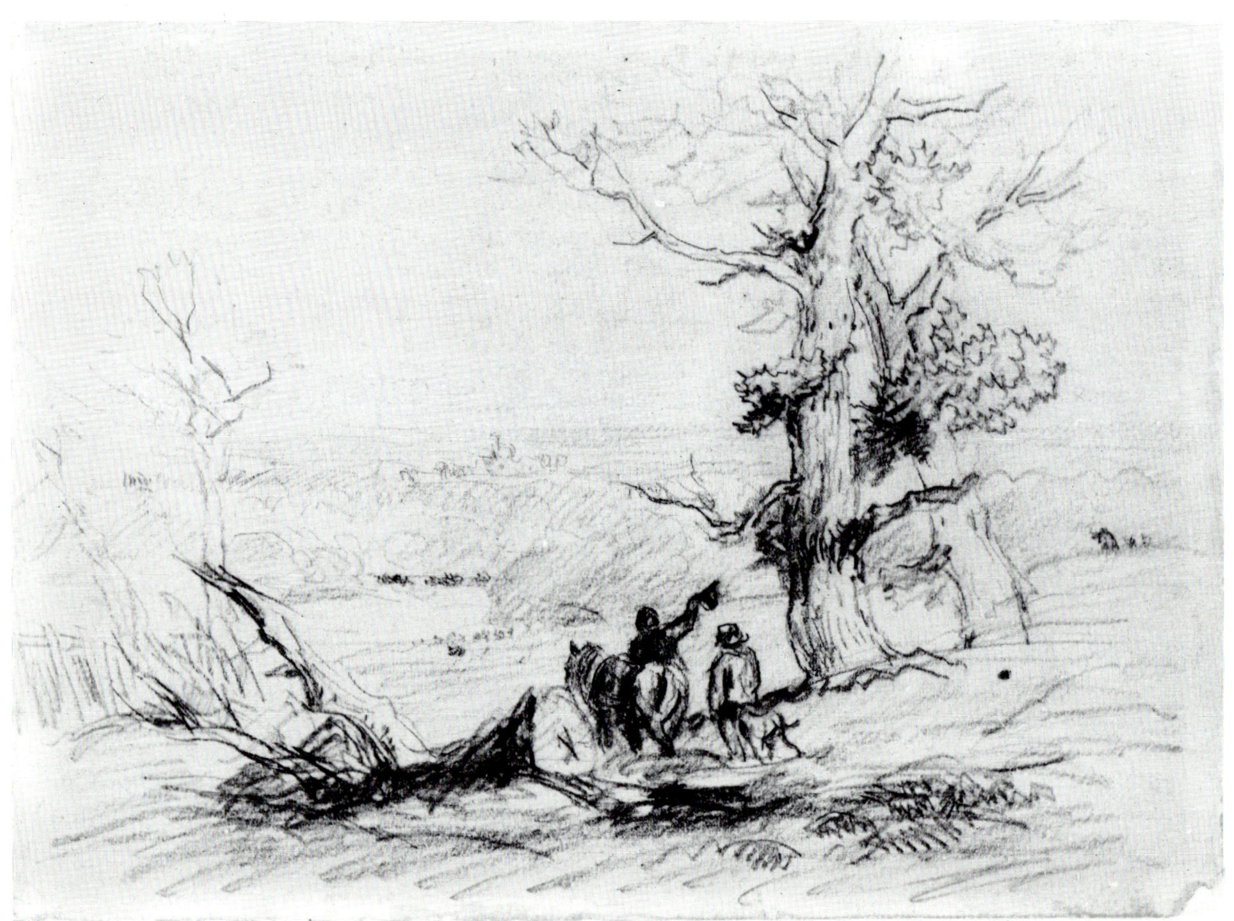

'Windsor – The Queen!' (cat. no. 74)

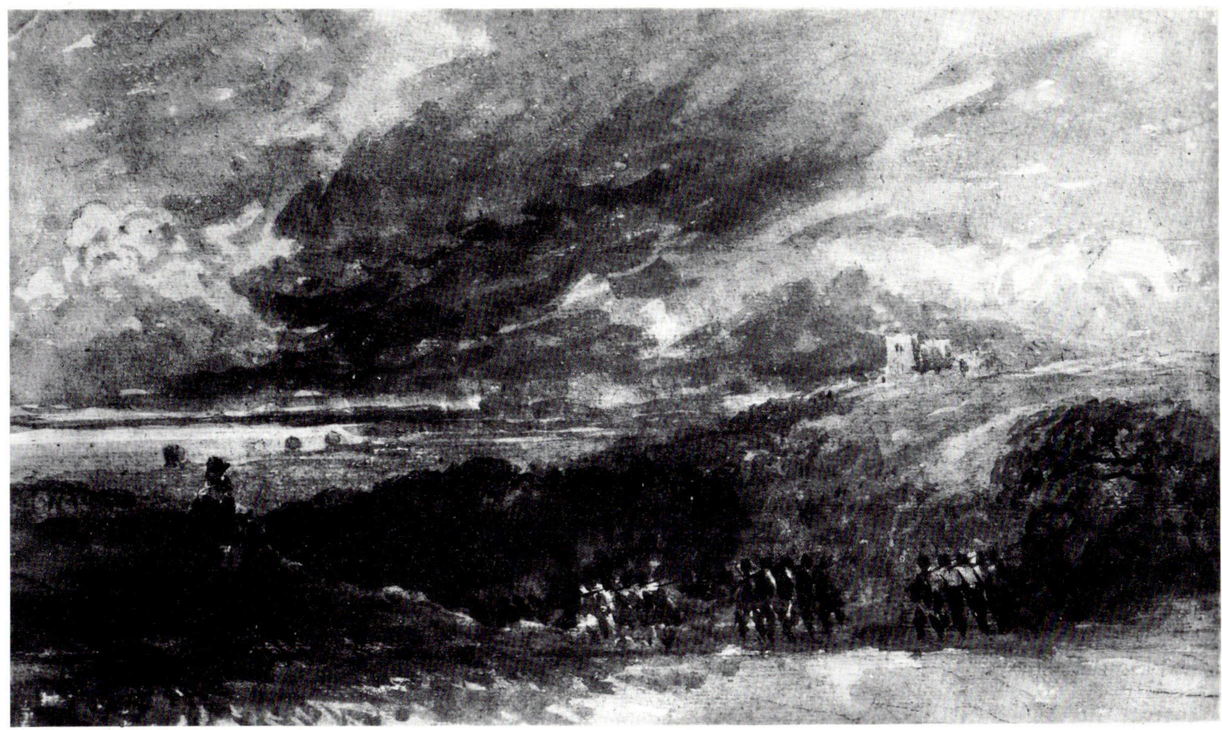

Peace and War: Lympne Church and Castle (cat. no. 77)

horizon, all achieved with broken handling, dabbing, scratching and scouring to bring out the texture of both paper and pigment.

Cox captured much of the same spirit of the watercolour in an oil version, dated 1845 (Aberdeen Art Gallery), painted for exhibition in London. The inconsistent titling of his pictures, both at the time and since, is brought out by the fact that the oil's present title, *Rain, Wind and Sunshine*, differs not only from the watercolour's but also from that given to it in a letter by Cox of 7 January 1846: 'I fear it will look very queer among such high-finished works as are usually sent to the Institution. I call my picture "Wind, Rain, and Sunshine" the size about 26 inches by 18 (canvas).' (Solly, p. 138)

76. Carting Home the Plough 1848

Watercolour, with scratching-out, on Scotch paper 27 × 37.1 (10⅝ × 14⅝).

PROV: James Orrock; presented by J. Arthur Kenrick 1925 (282'25).

EXH: BMAG 1890 (345).

LIT: A. G. Temple, *The Art of Painting in the Queen's Reign* 1897, p. 11.

Birmingham Museums and Art Gallery

In this glowing watercolour, A. G. Temple wrote, 'the warm brown earth seems to teem with richness and life.' It is a good example of the texture and absorbency of the so-called 'Scotch' paper – the wrapping paper manufactured at a Dundee mill, of which Cox was able to obtain a ream in 1836 – and the wheeling black flock on the right seems to confirm the apocryphal reply given by Cox on being asked how he dealt with the impure specks in the paper: 'Oh, I just put wings to them, and then they fly away as birds!' (Solly, p. 81)

77. Peace and War: Lympne Church and Castle

see p. 89

Watercolour over pencil on Scotch paper 28.2 × 46.4 (11⅛ × 18¼).
PROV: presented by J. Arthur Kenrick 1925 (272'25).
EXH: BMAG 1959 (58); Bourges 1970 (26).
LIT: Cox, p. 85, pl. 29.
Birmingham Museums and Art Gallery

Of all Cox's 'subject' pictures, *Peace and War* is perhaps the most enigmatic. Although the elements of the composition are simply enough explained in that title, the image conjures up memories of old conflicts and forebodings of new. Yet there is no historical association to be made: Cox accompanied his wife to Seabrook, near Hythe, for her health in 1838, and sketched at Saltwood and Lympne, close to the barracks at Hythe. The idea of contrasting labourers and soldiers was taken up in a different composition, and the setting transferred to Lancaster Castle, in an oil of 1846. Cox is said to have been greatly impressed by Müller's oil *The Baggage Waggon*, which he may have seen in progress when he took lessons from Müller. This watercolour appears to be unfinished; a large version, shown at the OWCS in 1848, is in the Lady Lever Art Gallery, Port Sunlight.

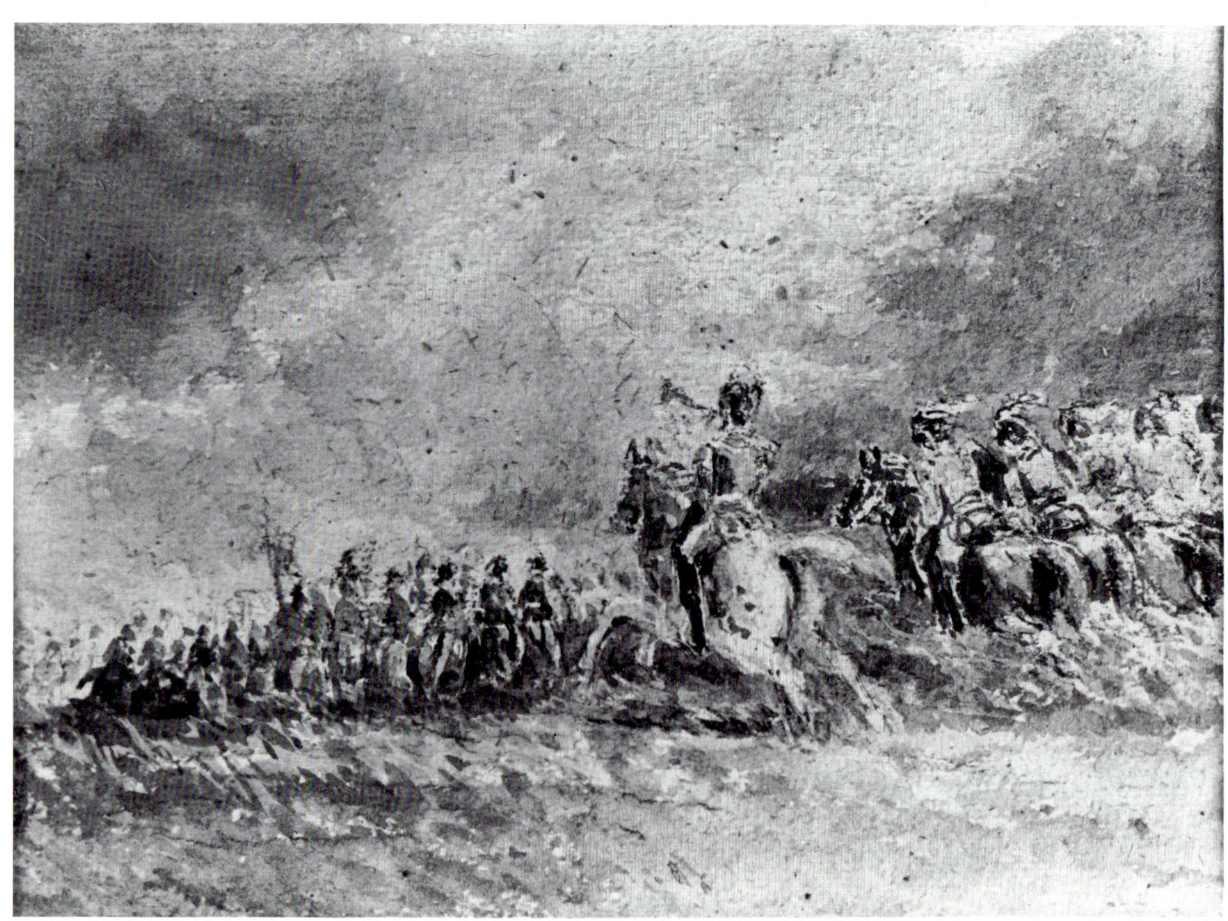

Cavalry Charge (cat. no. 78b)

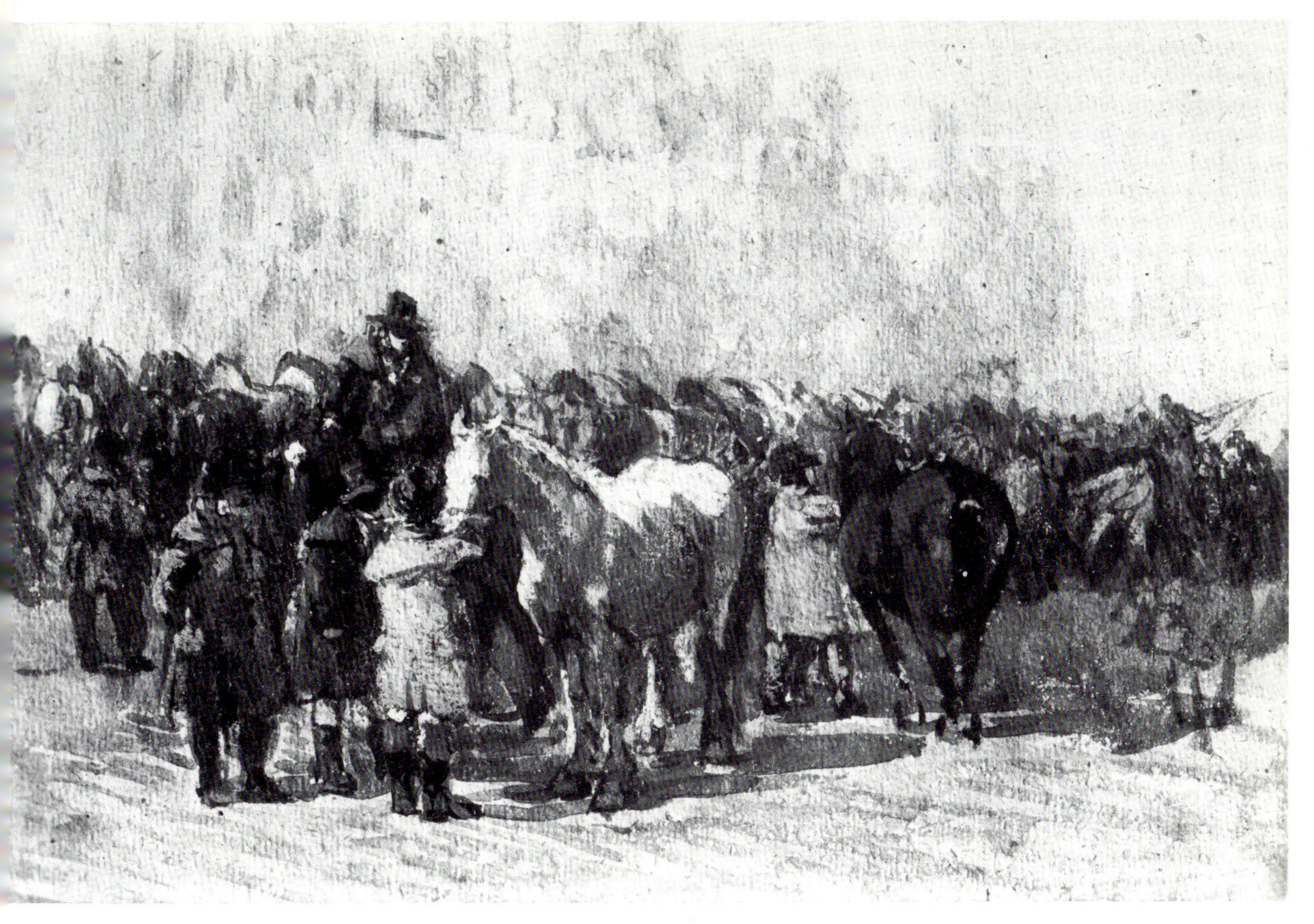

Birmingham Horse Fair (cat. no. 81)

78. (a) Battle Scene

Watercolour over soft pencil 11.5 × 18.5 ($4\frac{1}{2} \times 7\frac{1}{2}$).
PROV: W. Stone Ellis; Catherine Ellis; presented by M. B. Walker 1943 (9/1943).
Dudley Art Gallery

(b) Cavalry Charge

see p. 90

Watercolour over pencil on Scotch paper 12 × 16 ($4\frac{3}{4} \times 6\frac{1}{4}$).
PROV: as above (8/1943).
EXH: BMAG 1959 (140).
LIT: Cox, pp. 80–1.
Dudley Art Gallery

These sketches were both taken from a sketchbook belonging initially to David Cox's executor. On an unusually small scale, they still convey a sense of dramatic action, and little touches and details recall several full-scale works: the plunging horse in *The Night Train* (see below), the soldiers from *Peace and War*, even the cavalrymen that dash beneath the royal oak in the Bettws-y-Coed hotel's signboard.

79. The Night Train

see p. 11

Watercolour with scratching-out 28.5 × 38.1 ($11\frac{1}{4} \times 15$).
PROV: given by the artist to Charles Barber; presented by Barber's grand-daughters, the Misses Pritt 1925 (67'25).
EXH: BMAG 1959 (101); *Water-Colours by British Landscape Painters*, Norwich Castle Museum 1965 (26); *Victorian Painting*, Ottawa 1965 (25); *Art and the Industrial Revolution*, Manchester City Art Gallery 1968 (46); Bourges 1970 (40).
LIT: *Fraser's Magazine*, June 1859, p. 749; Cox, p. 109; T. S. R. Boase, *English Art 1800–1870*, 1959, pl. 17b.
Birmingham Museums and Art Gallery

There are three versions of this subject – another, with slight differences of detail, is in the Birmingham collection (125'23, known as *The Birmingham Express*), and a larger exhibition piece dated 1849, from the Nettlefold collection, is in Leeds City Art Galleries (OWCS 1849 [33]; Grundy I, p. 138). As so often in these instances (no. 77 is a case in point), the smaller, more compact composition is far more vibrant and powerful than the larger one. The work was probably conceived whilst staying at Charles Barber's house in Liverpool, the train therefore being the night express to Birmingham. Cox's life and work rarely display much contact with the Industrial Revolution, and it is not too unlikely to sense here an echo of Turner's *Rain, Steam, and Speed*, which Cox would have seen at the RA in 1844, and which is known to have impressed him. The title of *Sun, Wind and Rain* (no. 75), as well as its use of a similarly placed engine in full steam on the horizon, is perhaps another indication of indirect homage.

80. The Four Seasons

Each pencil, watercolour and bodycolour (all except *Spring* on Scotch paper) 27.3 × 18.2 ($10\frac{3}{4} \times 7\frac{1}{4}$).
PROV: bequeathed by J. R. Holliday 1927 (730'27–733'27).
EXH: BMAG 1959 (102).
LIT: Solly, p. 207.
Birmingham Museums and Art Gallery

Preparatory sketches for a set of oil paintings commissioned by his friend and patron Edwin Bullock in 1849, to decorate the summer house at Hawthorn House, Handsworth, Birmingham. Although the house still stands, the summer house has long disappeared, the paintings themselves apparently forming part of the sale of Bullock's pictures in 1870. The only comparable work of this kind by Cox was the fresco painted at the Royal Oak, Bettws-y-Coed (see section 8).

81. Birmingham Horse Fair

see p. 91

Watercolour and bodycolour on Scotch paper 18.7 × 29.6 ($7\frac{3}{8} \times 11\frac{5}{8}$).
PROV: William Quilter; presented by J. Palmer Phillips 1909 (55'09).
EXH: International Exhibition, London 1862 (1037); Swansea 1953 (62); *Rhodes Centenary Exhibition*, Salisbury, Rhodesia 1957 (220); BMAG 1959 (127); *Victorian Painting*, Ottawa 1965 (24); *Two Centuries of English Painting*, Prague and Bratislava 1969 (31); Bourges 1970 (41, repr.).
LIT: Solly pp. 260–61, 288, repr. p. 61; Roe 1946, pl. 24; Cox p. 109, pl. 30.
Birmingham Museums and Art Gallery

As Solly rightly says, 'considering that it is merely a rapid sketch, it is very powerful and complete', and has always been regarded as one of Cox's finest works. His habitually muffled figures are here perfectly suited to the crowded atmosphere of one of the city's liveliest markets. Its date is unknown, but when Rosa Bonheur paid her celebrated visit to Birmingham in 1856, where she was a guest of Edwin Bullock and was introduced to the artist, Cox 'produced it from his portfolio, saying that he also was an animal painter, and the lady expressed her admiration of it.'

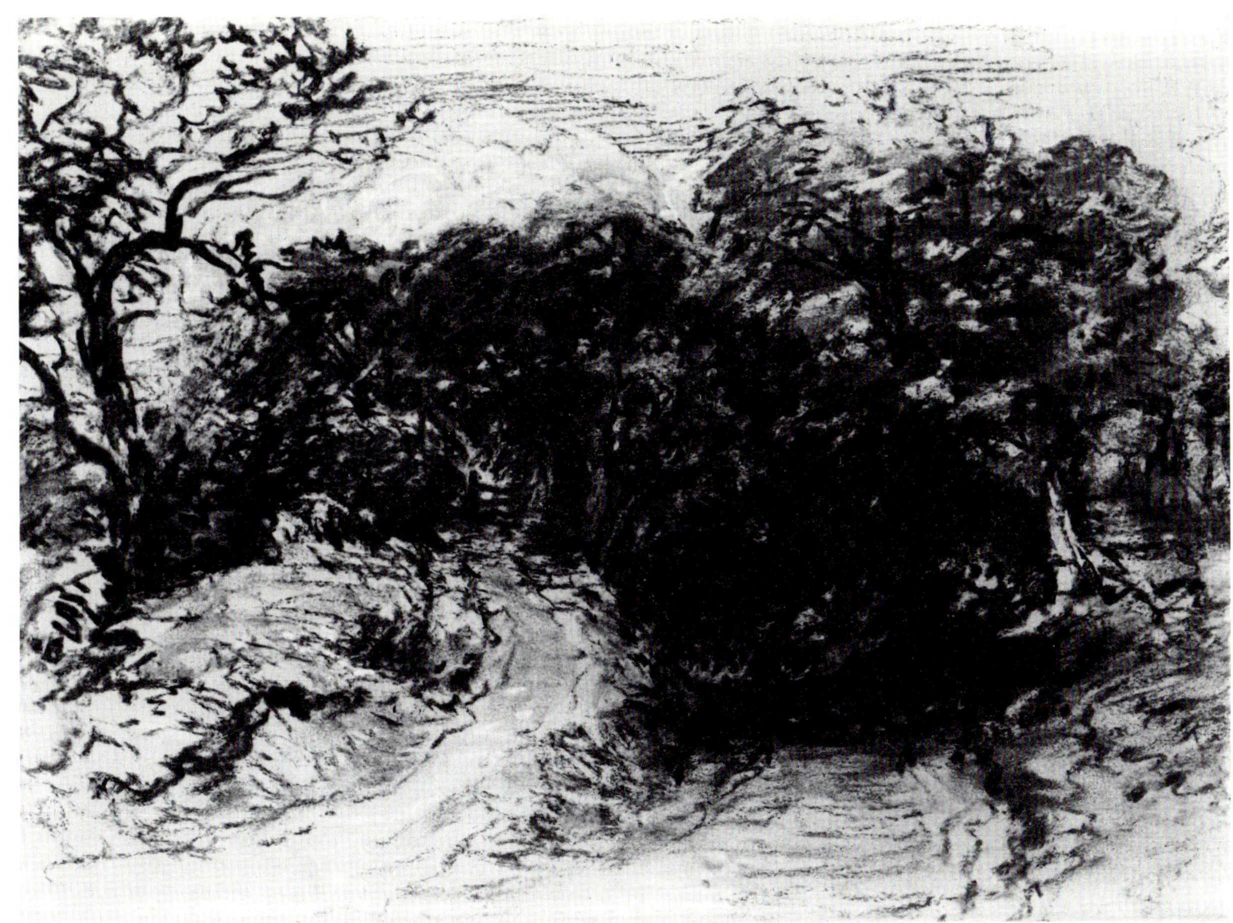

Hollow Lane near Harborne (cat. no. 82)

82. Hollow Lane near Harborne

Brown chalk and stump, touched with white, on buff paper 24.5 × 32.8 (9⅝ × 12⅞).
PROV: presented by Dyson Perrins 1919.
EXH: *Worcestershire Exhibition*, Worcester 1882.
The Visitors of the Ashmolean Museum, Oxford

83. Lane at Harborne 1849

Watercolour with heavy scratching-out 51 × 45.5 (20 × 17⅞).
PROV: presented by the Council of Guarantors of the Royal Jubilee Exhibition 1887 (D.19.1887).
LIT: *Catalogue of Water-Colour Drawings*, Whitworth Institute 1909, p. 44 (repr.).
Whitworth Art Gallery, University of Manchester

Although Cox's works generally derive from the inspiration found during summer and autumn sketching tours away from home, he could also find subjects near at hand, and made many drawings and watercolours of Harborne (and a few oils: there is a small *Harborne Church* in the National Gallery of Ireland, Dublin). Greenfield House then stood alone in a lane leading to the church, beyond which were meadows and open country. 'There were also many trees and undulating hills on this side, which became a sort of "home preserve" where Cox could always find subjects for sketches.' (Solly, p. 107)

84. Study of Fish: Skate and Cod

Oil on millboard 13 × 19.7 (5⅛ × 7¾).
PROV: David Cox junior; bought from the artist's grand-daughters by Augustus Walker; J. W. North; bequeathed by J. R. Holliday 1927 (666'27).
EXH: Swansea 1953 (81); BMAG 1959 (67).
LIT: Cox p. 94, pl. 24; BMAG Oils p. 35.
Birmingham Museums and Art Gallery

With the sole experience of a few small attempts in 1812 (nos. 10, 11), Cox took up the challenge of painting in oils in 1839, at the age of fifty-six. He was naturally doubtful about his abilities at first, those doubts often expressed in letters of the following years. Solly (p. 183) says that he would tell those who looked at his early work: 'Well, what do you see amiss? You must understand I am no great hand at oil-painting; it is not the work I have been used to.' There are very few references to work ascribable earlier than 1842, when growing confidence allowed him to sign and date his oils. This little still life has all the look of a skilled painter trying his hand at a new kind of work.

85. The Wyndcliffe, River Wye

Oil on canvas 34.9 × 45.7 (13¾ × 18).
PROV: Dr Archer, Birmingham; presented by Mrs Richards 1912 (3'12).
EXH: Liverpool 1875; *'Coming of Age' Exhibition*, Bradford 1925 (32).
LIT: BMAG Oils, p. 40.
Birmingham Museums and Art Gallery

The Wyndcliffe is an area of high ground above the River Wye, affording views of the river and Chepstow Castle in the distance (Tintern Abbey is just a little further up river). Cox painted a watercolour of this view in 1831 (Victoria and Albert Museum; reproduced in the catalogue of the Dixon Bequest, 1934), which he asked his son to send him in 1841 so that he might paint an oil version for the 1842 Birmingham Society of Artists exhibition. Signed but not dated, this is hardly the 'large oil' which Cox said he was intending, but it is probably of the same date; it is in a more highly-finished, 'watercolour' style than most later oils, and has a bright luminosity reminiscent of the small oils of Francis Danby, whose work Cox knew and admired.

86. Dudley Castle

Oil on canvas 34.3 × 42.5 (13½ × 16¾).
PROV: Mr Rodgett, Preston; bequeathed by Richard Newsham 1883.
LIT: Hibbert, no. 60; *Illustrated Catalogue*, Preston Corporation Art Gallery 1907, p. 26, repr.
Harris Museum and Art Gallery, Preston

The picturesque low mass of Dudley Castle atop its steep hill has long been a favourite subject for Birmingham and Black Country artists. As well as his contributions to Smith's *Dudley Castle* (1836), Cox made numerous other studies, the best being those from across the valley, with the lime-kilns in the foreground. He painted at least two other oils, dated 1846 (Murrieta sale 1892) and 1853 (Manchester City Art Gallery), of this view, in addition to this exquisite study.

87. Crossing the Sands 1848

Oil on panel 26.7 × 37.9 (10½ × 14¹⁵⁄₁₆).
PROV: bequeathed by Joseph H. Nettlefold 1882 (2487'85).
EXH: BMAG 1890 (76).
LIT: BMAG Oils, p. 38.
Birmingham Museums and Art Gallery

One of a number of jewel-like little oils on panel (*On the Sands*, BMAG 2514'85, is another) which capture the essence of previous successful watercolours (e.g. nos. 49, 51), but have their own singular freshness of treatment and magical liquidity of touch.

88. Sheep Shearing 1849 *see p. 96*

Oil on canvas 26.7 × 38.1 (10½ × 15).
PROV: bequeathed by Joseph H. Nettlefold 1882 (2508'85).
EXH: BMAG 1890 (93, repr.); *International Exhibition*, Glasgow, 1901 (334); BMAG 1959 (104).
LIT: *Studio*, Special Number 1903, pl. DC6; Cox p. 98; BMAG Oils, p. 38.
Birmingham Museums and Art Gallery

Cox's style in oils soon reached and equalled the maturity of his watercolour painting, so that this vigorously handled subject could be reproduced by the artist in the following year as a watercolour (British Museum, 1915-3-13-15), details such as the creamy impasto of the sheep's wool being matched by rich dashes of bodycolour.

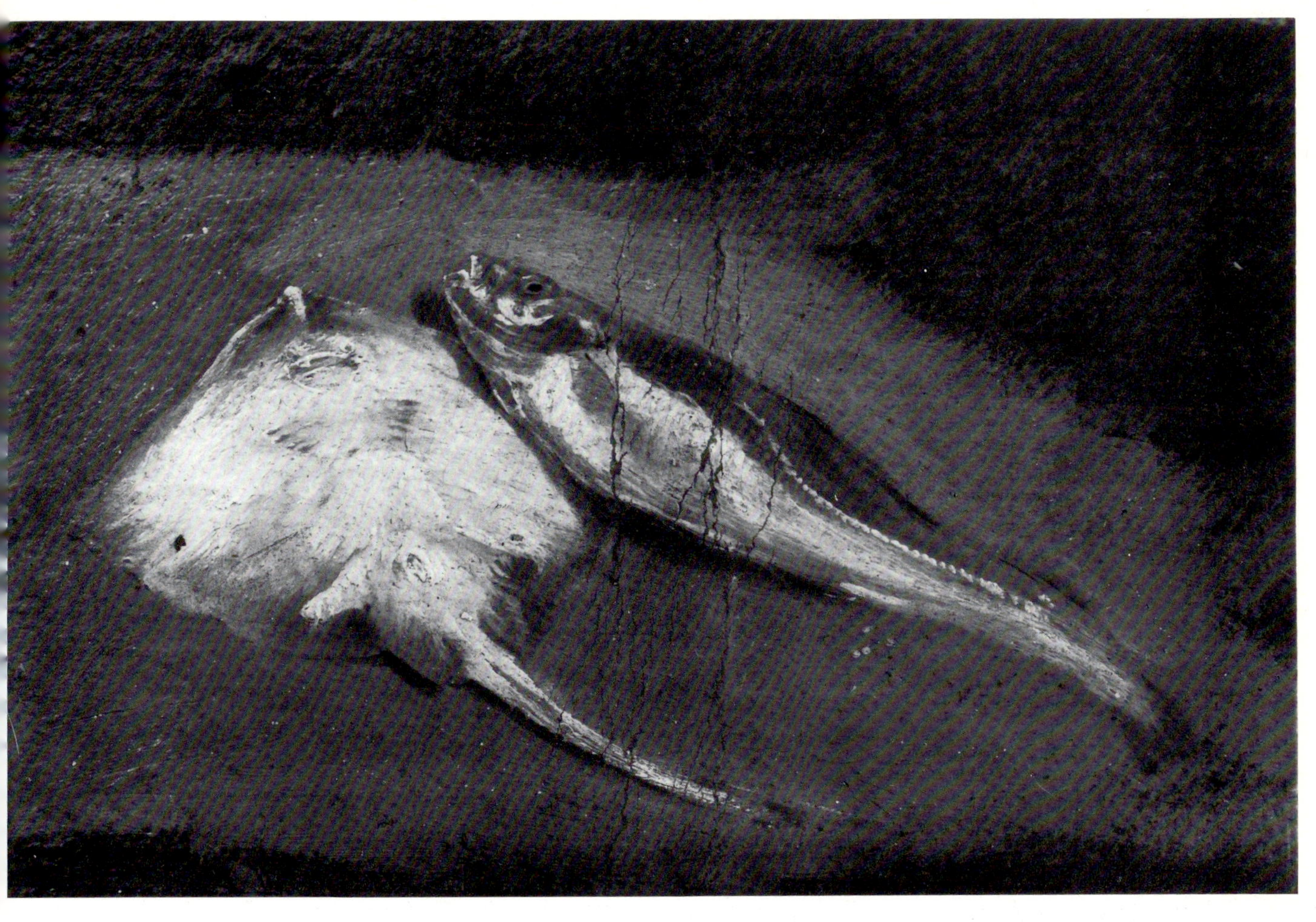

Study of Fish: Skate and Cod (cat. no. 84)

89. The Skylark 1849

Oil on canvas 71.1 × 91.4 (28 × 36).
PROV: bought from the artist by E. A. Butler for £40; Thomas Darby; Samuel Mayou; sold by him to Frederick J. Nettlefold for £2,300; presented by F. J. Nettlefold 1947 (P76'47).
EXH: Birmingham Society of Artists 1849; *Royal Jubilee Exhibition*, Manchester 1887 (831); *Loan Exhibition of Pictures from the City Art Gallery, Birmingham*, Agnew's 1957 (37); BMAG 1959 (99).
LIT: Solly pp. 153–54, 193–94, 218; Hall, pp. 140–44, 227, 231, 258; Grundy, I, pp. 136–38, repr.; Roe 1946, pl. 36; Cox p. 99; BMAG Oils, pp. 38–9.
Birmingham Museums and Art Gallery

'It is one of those subjects where the artist has concentrated all his thoughts and power on an idea which is so thoroughly realised that the spectator feels carried into the scene itself . . . the sky is unusually tender and full of *space*, and so is the distant landscape which stretches far away and melts into the sky at the horizon. The feeling conveyed is that of early summer, with perfect repose and enjoyment of out-door country life.' Solly's word-picture gives some idea of the appeal of this painting, which borders on the sentimental, to later Victorian taste. 'Who could ever cage a lark after looking on that picture?' asked Edward Radclyffe at the Cox exhibition banquet at Liverpool in 1875.

The increasing scale and brilliance of Cox's oils outshines the watercolours of this period. Certainly, *The Skylark* watercolour (23½ × 33½in, presented to Birmingham by the same donor in 1947), although now in a faded state, is rather drab and vacuous in comparison. The setting of the picture is said to be Harborne.

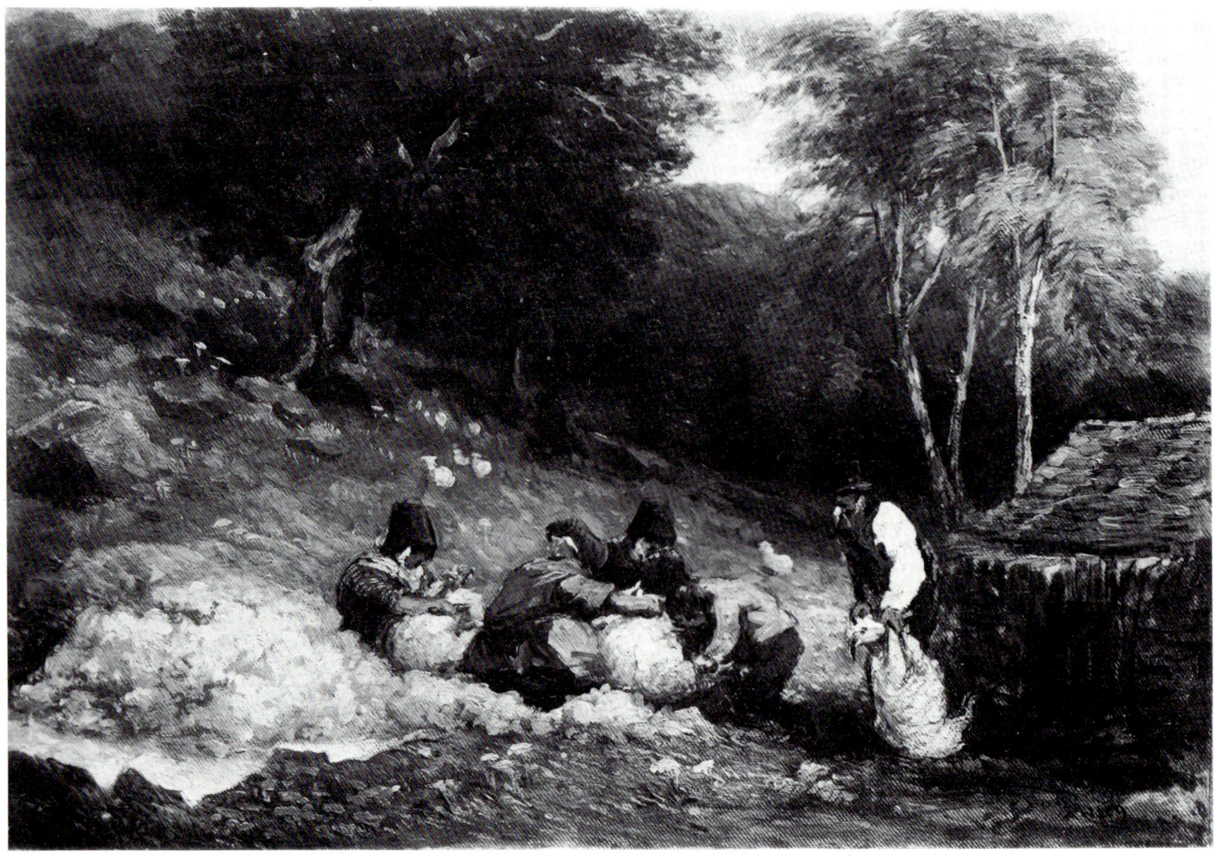

Sheep Shearing 1849 (cat. no. 88)

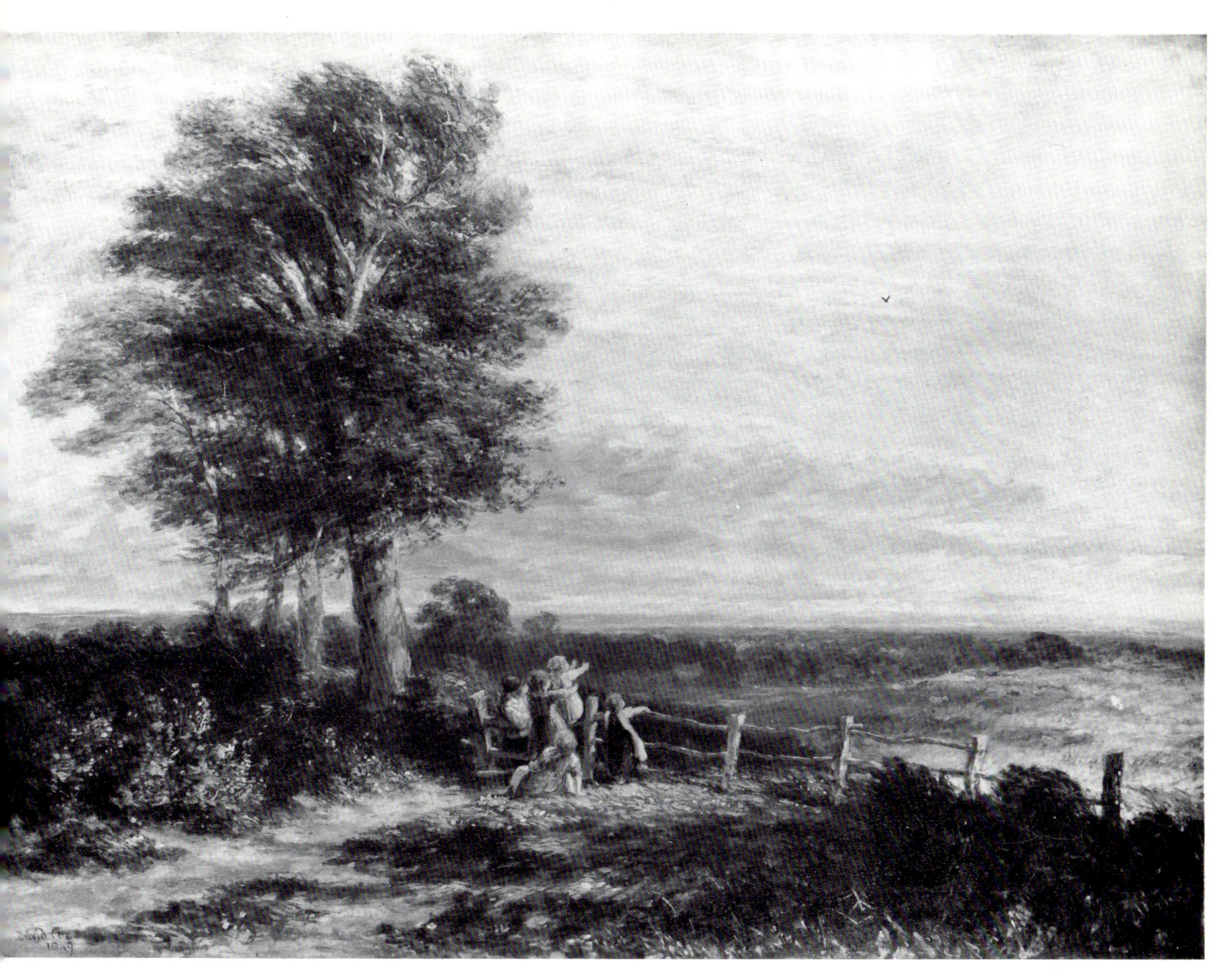

he Skylark 1849 (cat. no. 89)

90. The Vale of Clwyd 1849

Oil on canvas 90.5 × 142.3 (36⅝ × 56).

PROV: George Briscoe, Wolverhampton; Frederick Timmins; Mariano de Murrieta by 1873; T. J. Barratt; Barratt sale, Christie's 11/5/1916 (44), bt. Robson; bequeathed by Arthur William Young, 1936 (no. 1788).

EXH: *Loan Collection*, Guildhall Art Gallery 1897 (69); Winter exhibition, RA 1903 (117).

LIT: Solly, pp. 155, 190, 201; Hall, p. 118; James Orrock, *Cox's 'Vale of Clwyd'*, in *Magazine of Art*, Vol. 15, 1892, p. 385, repr.; B. Webber, *James Orrock, RI*, 1903, II, p. 66; J. Huskinson, Fitzwilliam Museum, *Catalogue of Paintings, III: British School*, 1979, pp. 57–8, pl. 35.

The Syndics of the Fitzwilliam Museum, Cambridge

Probably Cox's outstanding achievement as an oil painter, and one of the major works of the British landscape school of the 1840s, which has suffered such unjust neglect as a result of the extreme adulation of Constable during this century. Known from its provenance as the 'Timmins Clwyd', it has a sister version (the 'Sharp Clwyd', present whereabouts unknown), and these together with *Counting the Flocks* of the same dimensions (Manchester City Art Gallery) are the largest works in Cox's *oeuvre*.

It is all the more impressive, therefore, to see how Cox has preserved the freshness of the image and the spontaneity of treatment. As with Constable, and so often with Cox's own large exhibition watercolours, the immediacy of an original sketch is rarely translated intact onto the larger scale and greater degree of 'finish' of an exhibition work. Here, however, we have a wonderful evocation of British landscape, of light, and wind, and air, each element treated in Cox's own style, and yet coalescing into an harmonious whole. Built up, like Cox's watercolours, with short, dabbed brushstrokes, the surface is alive with light, carefully balanced colour, and movement, appropriately capturing the ripple of wind through the foreground foliage and the slanting sunlight carrying the eye into the breezy distance, with the sparkling water of the estuary and far-off blue-grey hills. The figures are perfectly scaled to fill the open side of the composition with quiet activity, and bear the final flickering touches of high-key colour, also scattered on the poppy heads below.

The river Clwyd runs through the former counties of Denbighshire and Flint, and into the sea near Rhyl. Cox made numerous drawings of the scenery of the valley, and *The Vale of Clwyd* was probably based on sketches made in 1844, according to Hall, from Sir John Williams's park at Bodelwyddan near St Asaph.

The 'Sharp Clwyd' remained unsold at eighty guineas in the Liverpool Academy exhibition of 1846, whilst Cox received only £95 (the second highest price he ever received for a work) for this even more powerful version. The later 19th-century appreciation of his work led to this work's changing hands twice for over £4,000 by 1916, but not for its monetary value was *The Vale of Clwyd* more than once called by critics 'the finest pastoral picture in the world'.

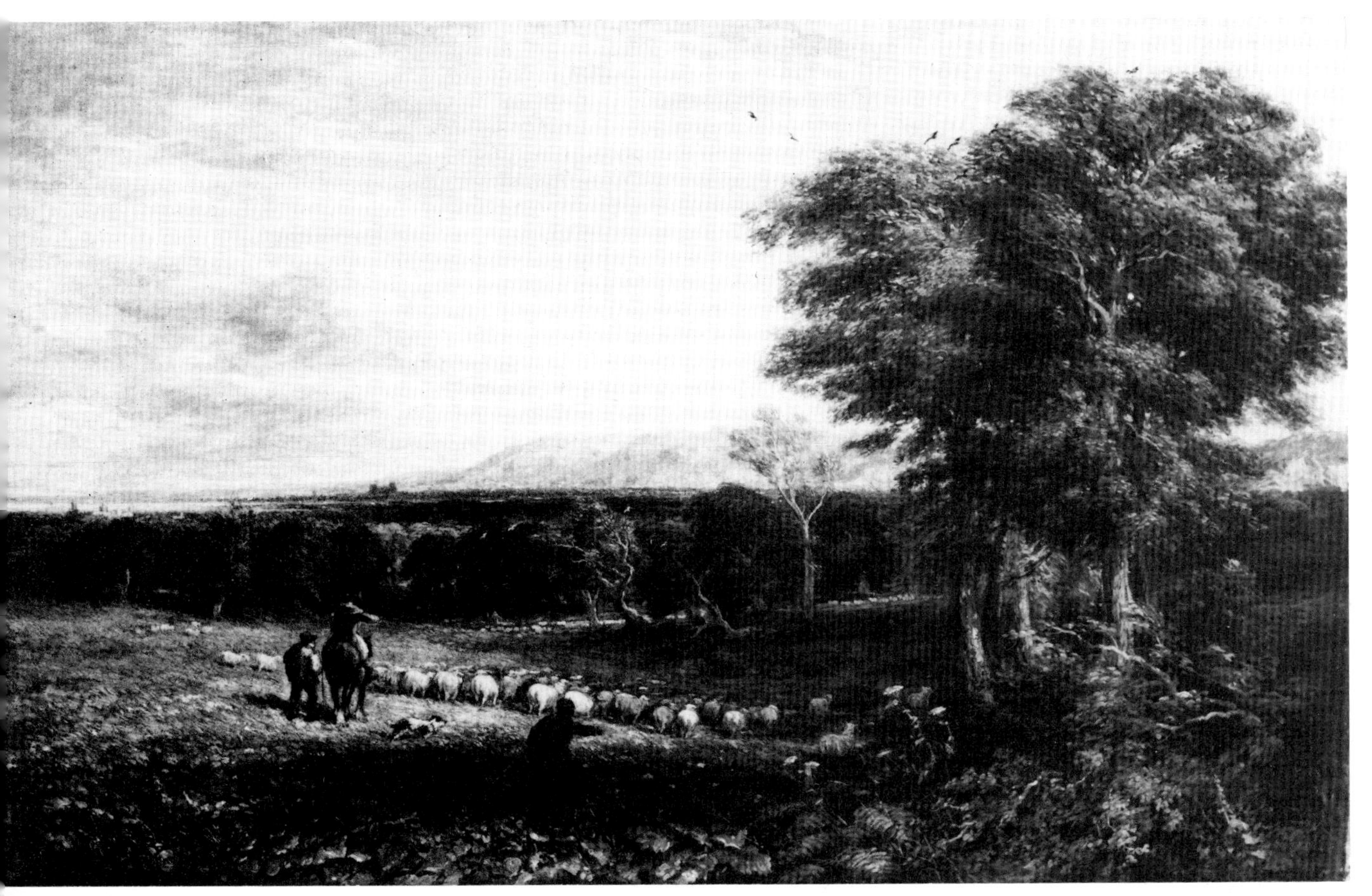

The Vale of Clwyd 1849 (cat. no 90)

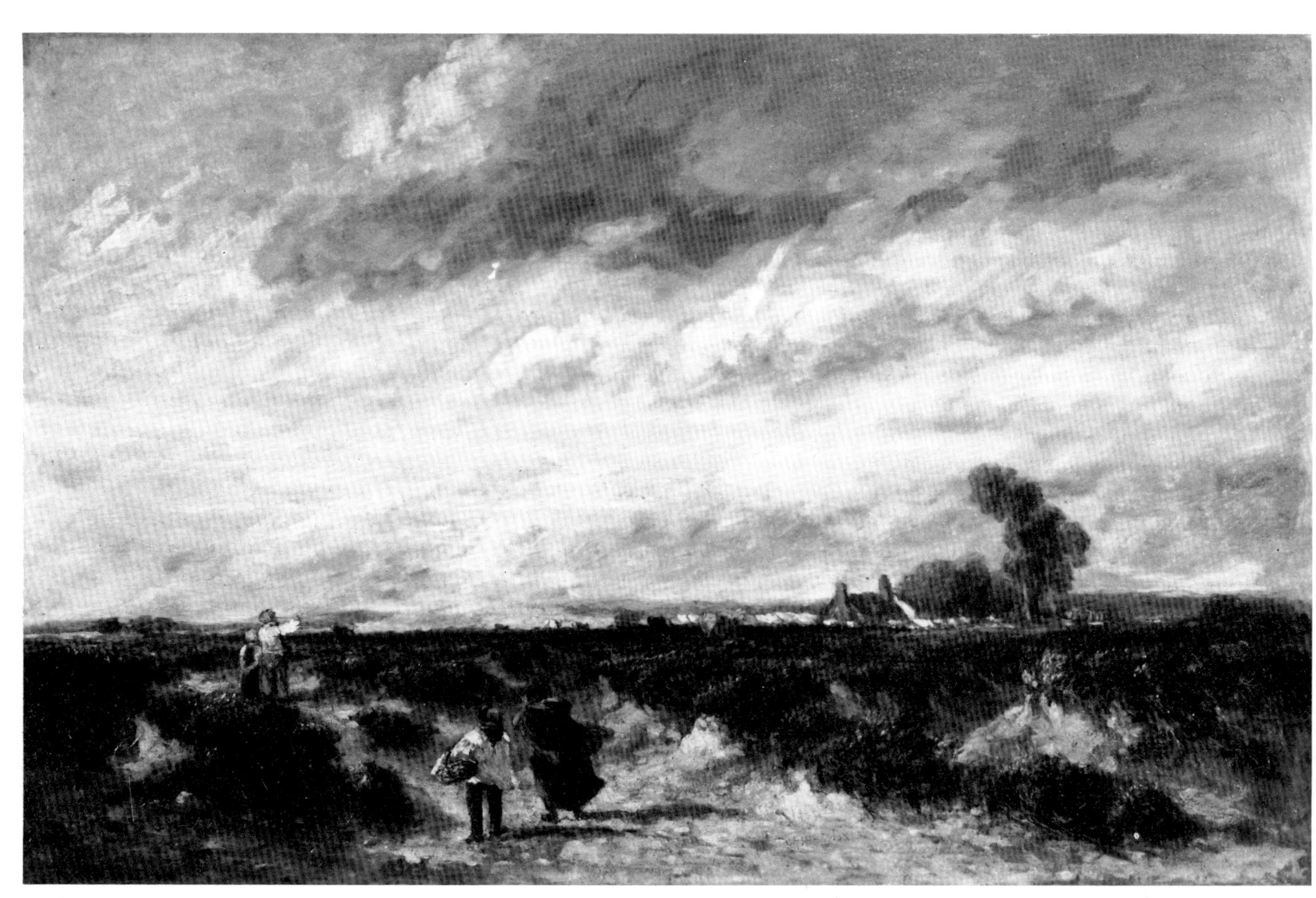

Flying the Kite – A Windy Day (cat. no. 92)

6. The Last Years 1850–59

By 1850, Cox was alone (his faithful Mary having died in 1845) but still at the height of his powers; indeed, he seems to have thrown new effort into his work during these years. In oils this meant a wide variety of scale and concept, from delicate little panels (no. 91) to the broadest of canvases (no. 93).

In the watercolours, a marked broadening of style is already evident by 1850, perhaps as a result of Cox's trying to infuse more vigour and life into what were often rather dull large exhibition pieces. However, he realised the dangers of a broad style developing into mere mannerism, especially on Scotch paper. 'My drawing upon the Scotch paper is so rough,' he wrote to his son, 'I fear I shall bring down all against me.' When under calm but firm control (as in nos. 98, 99), his manipulation of the opportunities afforded by his unique medium is very impressive.

Cox survived the traumatic year of 1853 surprisingly well. Between the bout of bronchitis that sapped his usually robust health and the stroke from whose effects he was never to recover fully, he suffered the mental anguish of criticism of his work. Like the proud protagonist of The Challenge *(no. 102), he was prepared to stand his ground: 'They forget they are the* work of the mind, *which I consider very far before portraits of places . . .'*

91. The Cross Roads 1850

Oil on panel 16.5 × 75.4 (6½ × 10).
PROV: ?Edwin Bullock (1870 sale, as *Inquiring at the Cross Roads*); bequeathed by Joseph H. Nettlefold 1882 (2502'85).
EXH: BMAG 1890 (100); Swansea 1953 (85); BMAG 1959 (106).
LIT: Solly, p. 221; BMAG Oils, p. 39.
Birmingham Museums and Art Gallery

Another of the small but infinitely delicate little oils (see no. 87) which synthesize subjects so often previously treated in watercolours and drawings. With a few tiny brushstrokes, Cox again pits one of his windswept country women against the elements. The image of the traveller lost, in mid-journey, or seeking the right road or crossing, Cox made very much his own (see nos. 49, 73, 101).

92. Flying the Kite – A Windy Day 1851

Oil on Canvas 47.6 × 73 (18¾ × 28¾).
PROV: Holbrook Gaskell, by 1875; Christie's 24/6/1909 (12); Lt Col James B. Gaskell; Christie's 30/4/1926 (110); presented by F. J. Nettlefold 1948 (no. 1194).
EXH: Liverpool 1875 (22); Glasgow 1888 (248); BMAG 1890 (117); *British Art*, RA 1934 (667); BMAG 1959 (113).
LIT: Grundy, I, p. 444, repr. colour; Roe 1946, colour pl. 10.
Walker Art Gallery, Liverpool

A Windy Day is the simple title of the small oil, dated 1850, in the Tate Gallery (no. 2666), and was used as the subtitle for a number of little paintings between 1846 and 1853. It emphasises the greater part which the sky, usually heavily filled with clouds, plays in these oils rather than in the watercolours from which any of them might derive or which were to follow (the closest parallel to *Flying the Kite* is the watercolour of that title in the British Museum, dated 1853, which is varied by the addition of two figures to the group of children). The streaming line of washing, which mixes subtly with wandering cattle to mark the horizon line, is also a familiar motif (going back at least to Wolverhampton Art Gallery's *Cottage at Dulwich – A Windy Day* of 1846).

93. Rhyl Sands 1854–5

Oil on canvas 74.3 × 135.3 (29¼ × 53¼).
PROV: sold by the artist for £100; Croft; R. Adams, Birmingham, by 1859; Albert Levy; Christie's 1/4/1876 (252); bequeathed by Joseph H. Nettlefold 1882 (2489'85).
EXH: German Gallery 1859 (1); Burlington House 1875 (20); *Jubilee Exhibition*, Manchester 1887 (832); BMAG 1890 (103, repr.); Swansea 1953 (87); BMAG 1959 (124).

LIT: Solly, p. 195; Roe 1924, p. 126; Roe 1946, pp. 81–3, pl. 43; Cox, pp. 73, 98, pl. 26B; BMAG Oils, p. 41.
Birmingham Museums and Art Gallery

Rhyl Sands is amongst the best-known of Cox's compositions, but more from the spontaneous oil sketch belonging to Manchester City Art Gallery, the quick, nervous handling of which has often provoked comparison with Boudin and Impressionism, than through the finished work. Certainly this and other related sketches (for which see Manchester City Art Gallery, *David Cox Catalogue* 1982, no. 5, and no. 100 below) are, for their date, unusually direct and modern in feel, but the finished oil, too, is compelling. With its composition dramatically extended from the safety of the shore into a turbulent sea, it draws the spectator into its airy expanses.

This feeling of depth beneath apparent simplicity was finally recognised by Cox's contemporaries towards the end of his life, and his position in the hierarchy of British painting judged accordingly. No apology is therefore offered for quoting in full the appreciation of *Rhyl Sands* which appeared in the *Fraser's Magazine* review of the 1859 German Gallery exhibition: 'As a landscape painter there are not a few who would deliberately prefer the works of Cox to those of Turner, because, although not of such astonishingly varied a character or diversity of theme as the former, neither of such vast scope of intellectual grasp – yet, nevertheless, there is a sturdy simplicity of truth, the honest genuineness of which rises far above the prosaic – for the same reason that the homeliest things are oftentimes the most poetical; which never fails to win admiration, and this after a little time deepens into the profoundest astonishment and delight as the accustomed eye discerns new wonders of truth and marvels of perfect success in representations of nature. Thus we say, in looking at a picture like "*Rhyl*" we see but a low-toned work of moderate effectiveness; hundreds of casual observers might pass it by thoughtlessly; but let us stay a moment to look along that low stony beach, over-driven by a world of fleecy clouds that roll past heavily upon a strong breeze. In an instant the whole picture seems to open, deepening and clearing before the eye, much as a stereoscope does when we look intently. That which looked composed dun sea is now a hurrying tormented mass of water that fretfully chafes beneath the persisting wind, and wreaks its angry will upon the rocky shore, in irregular ungathered masses, where the tide and the wind are at strife. Over the yeasty petulant waters the long winged gulls fly low and dip their flashing glancing wings – wings that shine in the transient gleam of light through the cloud-gaps above – which, parted in their hasty flight, reveal the grey blue sky of spring. On a sudden it seems a veil has been withdrawn, not from the picture, but from our sight; for now the clouds have that multitudinous motion which seems to carry them in an universal creeping swiftness, where thousands are moving like one to dip far off down behind the horizon, just as the sun goes down behind a cliff. It is fairy work indeed: and yet all this is no more than a rugged stony beach, whereon promenade some people dressed in forgotten fashions; a long greyish dun stretch of yeasty sea; and overhead the nations of the clouds careering on.'

94. (a) The Skirts of the Forest 1843

Oil on canvas 69.8 × 90.2 (27½ × 35½).
PROV: painted for William Roberts; Joseph Gillott; his sale April 1872; E. Crompton Potter; his sale, Christie's 22/3/1884; W. Cuthbert Quilter; B. Schroder; Christie's 29 February 1980 (188).
EXH: ?RA 1843 (1189); Liverpool 1875 (19); Birmingham 1890 (229).
LIT: Solly, pp. 119–20, 202.
Private Collection

(b) The Skirts of the Forest 1855–6

Oil on canvas 70.5 × 90.2 (27¾ × 35½).
PROV: painted for David Jones for £40; sold by his widow, with the Welsh Funeral of 1850, to Joseph H. Nettlefold for 3000 gns; bequeathed by him 1882 (2484'85).
EXH: Liverpool 1875 (40); BMAG 1890 (77, repr.); BMAG 1959 (126).
LIT: Solly, p. 201; Redgrave, p. 53, repr.; Roe 1946, pl. 44; Cox, p. 98; BMAG Oils, pp. 41–2.
Birmingham Museums and Art Gallery

Cox occasionally moved from the open fields and hills into the woods and forests of England, notably for chiaroscuro effects in chalk in the woods at Harborne or Bolton Abbey, but also for sombre yet tonally dramatic oils such as *The Skirts of the Forest*. The 1843 version, painted for William Roberts, was originally entitled *Outskirts of a Wood, with Gipsies*,

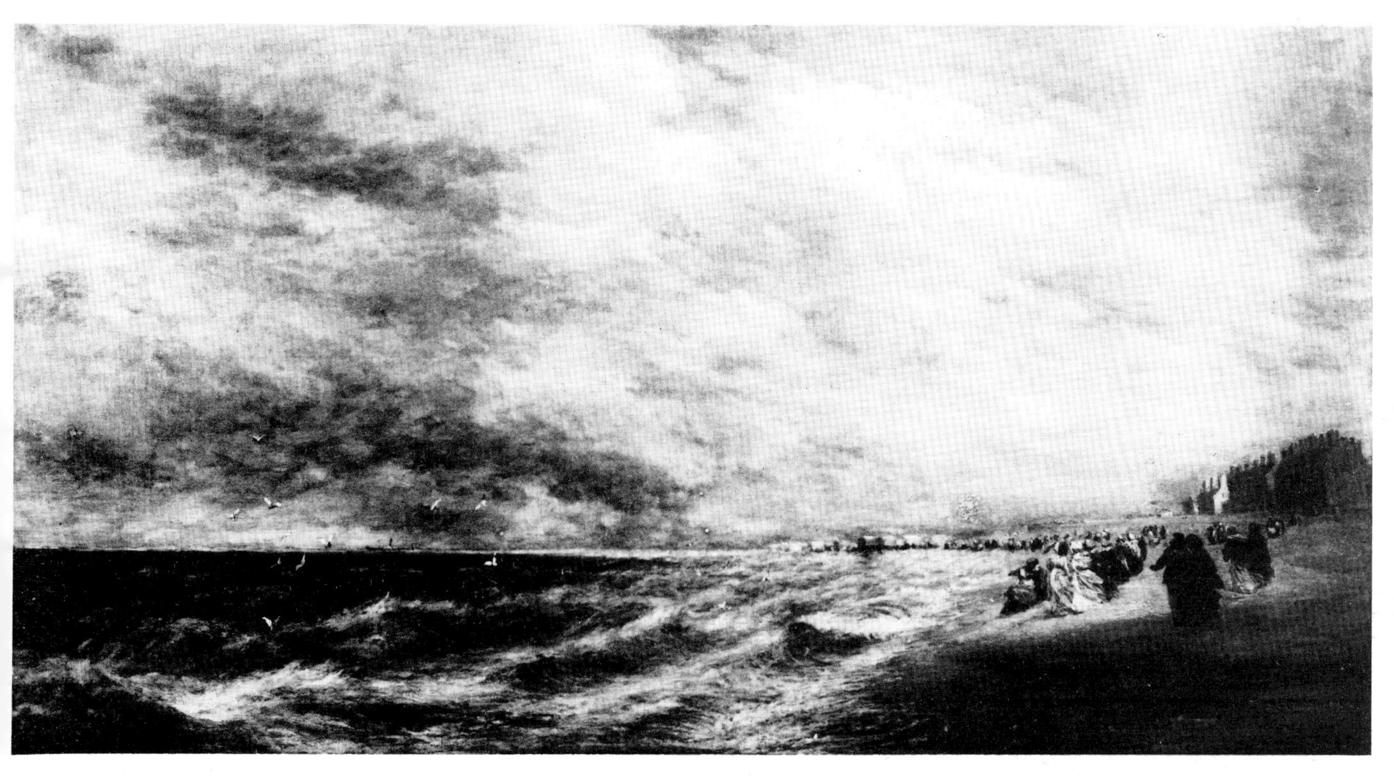

Rhyl Sands 1854–5 (cat. no. 93)

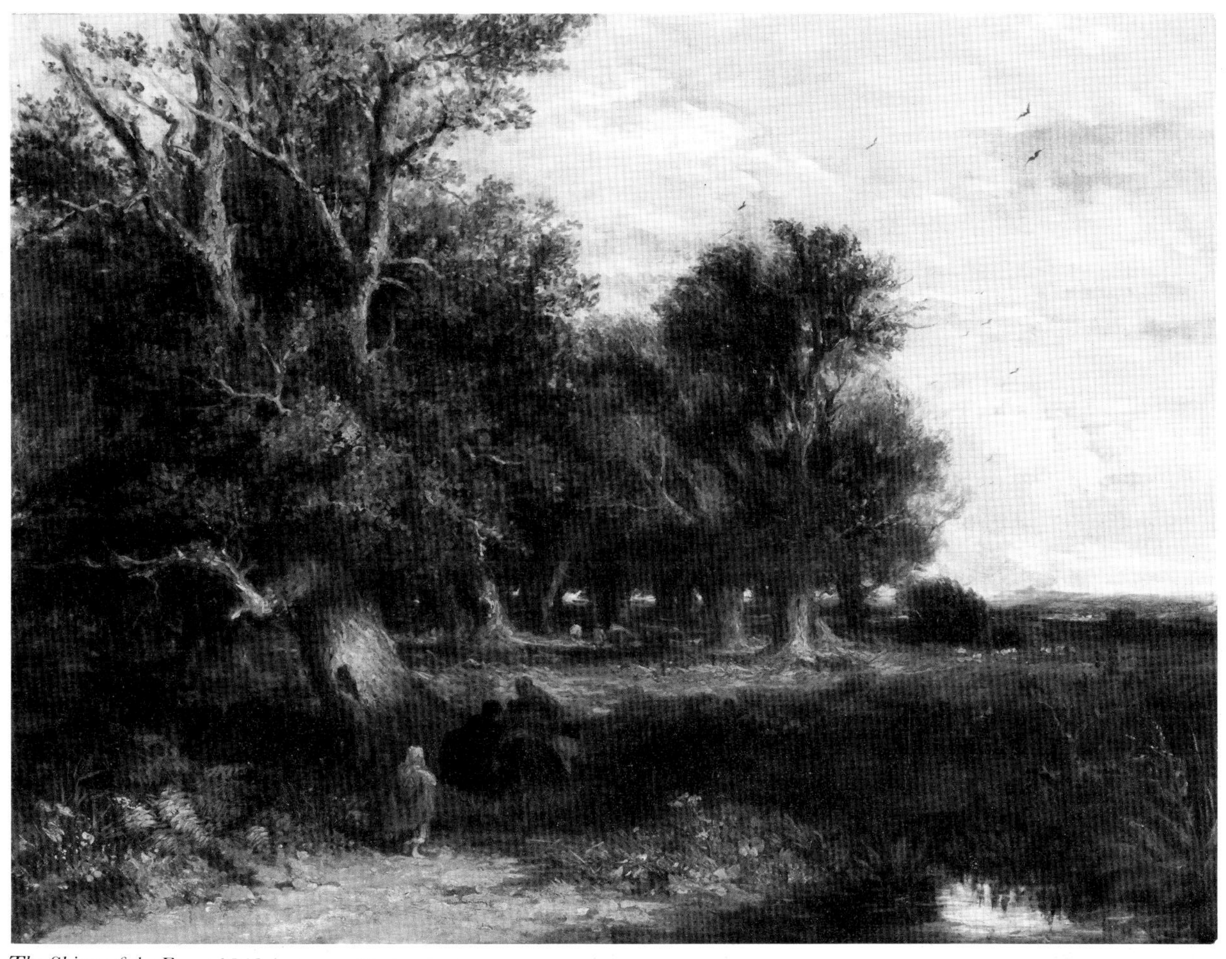

The Skirts of the Forest 1843 (cat. no. 94a)

and it is instructive to compare it with the later work, painted in Cox's declining years but showing interesting changes of detail and tonality that would certainly accord with the strength of character and purpose required for such taxing work. In the first version, the figures of the gipsies are thrown into perhaps a symbolic shadow, befitting their restless life, whilst, in the manner of his early oils, the foliage is delicately picked out in a mosaic of subtle greens. In the later work, Cox goes for an altogether bolder treatment, and earth, sky, wood and figures are treated with total solidity, the contrast of highlights and dark tones being especially brought out in the foreground oak and in the almost as solid shawled figure, as well as in the shafts of light between the oaks of Sherwood Forest.

95. The Broom Gatherers

Watercolour over black chalk, on Scotch paper 40 × 54 ($15\frac{3}{4} \times 21\frac{1}{4}$).

PROV: bequeathed by Richard Newsham 1883.

LIT: Hibbert, no. 101.

Harris Museum and Art Gallery, Preston

A powerful study, in freshly preserved colours, showing the extraordinarily broken handling and hard-edged contours of the kind of work of the early 1850s which Cox knew would be found too 'rough' for popular taste. His groups of open-air labourers gathering peat, fern or blackberries are amongst the most impressive of his realist images, sympathetically drawn from the rural folk of England.

96. An Impression: The Crest of a Mountain

Watercolour over pencil 27 × 38 (10⅝ × 15).
PROV: presented by J. Arthur Kenrick 1925 (329'25).
EXH: Swansea 1953 (57).
Birmingham Museums and Art Gallery

It is not certain that the title of 'impression' for this sketch is a contemporary one, but this could well be added to the list of works in which critics have observed Cox attempting to capture a transient moment of natural beauty – 'effect' would have been his term – in a way that has since been labelled 'impressionist' and identified with French painters of a succeeding generation. It might well be related to the *Summit of a Mountain* which Cox showed at the OWCS in 1853, and which he thought was worth £100, if any of his works were; Solly described it as 'a remarkably fine out-of-doors sketch'.

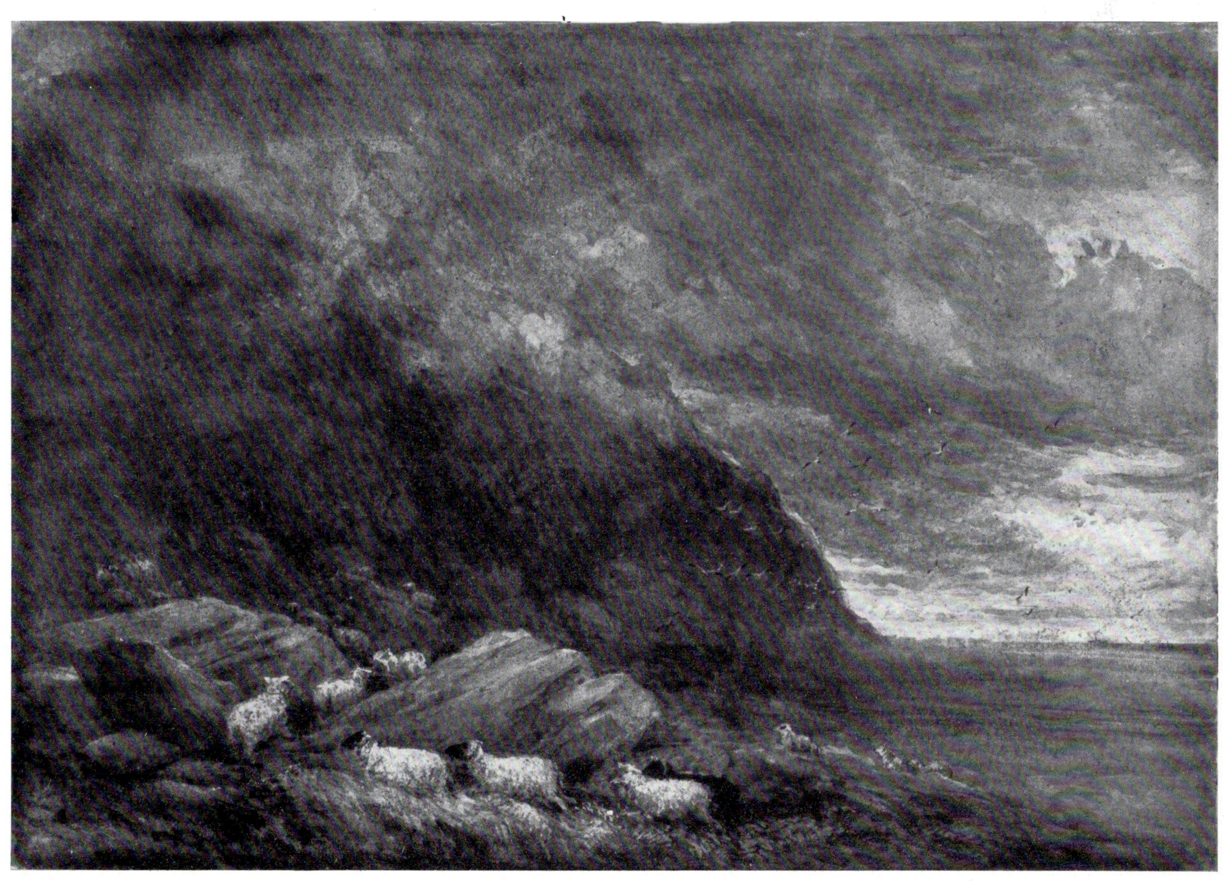

Penmaen Bach 1852 (cat. no. 99)

97. Two landscape studies

(a) black chalk and stump 16.4 × 25.3 (6½ × 9⅞).
(b) black chalk and stump 16.9 × 26.9 (6⅝ × 10½).
PROV: presented by Dyson Perrins 1920.
LIT: Hall, p. 226.
The Visitors of the Ashmolean Museum, Oxford

Two remarkable atmospheric studies showing Cox's power of abstracting the elemental structure of landscape – in such a physical representation as to include a weighty thumb-print in its manufacture!

98. Stokesay Castle 1852 *see p. 14*

Watercolour over soft pencil, on Scotch paper 27.2 × 38.7 (10⅝ × 15¼).
PROV: presented by J. Arthur Kenrick 1925 (284'25).
EXH: *Artists of Victoria's England,* Jacksonville, Florida 1965 (16).
Birmingham Museums and Art Gallery

In this instance as in no. 72, Cox achieved an almost tactile richness in quite small-scale compositions on Scotch paper, exploiting its absorbency with full brushes of deep colour over heavy, earthy under-drawing. Like many other works with a topographical title, the subject is less the place – one recalls Cox's abjuring mere 'portraits of places' – than the time and place of the artist's observation and his subsequent idea for the picture.

99. Penmaen Bach 1852 *see p. 105*

Watercolour and bodycolour over traces of pencil with scratching-out, on Scotch paper 57.1 × 82.5 (22½ × 32½).
PROV: Sir Josiah Mason; presented by Martyn Smith 1882 (2489'85).
EXH: RBSA 1873 (107); Liverpool 1875 (151, as *Mountains and Sheep*); Bourges 1970 (38).
Birmingham Museums and Art Gallery

Conceived on an altogether grander scale, this combines the simplest of subjects – sheep scurrying towards the cliff on the remote north coast of Wales – with great elaboration of technique to fill the wide expanse of the paper with an unsurpassed impression of imminent rain upon a bleak landscape. As well as the 'mosaic' of little strokes that are characteristic of his style – for instance, in the sheep's wool – Cox has used broad washes for the solid, wet rocks, a sponged

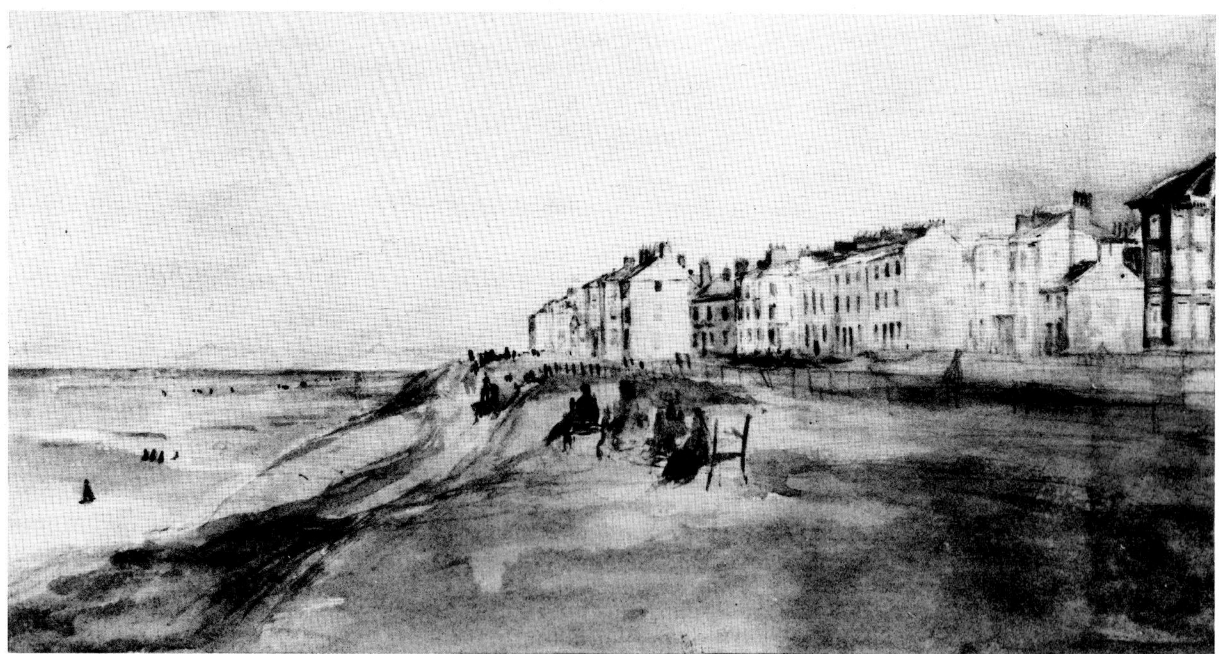

Rhyl Sands (cat. no. 100)

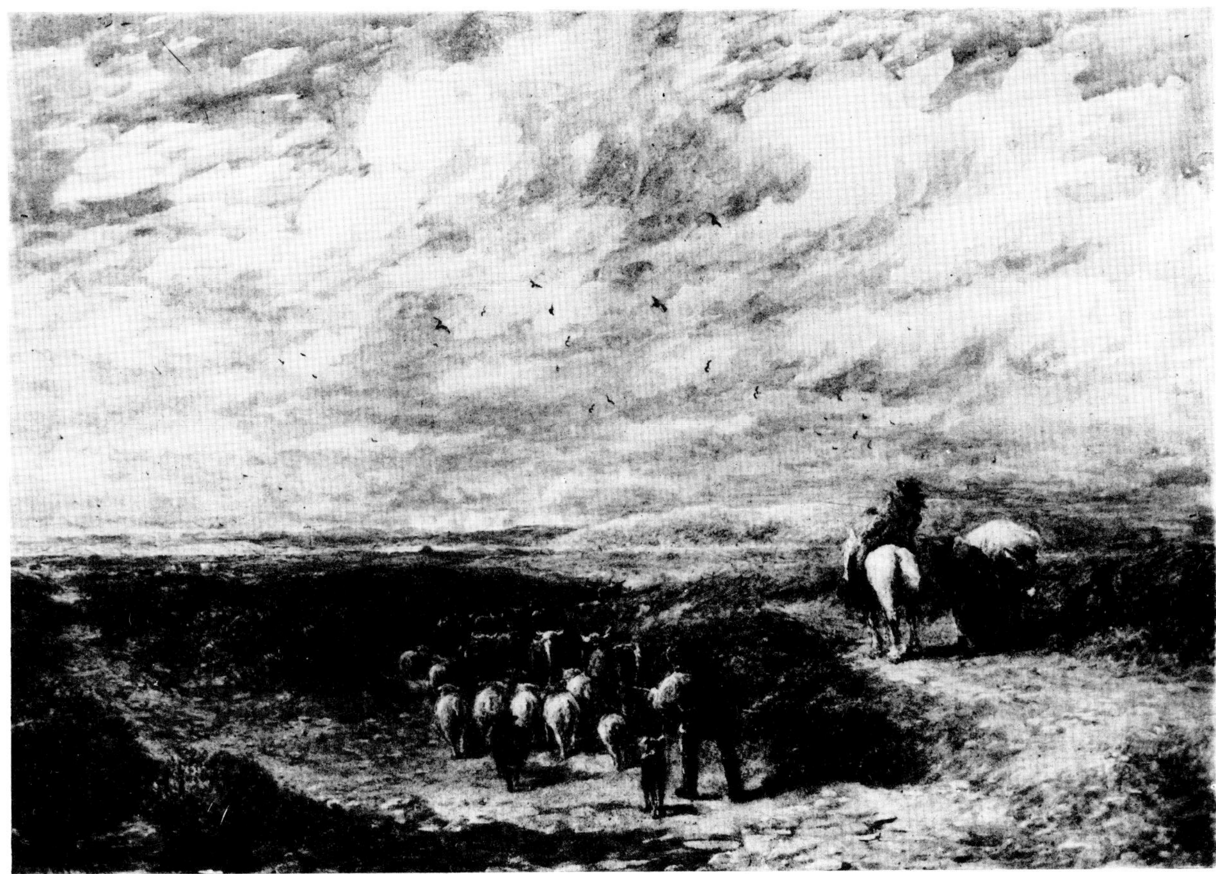
Keep the Left Road 1854 (cat. no. 101)

and scraped accumulation of greens and blues for the dark hills and threatening sky, and an instinctive combination of bodycolour and scratching-out to indicate the wheeling gulls. All this, whilst adhering to one of the fundamental techniques of English watercolour, in leaving the whiteness of the paper (for Scotch, in reality, a greyish tone) to act as the source of light for the whole composition.

100. Rhyl Sands

Watercolour over pencil 19.1 × 36.7 (7½ × 14½).
PROV: Mr and Mrs W. Spooner; Spooner Bequest 1967 (S.27).
LIT: *Apollo*, July 1968, p. 57 (repr.).
Courtauld Institute Galleries

Cox visited Rhyl in August 1854, and the expansive oil *Rhyl Sands* (no. 93), dated 1854–5, must have been conceived on that visit. He also exhibited watercolours of Rhyl from 1843, however, so it is difficult to determine the precise date of the various surviving sketches. This one may well date from the 1854 visit, and has slight architectural sketches, including the door of the Royal Hotel, on the reverse.

101. Keep the Left Road 1854

Watercolour and bodycolour, with scratching-out, on Scotch paper 72.7 × 100.7 (28⅝ × 39⅝).
PROV: Henry Jephson; presented by J. Arthur Kenrick 1925 (266'25).
EXH: OWCS 1854 (164); *The Watercolour art of the 19th century*, Fine Art Society 1901 (91).
Birmingham Museums and Art Gallery

A fine climax to the lifelong series on the 'lost traveller' theme, and one of the best examples of the successful translation of a sketchbook 'incident' onto a really large scale. The shaky signature betrays the effect on the artist of a stroke suffered the previous year, but it is difficult to imagine that he would not have carried out a good proportion of the work on such an important watercolour close to the sending-in date in the following spring. There is a rather vague sponginess to the landscape, but no lack of skill in the handling of the sky, and in such neat details as the highlighting of the horse's rump with a thick blob of bodycolour, or the drover's arm and his dog's head with a deft stroke of the knife. The colours in this work are extremely well preserved.

102. The Challenge 1856

Watercolour and bodycolour 45.5 × 66.6 (17⅞ × 26¼).

PROV: Rev. Chauncey Hare Townshend; bequeathed by him 1869 (1427–1869).

EXH: OWCS 1856 (179); *Forty-two Watercolours*, Victoria and Albert Museum 1977 (34, repr.); *The Exhibition Watercolor 1770–1870*, Yale 1981 (49, as *On the Moors*, repr.).

LIT: Solly, p. 286; Cox, p. 110, pl. 32; Hardie, Vol. II, pl. 190; Lambourne, p. 87, col. pl. 20.

Victoria and Albert Museum

The title of *The Challenge* is more strictly reserved for the large watercolour shown at the OWCS in 1853 (Ashmolean Museum, Oxford), of two bulls in confrontation across a wild ravine, but its title has generally been appropriated by this work (inscribed on the reverse, *On the moors near Bettws-y-Coed*). The

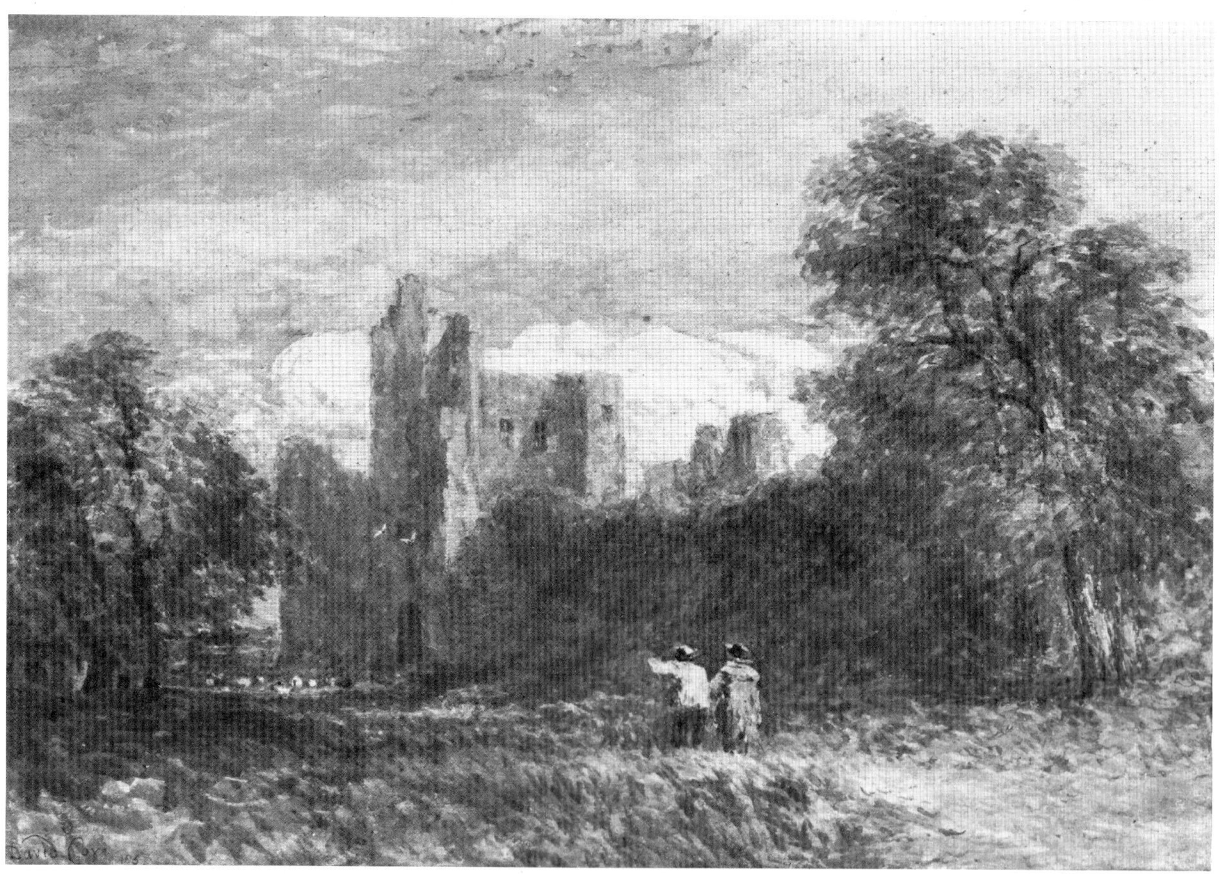

Kenilworth Castle 1857 (?) (cat. no. 103)

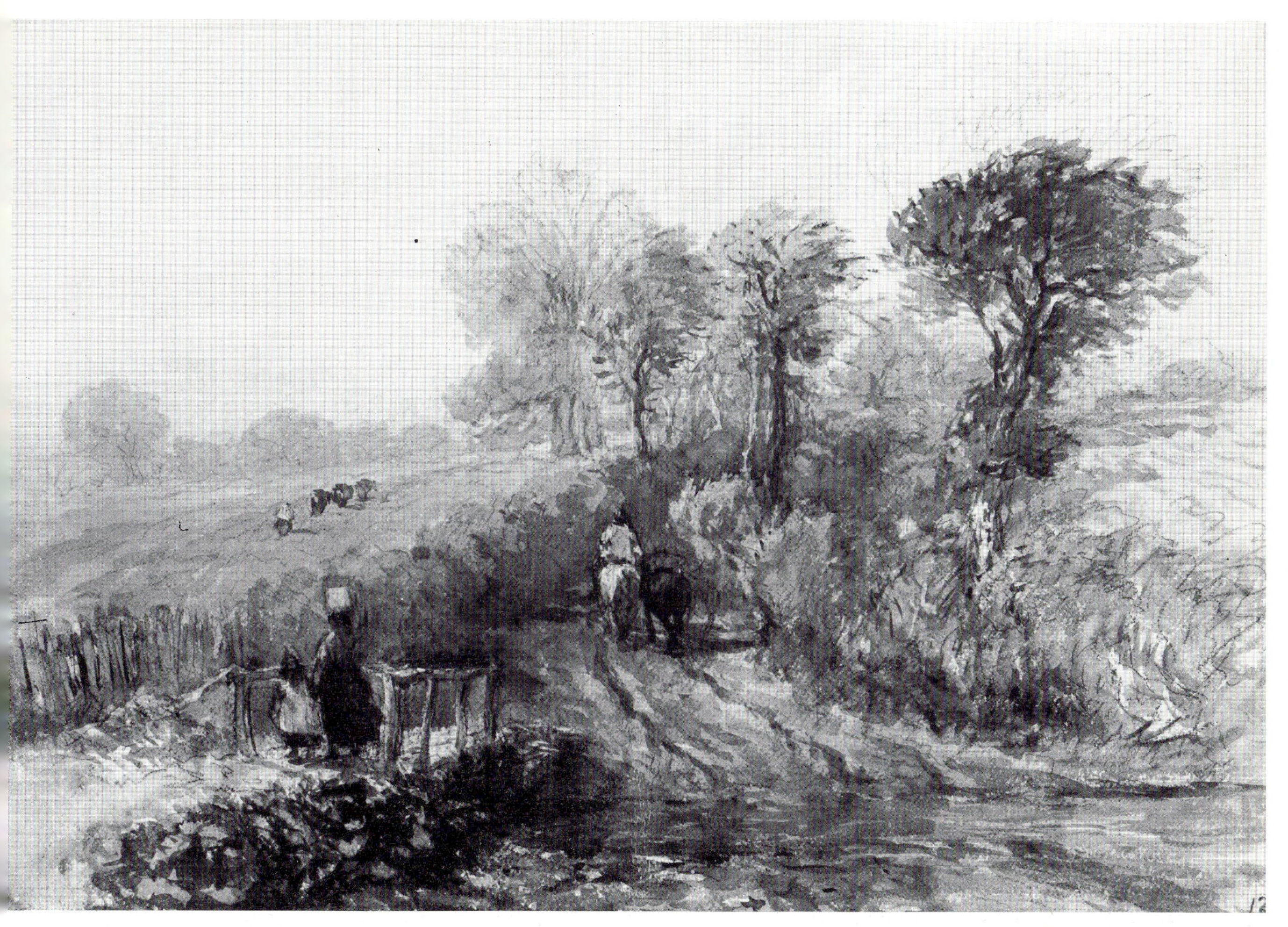

Vater Lane, Harborne (cat. no. 104)

challenge here is of a more passionate kind, of the animal power of the lone bull against the elemental forces of nature; John Murdoch has rightly cited this as one of the artist's most celebrated embodiments of the 18th-century notion of the sublime. As in *Penmaen Bach*, Cox has depicted his vast, gloomy, storm-beaten landscape through appropriately rough but powerfully coherent execution.

103. Kenilworth Castle 1857 (?)

see p. 108

Watercolour over pencil on Scotch paper 51 × 72.7 (20 × 28⅝).
PROV: purchased at OWCS exhibition by Rev. C. J. and Mrs Sale; Sale Bequest 1915.
EXH: OWCS ? 1858 or 1859.
LIT: Solly, pp. 292–93; *Sale Bequest*, no. 13.
Worcester City Museum and Art Gallery

A very grand finale to a subject which Cox painted from the earliest period (no. 3). The ghostly figures still haunt the foreground, but instead of heralding the dawn they now make their way beneath the twilit mass of the castle, dimly perceived but omnipresent, like a gateway into the beyond.

There is a little doubt as to whether this is the watercolour shown at the OWCS in 1858 (it appears to be signed 1857, and the Society's register records the purchase in that year of this subject by Mrs Sale) or in 1859 (the Sale Bequest catalogue gives this year as the date of acquisition). In either case, it was a work well received, as were all the last exhibited watercolours. 'Each of these was beautiful and grand in its way, proving that in spite of ill-health and increasing years there was no failing in the artist's deep feeling for nature, nor in his powers of expression.' (Solly, p. 293)

104. Water Lane, Harborne

see p. 109

Watercolour over black chalk, with scratching-out, on coarse paper 46.5 × 65.6 (18¼ × 25¾).
PROV: Rev. C. J. and Mrs Sale; Sale Bequest 1915 (1915-3-13-21).
The Trustees of the British Museum

Just as Cox had recourse, in the last years at Bettws-y-Coed, to objects close at hand, so he found views capable of majestic, dramatic treatment in the lanes around his house in Harborne. Each of the elements of this composition, which might well have been encompassed in a 7 × 10 inch sketch in former years, has been expanded by the desperate but majestic breadth of the artist's declining powers into a noble grandeur, whilst the astonishing freedom of the drawing is matched only by the bold strokes of glowing colour, creating a strangely unified whole and as complete a work of art as any of the preceding fifty years.

7. 'Dear Old Haddon'

For a detailed examination of Cox's association with Haddon Hall, see above, p. 29.

105. Haddon Hall 1838

Watercolour and bodycolour 45.8 × 62.2 (18 × 24½).
PROV: presented by the Council of Guarantors, Royal Jubilee Exhibition, Manchester 1887 (D.27.1887).
EXH: ?OWCS 1838 (18).
Whitworth Art Gallery, University of Manchester

106. Haddon Hall from the Park

Watercolour over pencil, with scratching-out 27.6 × 40.3 (10⅞ × 15⅞).
PROV: John Muir Hetherington; Christie's 1/5/1908 (43); presented by J. Palmer Phillips 1908 (30'08).
EXH: BMAG 1959 (40).
Birmingham Museums and Art Gallery

Amongst Cox's great number of drawings of Haddon, surprisingly few are of large size; most are

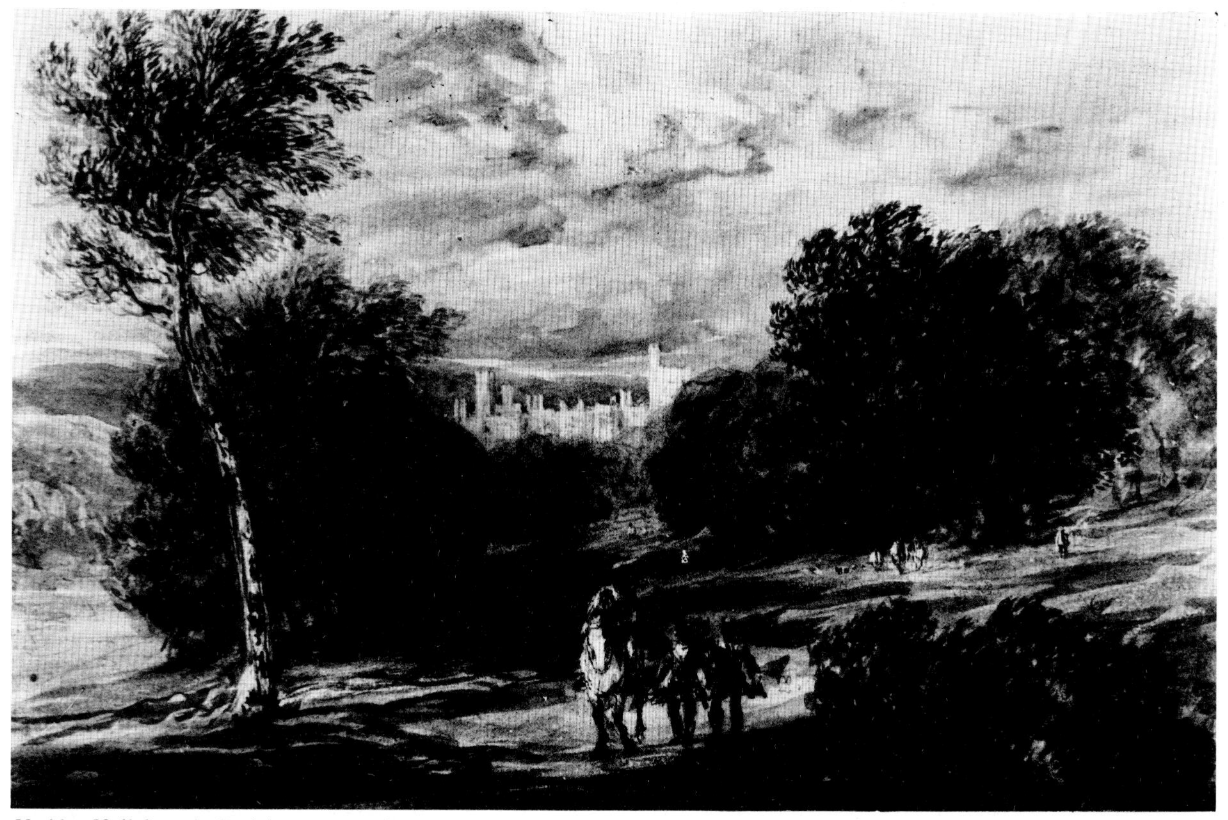

Haddon Hall from the Park (cat. no. 106)

of the small type, and in the popular middle period style, of no. 106. The largest watercolour would seem to be that of *The Terrace* (24 × 29½ inches, Royal Albert Museum, Exeter), whose composition Cox also adopted for what appears to be the only oil of Haddon (Ashmolean Museum, Oxford, dated 1849). Two other late, substantial works are *The Park at Haddon* of 1853 (described by Solly, p. 271), and the unusual vertical composition, *Rook Shooting*, dated 1850 (reproduced in W. Roberts, *Memorials of Christie's*, 1897, opp. p. 294).

The present work (no. 105) is perhaps to be identified with the subject *Returning from Hawking – Haddon Hall*, shown at the OWCS in 1838. It is certainly the most elaborate recreation of a setting 'in the olden time', with figures reminiscent of Bonington's Vandyckian staffage.

107. The Great Hall

see p. 28

Watercolour over pencil, on two joined sheets of paper 26 × 46.3 (10¼ × 18¼).
PROV: presented by J. Arthur Kenrick 1925 (316'25).
EXH: ?OWCS 1832 (100).
Birmingham Museums and Art Gallery

108. Bedroom

Watercolour over pencil 26 × 37.3 (10¼ × 14⅝).
PROV: presented by J. Arthur Kenrick 1925 (320'25).
EXH: ?OWCS 1832 (283).
Birmingham Museums and Art Gallery

Although having the appearance of hasty sketches, these drawings do capture the airy, romantic atmosphere of Haddon, and it is remarkable how little has changed to this day (even to the antler trophies and fire irons). There is another similar study, *The Great Chamber*, in the Birmingham collection (317'25), and these would seem to be part of a series – if not those exhibited at the OWCS in 1832, then perhaps the sketches drawn for William Ellis in 1845, which Solly described as 'powerful and admirable in arrangement and colour'. An identical but smaller view of the *Bedroom*, sold at Christie's (18/6/1980 [109]), interestingly contains costumed figures.

109. The Terrace, with figures

Watercolour and bodycolour, with scratching-out 19.2 × 27.1 (7½ × 10⅝).
PROV: presented by J. Arthur Kenrick 1925 (291'25).
EXH: ?OWCS 1834 (386); Bourges 1970 (13).
LIT: Cox, pl. 1.
Birmingham Museums and Art Gallery

110. The River Steps

Watercolour over soft pencil 24 × 31.6 (9⅜ × 12⅜).
PROV: bequeathed by J. Palmer Phillips 1919 (103'19).
EXH: *Canadian National Exhibition*, Toronto 1935 (44).
LIT: OWCS Club, Vols X, 1932–3, pl. III, and XVI, 1938, pl XV.
Birmingham Museums and Art Gallery

A contrast in styles in two depictions of the famous 17th-century stone terraces of the gardens at Haddon, dropping by degrees down to the River Wye. This gives a good idea of the development of Cox's work between the early visits to Haddon in the 1830s (if no. 108 is to be identified with *A Terrace, with figures*, shown at the OWCS in 1834) and his later expedition of 1845. The incessant wet weather which he encountered on this latter visit may explain the lushness of the colouring of no. 109, which is one of the best-preserved examples of the artist's use of a heavily-laden swansquill brush over vigorous preliminary drawing.

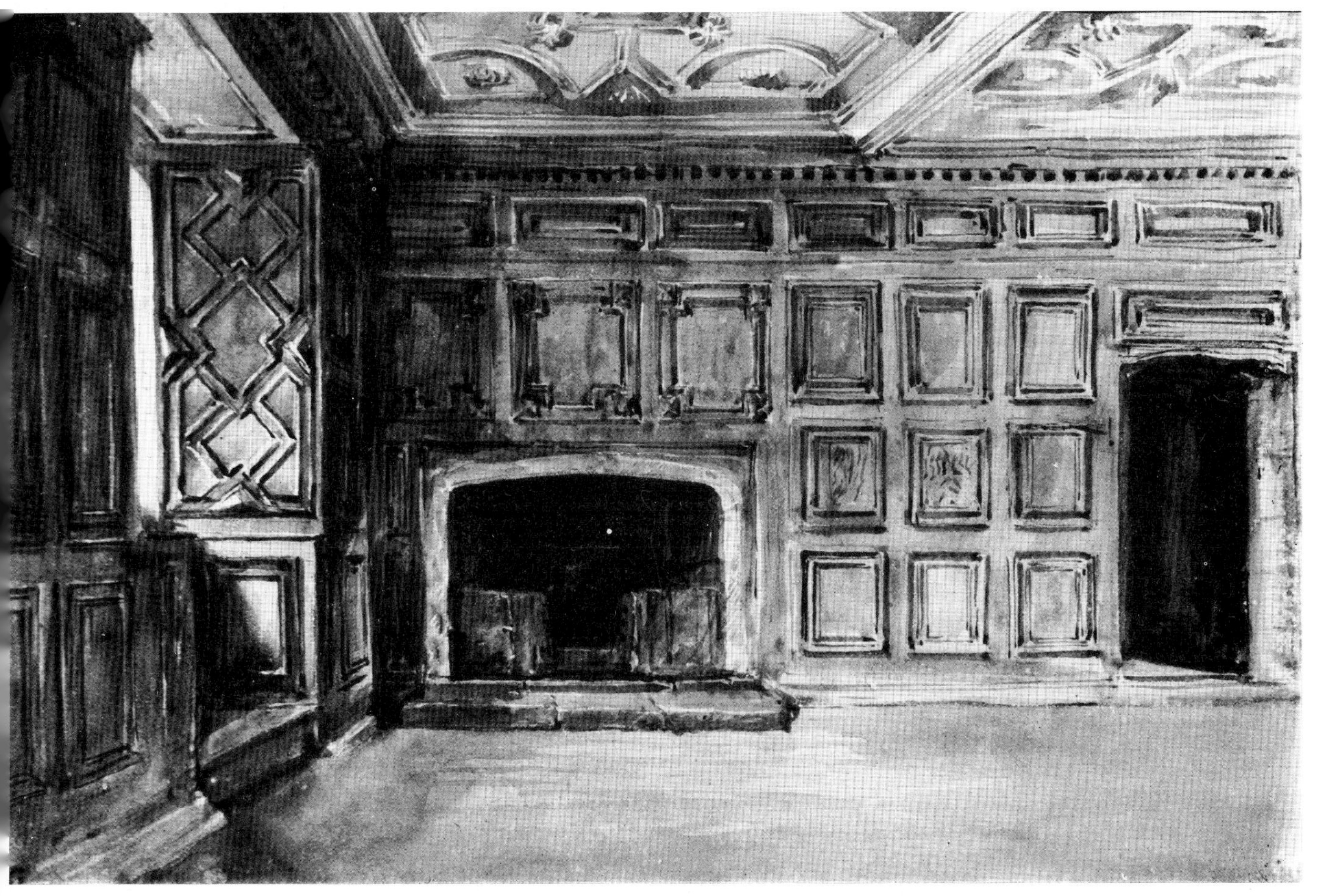

Bedroom (cat. no. 108)

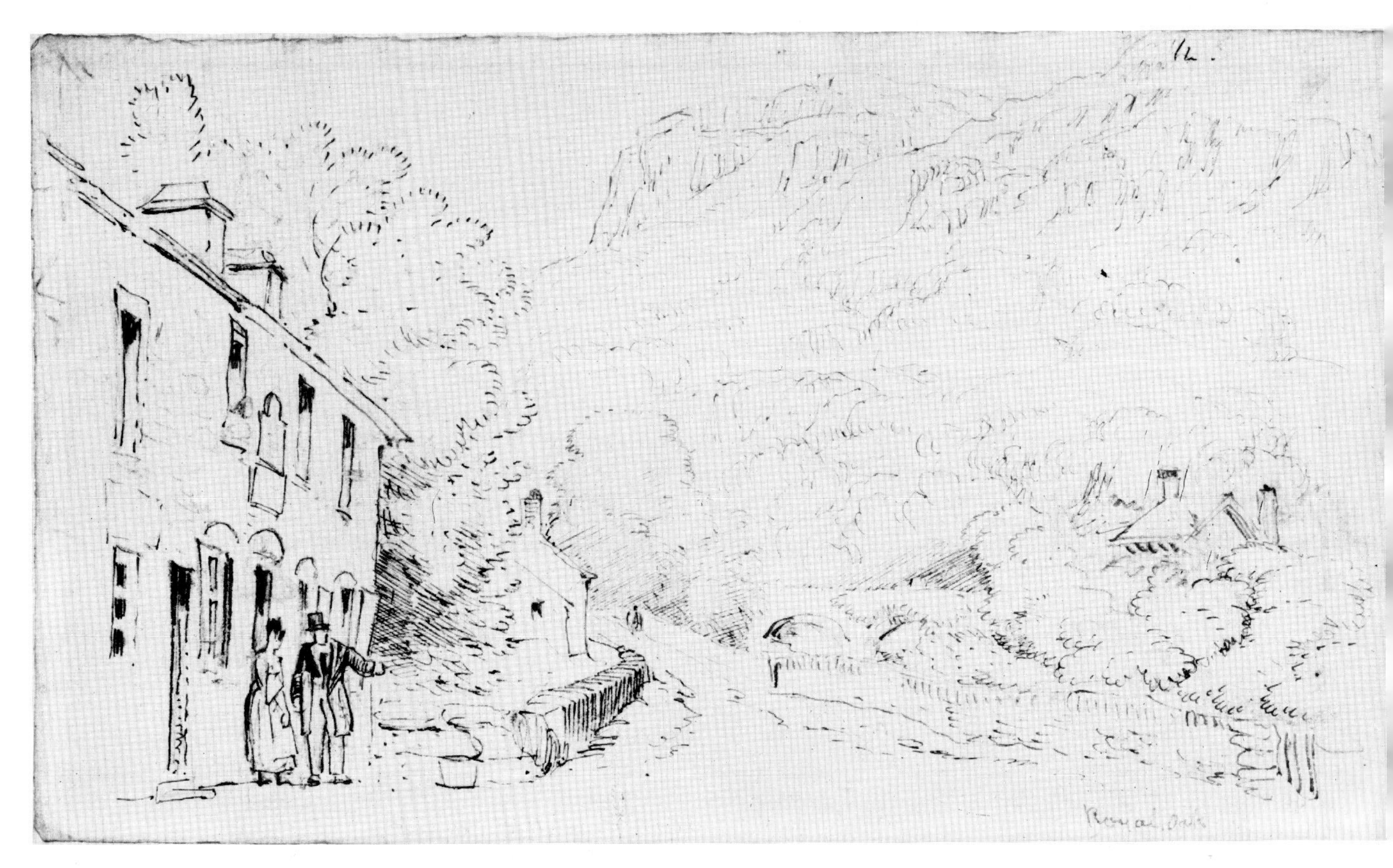

The Royal Oak Inn (cat. no. 111)

8. Bettws-y-Coed 1844–56

Although Cox made several earlier short tours of Wales, notably in 1816, 1818 and 1836, the annual summer visits to Bettws-y-Coed and vicinity from 1844 to 1856, when poor health finally prevented long travel, mark his most important association with any one area of the kingdom.

The small Caernarvonshire village (little larger today than in the 1840s) is situated at the junction of three rivers – the Conway, the Lledr and the Llugwy – and its unusally varied and beautiful scenery became increasingly attractive to English landscape painters as the century progressed. Girtin, Ibbetson and Varley exploited its picturesque possibilities during their Welsh tours at the turn of the century, but it was probably on the recommendation of his mentor in oil painting, W. J. Müller, that Cox first went to explore Bettws.

Equally, Cox was to find in and around Bettws plenty of subjects for treatment in watercolour, suitable for his now established facility of capturing Nature's moods. The flat meadows between the rivers Conway and Llugwy provided the setting for such large-scale pieces as Changing Pastures *and* The Big Meadow*; the rushing rocky streams for* The Old Mill *and* Pont-y-Pair*; the towering hills gave endless inspiration for broad, craggy landscapes, whilst the quiet, yew-shadowed old church became the focus for his most famous painted work,* The Welsh Funeral *(nos. 115, 116).*

He first stayed at the Swan Inn, arriving in July 1844 in the company of his young Birmingham artist friend Harry Johnson. After only a few days, he was writing enthusiastically to his son that 'we agree to stop a week; there is no end of the fine river scenery and rocks and mountains' (Solly, p. 162). In later years he took to the Royal Oak Hotel, with its hospitable landlord Edward Roberts, and would set out from Birmingham by the old Grand Junction Railway, travelling via Chester and Rhyl to Conway, where he would be met by an open Welsh car sent by the Royal Oak. Solly (pp. 178–9) describes the artist's typically methodical and domestic routine: 'He used to get up at eight to breakfast, and if fine he would go out sketching till dinner, at one o'clock. After dinner, a good rest and a nap, followed by an early cup of tea, quite refreshed him, and he would sally out again to see and take notes of the evening effects, and especially the sunsets, which he never liked to miss. At eight, or sooner, he returned home to a light supper, and then to bed, about nine o'clock.'

His friendly association with the Royal Oak produced two rather unsual works. On one particularly wet day, according to Hall, 'Cox embellished the parlour with a large picture in water-colour on the bare plaster of a bricked-up doorway – Catherine Douglas Barring the Castle Door with her Arm – after Redgrave. It was effectively painted, and surprised many a stranger on first entering the room.' This has, of course, long succumbed to time, but the signboard which Cox repainted in 1847 (a heavily impastoed impression of King Charles II hiding in the oak from Roundhead pursuers) is still happily preserved within the hotel.

The increasing number of artists arriving yearly at the Royal Oak induced Cox to transfer his headquarters across the road to the farmhouse belonging to the hotel. This became useful in his last years of visiting Bettws, when he could only just summon the energy for a short walk to the riverside or meadow to fix upon a subject. Just before leaving for home, on 22 September 1856, he signed his name in the visitors' book at the Royal Oak for the last time, and was never to visit 'dear old Bettws' again.

111. The Royal Oak Inn

Pen and ink over pencil 16.8 × 27.1 (6⅝ × 10⅝).
PROV: bequeathed by J. R. Holliday 1927 (no. 1328).
The Syndics of the Fitzwilliam Museum, Cambridge

Considering his associations with the inn, the Royal Oak appears but rarely in Cox's drawings of Bettws-y-Coed. Another drawing of the inn, road and river, in black chalk, is in the Ashmolean Museum, Oxford. Both drawings show the low, stone building whose increasing popularity (partly engendered by Cox's annual presence) led to its eventual rebuilding in 1861 as a gabled, three-storey structure; this, in turn, has been extended and considerably altered, with

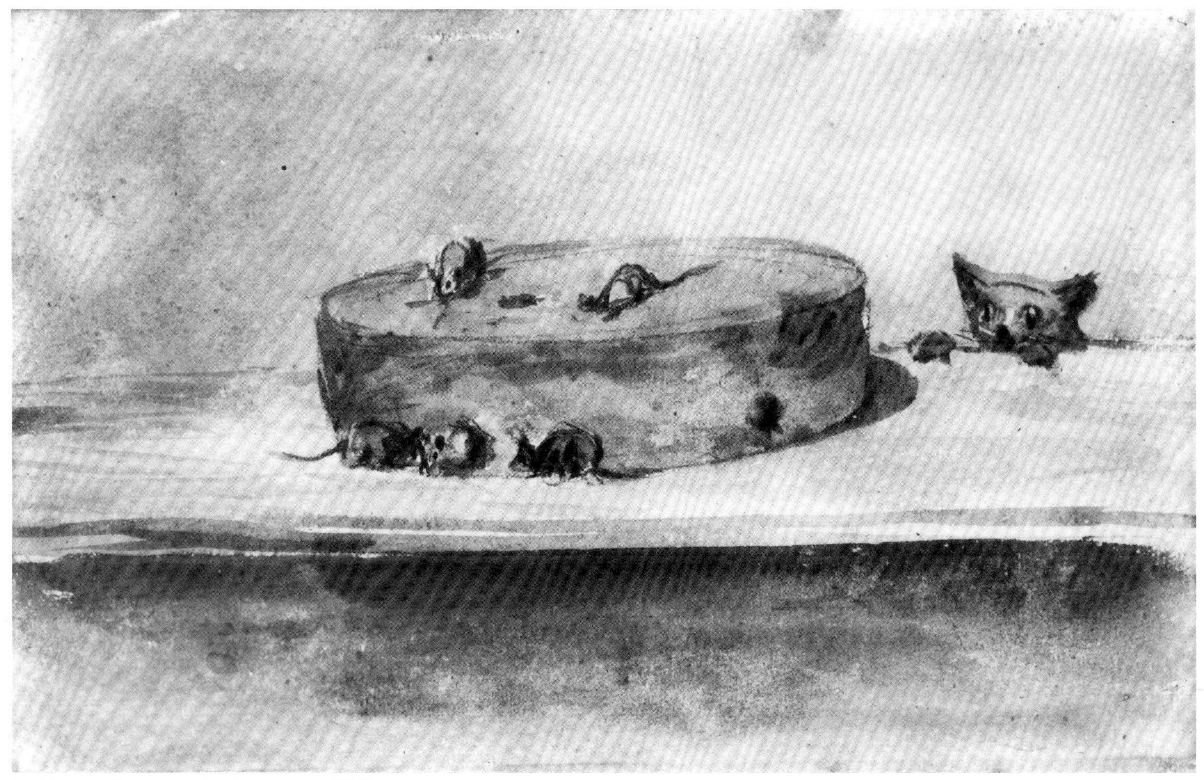

Incident at Bettws-y-Coed (cat. no. 112)

only the signboard within acting as a reminder of the days of David Cox.

112. Incident at Bettws-y-Coed

Pencil and watercolour 14.6 × 23.5 (5¾ × 9¼).
PROV: C. T. Parsons; Mr and Mrs Cyril Fry.
EXH: BMAG 1890 (447).
Mr and Mrs Cyril Fry

'This sketch was made by Cox at the Royal Oak Hotel, Bettws-y-Coed. The artist and Mr William Bullock were dining together, when, hearing a slight commotion, they found it was caused by the sudden flight of several mice, who, while feasting on the cheese, had been distressed by the cat's head appearing above the table. Cox seized his brushes and dashed off this sketch in a few minutes.' (1890 Catalogue)

113. Cottage Interior, Trossavon, near Bettws-y-Coed

Oil on board 27.9 × 39.1 (11 × 15⅜).
PROV: bequeathed by Joseph H. Nettlefold 1882 (2494'85).
LIT: Solly, p. 128; Hall, p. 108; Cox, pl. 23; BMAG Oils, p. 36.
Birmingham Museums and Art Gallery

Hall records that 'cottage interiors – of which there were several within easy reach, and extremely good subjects – were of course the chief places of resort on wet days, and Cox made some admirable studies from the more picturesque of them', whilst Solly remembered having seen 'several drawings by him of curious Welsh kitchens, with the broad, open fireplaces, clothes hanging from the walls, three-legged stools, and marvellously old dressers'. Cox's attention to the picturesque qualities of cottage interiors, particularly as subjects for oil sketches such as this, may well have been drawn by W. J. Müller's studies in both watercolour and oil, made in Wales in the 1830s and 1840s. Solly, in his *Memoir* of that artist, describes several such 'thoroughly Welsh' works, likening them to Dutch genre pictures. Bristol City Art Gallery has a typical small oil study by Müller of this kind, an *Interior with goats, Bettws-y-Coed*.

114. The Old Mill, Bettws-y-Coed 1847

Oil on canvas 68.5 × 88.9 (27 × 35).

PROV: painted for Marshall Carritt, for £40; Joseph Gillott, July 1865; Thomas Darby; Thomas Wrigley; presented by his children 1897.

LIT: Solly, pp. 147, 196–97; Hall, p. 120; Bury 1901, p. 26, repr.

Bury Art Gallery

An unusually expansive composition, showing mature trees in their full height instead of as a framing device, this is one of the most beautiful and impressive of Cox's mature oil style, the overall short brushstroke blended and varied between the treatment of foreground, tonally contrasted middle ground and very lightly painted hills. The little dabs of pink on the mill roof make a particularly vibrant focal point, to set against the noisy incident below; the boy chasing geese appears in several other works by Cox, and geese appear again in the watercolour *Watermill near Bettws-y-Coed* in the Victoria and Albert Museum.

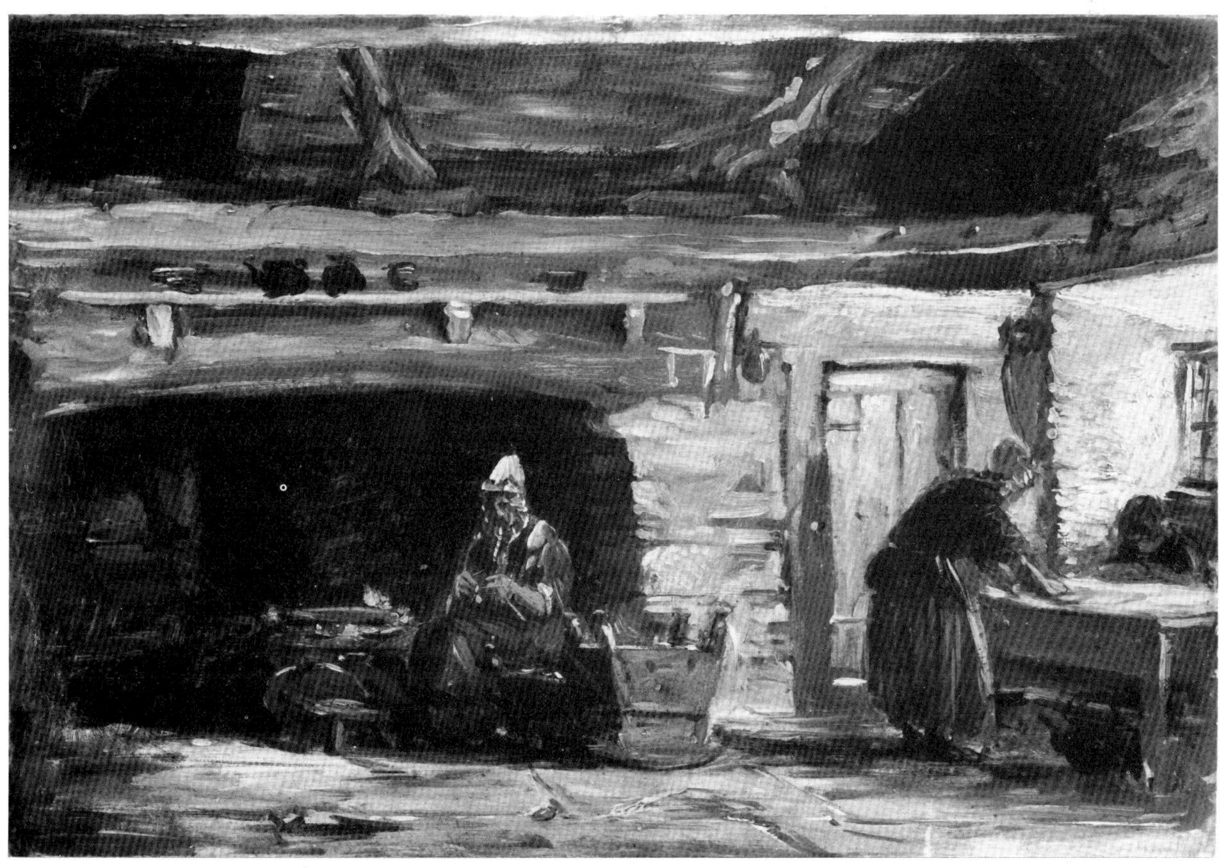

Cottage Interior, Trossavon, near Bettws-y-Coed (cat. no. 113)

115. The Welsh Funeral 1848 *see p. 17*

Oil on canvas 46.4 × 71.1 (18¼ × 28).
PROV: painted for Charles Birch; at sale 1857, 1892; John Betts; C. P. Forster; presented by H. Dean Esq 1943 (3′43).
EXH: ?Liverpool Academy 1848 (79, as *Funeral at Bettws-y-Coed*); RBSA 1849 (280); Liverpool 1875 (21); BMAG 1890 (123); BMAG 1959 (95); *Liverpool Academy 1810–1867*, Liverpool 1967 (55).
LIT: Solly, pp. 174–75, 195, 200, 251–52; M. Davies, National Gallery Catalogue, *British School*, 1946, p. 43; Cox, pp. 99, 101, colour pl. IV; BMAG Oils, pp. 37–8.
Birmingham Museums and Art Gallery

This is the premier version of the touching subject by which Cox is still perhaps best remembered as a painter in oils. It was suggested to the artist by his being present at the funeral of a young Welsh girl, a relative of the landlord of the Royal Oak, whilst he was staying there (presumably in 1847). The ceremony took place in the evening, as was the custom in North Wales, and Cox has caught the effect of evening light on the bellcote, shining out through the dark, yew-lined avenue leading to the old church at Bettws. This, together with the open foreground where some children pause but others continue their quest for gay wild flowers, relieves the sombre mood of the occasion and gives the whole picture an added poignancy. Solly's identification of the figure with the stick as Cox himself as onlooker, and his reporting of the symbolical inclusion of poppies (more noticeable in the large watercolour of 1850, untraced) should probably be regarded as romantic embellishments. There is, however, no doubting Cox's creation of a lasting and noble image, that may stand beside Courbet's *Burial at Ornans* and Turner's *Peace: Burial at Sea*.

116. The Welsh Funeral 1852

Oil on canvas 26.6 × 35.5 (10½ × 14).
PROV: Edwin Bullock; his sale May 1870; bought from Agnews June 1870 by Thomas Wrigley; presented by his children 1897.
LIT: Solly, p. 200; Bury 1901, p. 27.
Bury Art Gallery

Versions of *The Welsh Funeral* are numerous, and well described in the literature cited for no. 115. This particularly attractive small oil, however, overall lighter than its progenitor, and displaying Cox's delicate touch and keen eye for colour balance, seems to have escaped attention.

117. (a) The Welsh Funeral

Black chalk and stump on buff paper 17.7 × 28.1 (7 × 11⅛).

(b) Churchyard Yew, Darley, Derbyshire

Brown chalk and wash on buff paper 17.4 × 29.3 (6⅞ × 11½).
PROV: both presented by Dyson Perrins 1920.
Visitors of the Ashmolean Museum, Oxford

There are several studies, in many media, of Bettws-y-Coed church and its surroundings (and see no. 120), but this strong chalk sketch must either be considered as a preparatory drawing for the series of oils, or possibly one of the memory drawings which Cox was accustomed to make late in life. It captures in a few bold strokes the essential details of the composition, concentrating on the foreground 'incident'.

The subject of Darley Churchyard is appropriately linked in the mounting together of these two drawings. The pale filtering of light through dense yews (an effect also observed in some Bettws-y-Coed church scenes) provided inspiration for a number of late works. Worcester City Art Gallery has the gritty watercolour shown at the OWCS in 1859, which neither Cox nor his son would part with, and the Graves Art Gallery, Sheffield, has the 1850 oil which Solly (p. 215) graphically describes: 'A large yew occupies the centre, tombstones are clustered around its base, some in deep shadow, and some in half light, which give breadth to the composition. On the left some steps lead up to the church, the upper part being illumined by the glow of evening. Some girls seated on these steps assist cleverly in carrying the light across. The sky is bright, yet powerful. *Power* and brilliancy are the chief characteristics of this picture, as, indeed, of all his best works. He loved power almost beyond everything else.'

118. Welsh girl blowing a horn

Watercolour over pencil 26.7 × 16.7 (10½ × 6⅝).
PROV: bequeathed by J. R. Holliday 1927 (P80′61).
LIT: Solly, p. 58.
Birmingham Museums and Art Gallery

Solly, in describing one of the Roscoe illustrations, points out a figure of 'a girl blowing a cow's horn. Cox used to be summoned to dinner in this way when staying in a remote part of North Wales, and

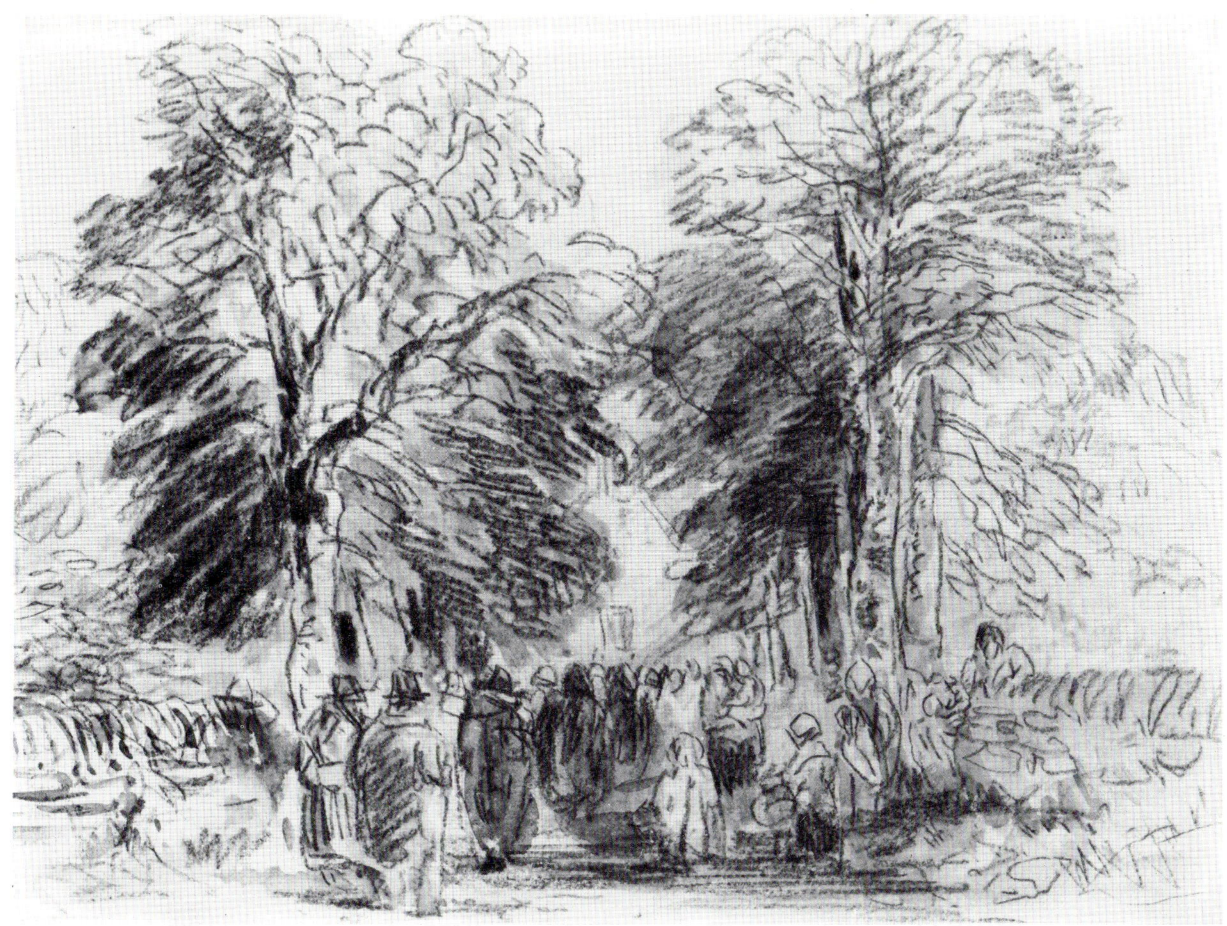

The Welsh Funeral (cat. no. 117a)

he painted a figure subject of the girl with her horn from nature.' There is a drawing of Dolbenmaen church at Hereford City Art Gallery, and the watermill there formed the subject of the watercolour bought by John Ruskin at the OWCS in 1837.

119. Stone Bridge, Wales

Watercolour over black chalk 27.6 × 37.9 (10⅞ × 14⅞).
PROV: presented by subscribers 1907 (337′07).
EXH: *Peinture anglaise (XVIII et XIX siècle)*, Musée Moderne, Brussels 1929 (47); Swansea 1953 (38); *Art in Wales* [1962] (210).
LIT: Hardie 1967, p. 207.
Birmingham Museums and Art Gallery

Martin Hardie has pointed out that in freely-handled late studies such as this, Cox 'painted the hills of Wales with a new intensity and vigour, as if he were seeing them for the first time'.

120. Bettws-y-Coed

see p. 121

Watercolour over soft pencil, with scratching-out, on Scotch paper 37.5 × 55.5 (14¾ × 21⅞).
PROV: presented by subscribers 1907 (321′07).
Birmingham Museums and Art Gallery

An unusually tranquil scene, showing the churchyard at Bettws with the broad river Conway to the right, but typical of the large sweeping views of spots close to the Royal Oak, which were as far as Cox could walk in his last years' visits.

121. Llanrwst

Pencil 20.2 × 28 (8 × 11).
PROV: bequeathed by J. R. Holliday (753'27).
EXH: BMAG 1959 (74).
LIT: *Drawings*, pl. XVI; Roe 1946, pl. 26; Cox, p. 81, pl. 17A.
Birmingham Museums and Art Gallery

Llanrwst is a village just north of Bettws-y-Coed, where many visitors (including at times, Cox himself) stayed in the summer if they found the Royal Oak full. This drawing is typical of the lively, individual drawings in pencil, charcoal or chalk (the Birmingham collection has a fine group) that remain a much-admired part of Cox's work.

122. Watermill at Trefriw, near Llanrwst

Watercolour and black chalk with wash 19.4 × 27.6 ($7\frac{5}{8} \times 10\frac{7}{8}$).
PROV: Guy Bellingham Smith; Colnaghi; J. Leslie Wright Bequest 1953 (P129'53).
EXH: *Masters of British Water-Colour: the J. Leslie Wright Collection*, RA 1949 (199); *English Watercolours and Drawings: the J. Leslie Wright Bequest*, Birmingham 1980 (18, repr.).
LIT: *Drawings*, pl. XIII.
Birmingham Museums and Art Gallery

It is interesting to compare such a study, with its light washes of watercolour over a firmly-drawn outline, with works of a very similar type executed by Samuel Palmer during his Welsh tour of 1836.

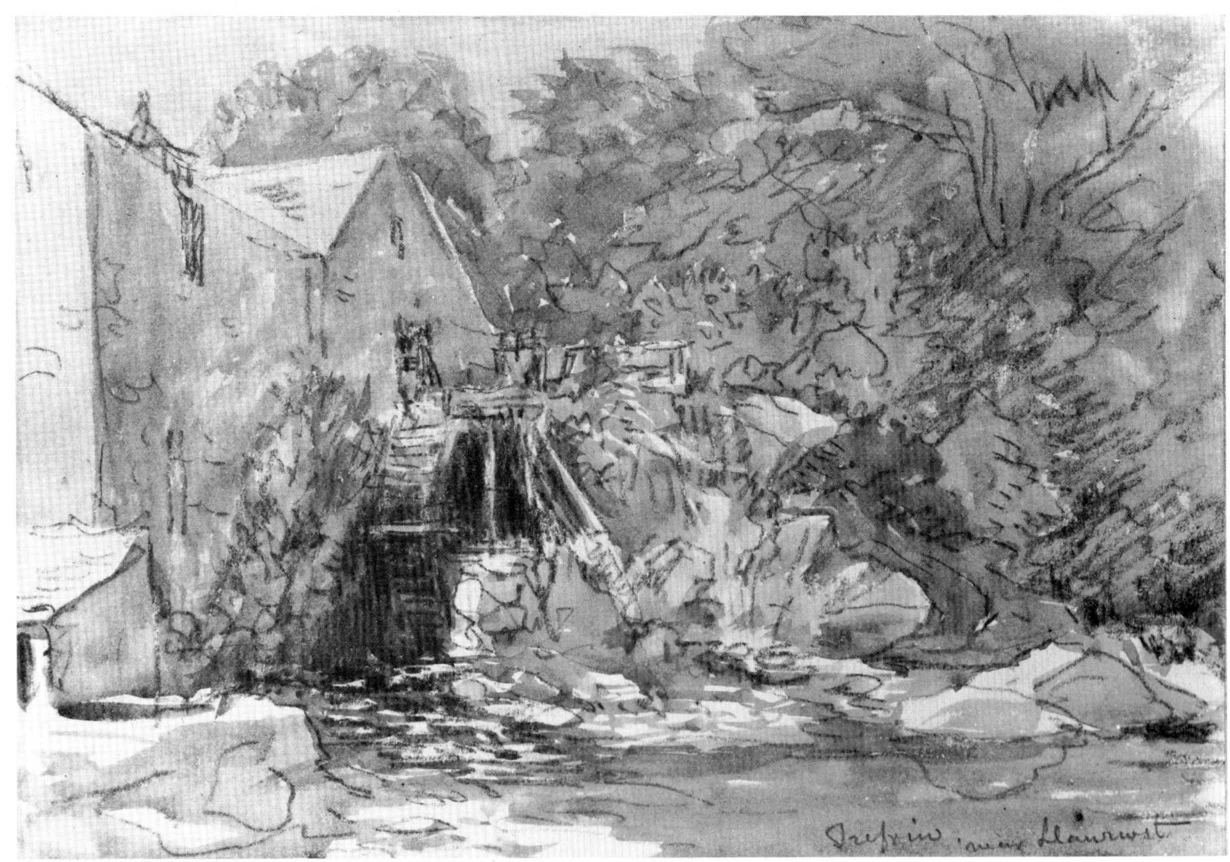

Watermill at Trefriw, near Llanrwst (cat. no. 122)

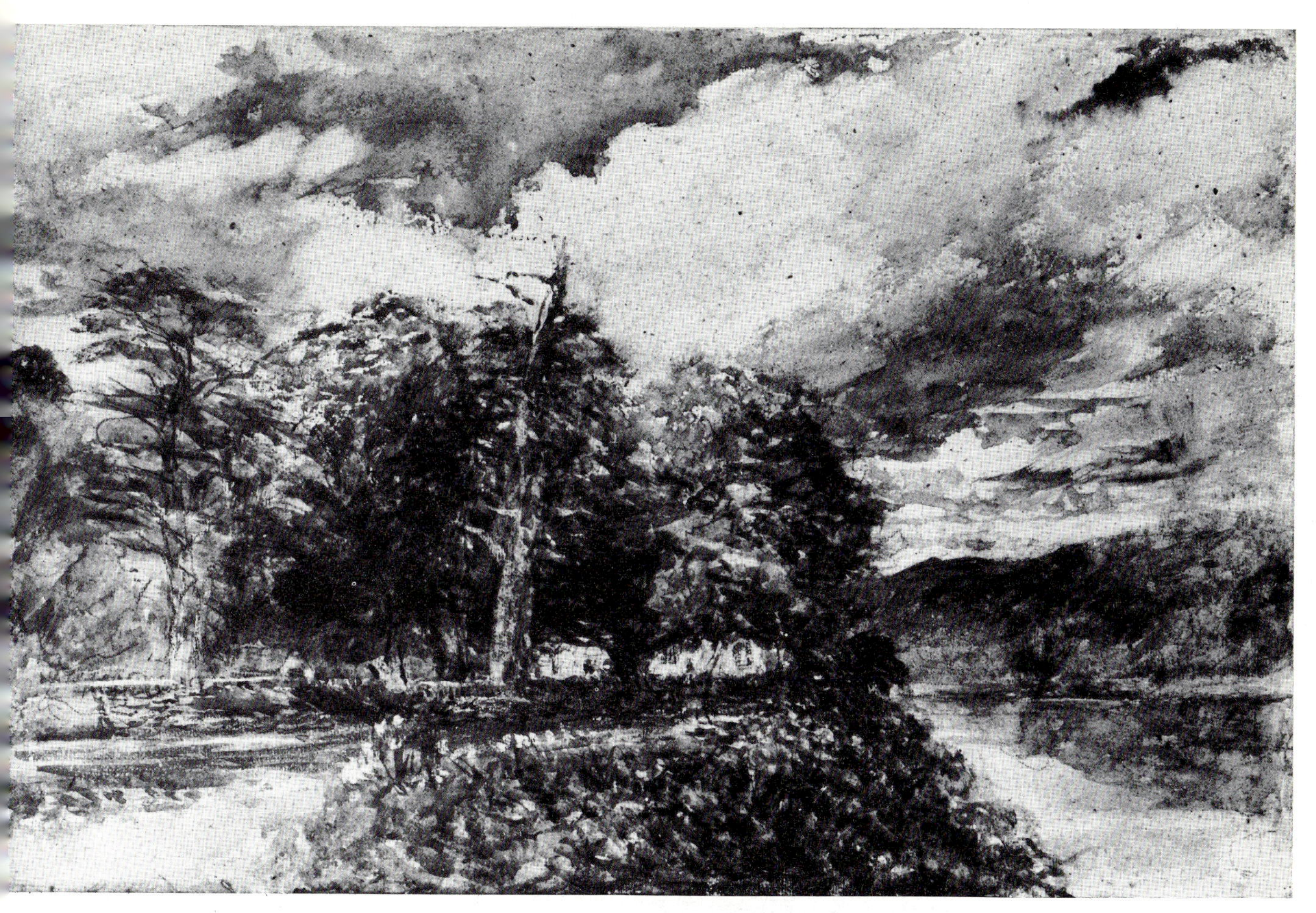

Bettws-y-Coed (cat. no. 120)

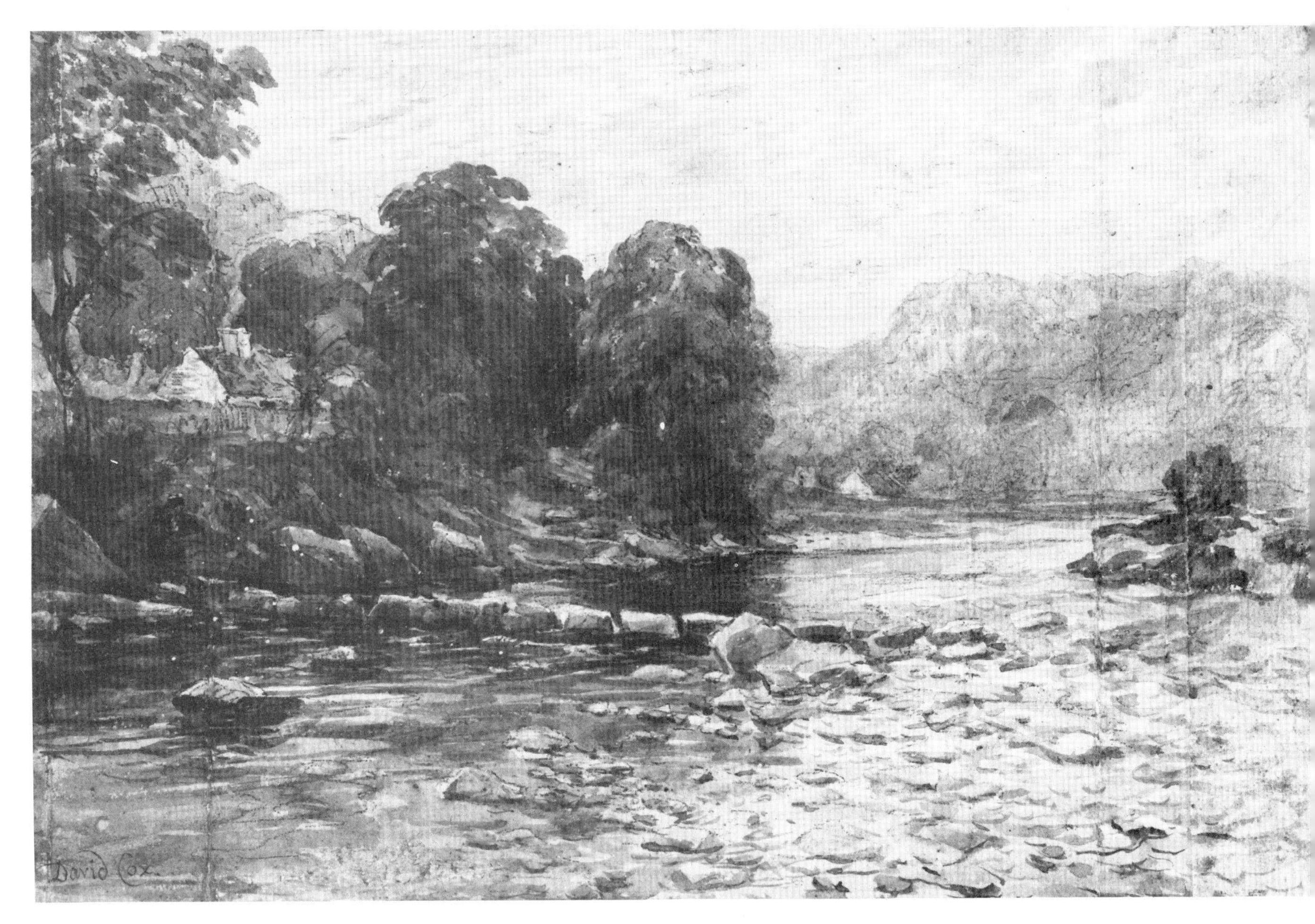

Stepping Stones, Bettws-y-Coed (cat. no. 124)

123. View near Bettws-y-Coed

Watercolour over black chalk, on Scotch paper; dated 14 August 1846 47.2 × 74.6 (18½ × 29⅜).

PROV: T. N. Sherrington; presented by J. Palmer Phillips 1908 (32′08).

LIT: Solly, p. 165; Cox, p. 116.

Birmingham Museums and Art Gallery

This and *Stepping Stones, Bettws-y-Coed* (Birmingham collection, 31′08) were painted for T. N. Sherrington of Yarmouth, who was staying at the Royal Oak in the summer of 1846, and making sketching expeditions with the artist. Mr Sherrington gave Cox a commission for four drawings. Cox wrote to William Roberts on 13 August: 'I have received a very kind letter from Mr Sherrington, wherein he expresses a wish I would make him a sketch as large as the one I made at the Stepping Stones, up in the Dolwyddelan Vale; but I do not think the weather will permit if I should stay long enough.' (Solly, p. 165)

In two unpublished letters, dated 28 August and 3 September 1846, addressed to Mr Sherrington and accompanying the drawings, Cox gives the following account of them. In the first he writes: 'I ought to have acknowledged the receipt of a very kind letter from you whilst I was at Bettws-y-Coed, but as I wished to accomplish a sketch in the Vale of Dolwyddlan as you had requested I postponed writing until my return home . . . After you left me I had very bad weather for nearly the whole time, three weeks, so I have made but few sketches in addition to those you saw. I shall by rail of this day send off the sketches you were so kind as commission'd me to make. I was certainly fortunate in having a fine day to make the sketch in Dolwyddlan, which I hope you will like, together with the Stepping Stones, one at Llyn Cramant, and one near Penmachno Mill; the four I charge you nineteen pounds, thus—

the two large ones £8 each	£16
the two small ones	£3
	£19

I trust I have not charged too high, and that they will meet with your approval.'

On 3 September he wrote again, thanking Mr Sherrington for his cheque and adding: 'I am delighted to find you are so much pleased with the scenery of N. Wales, and shall be most happy to have the pleasure of your kind company. Indeed, I wish we could have you down here for a while to talk over our trip and suggest new subjects for next year's exhibition. I saw one or two very fine stormy effects after you left me, but so transient I had not a moment to paint them, so must trust to a remembrance of the impression they made.'

124. Stepping Stones, Bettws-y-Coed

Watercolour over black chalk, with flecks of bodycolour, on two joined sheets of Scotch paper 36 × 52.6 (14⅛ × 20¾).

PROV: bought from the artist, 1859, by Mr and Mrs Sale; Sale Bequest 1915 (1915-3-13-19).

LIT: *Sale Bequest*, pp. 7, 12.

The Trustees of the British Museum

The almost reckless handling, colouring and sheer power of this watercolour, together with the almost accidental splashes of bodycolour on its surface and the venerable florid signature, testify to its being one of the last works from David Cox's hand. According to the catalogue of their bequest, 'Mr and Mrs Sale paid David Cox a last visit at Harborne in April, 1859, a few weeks before he died, and bought four water colours from him. He was very feeble then and confined to his room'. The works in question are *Richmond* (Worcester City Art Gallery), *Church Pond: Bettws-y-Coed, A Windy Day* and *Stepping Stones* (all British Museum), the fourth being said to be Cox's very last work. 'Mr Sale paid £40 for the lot, and Mrs Sale knelt by the side of David Cox, and handed him the drawings for his signature.'

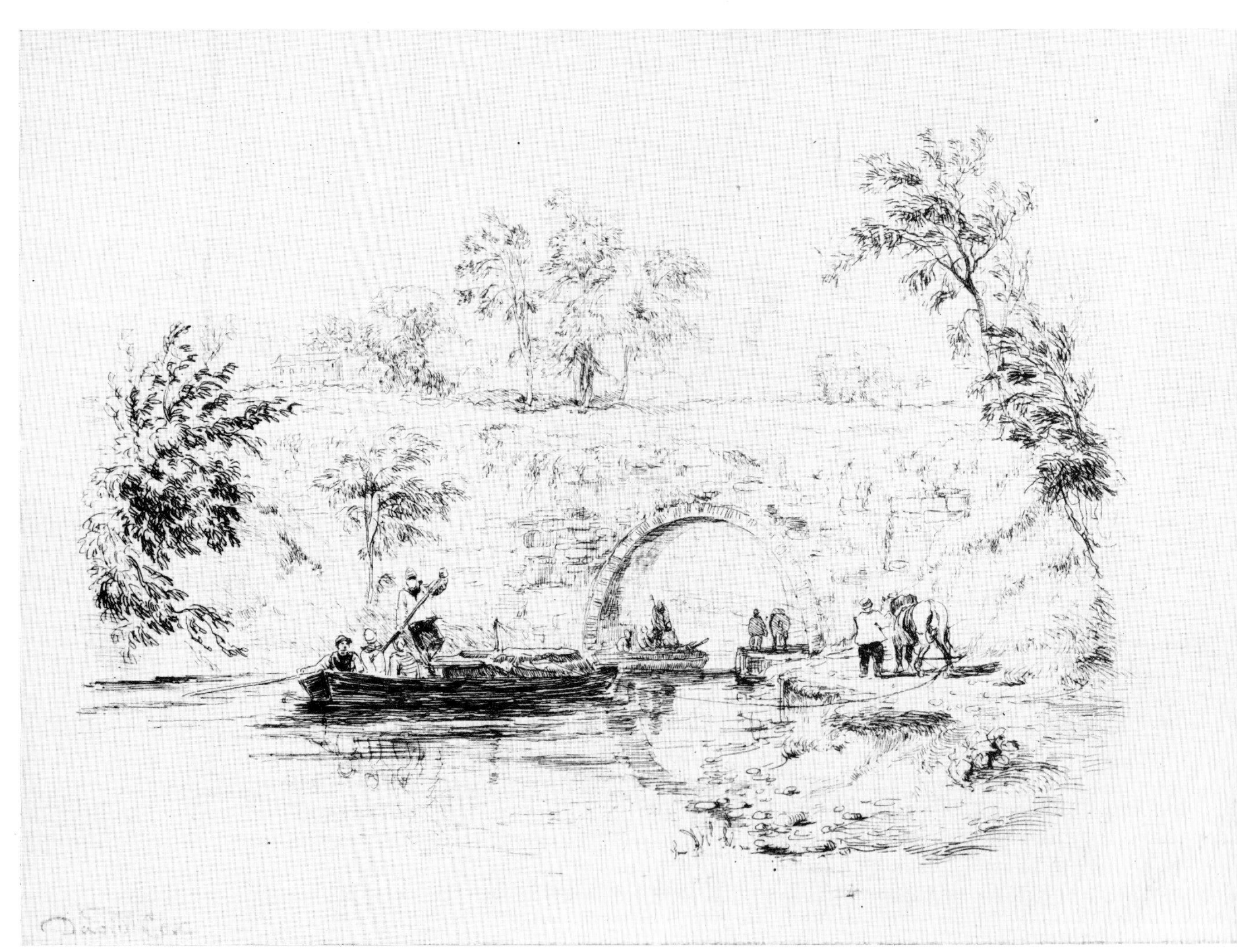

On the Canal, near Birmingham (cat. no. 125b)

9. Engraved Work

Whilst many other drawings made for reproduction are shown elsewhere (Sections 2 and 3 especially), a few for particular books typical of Cox's skilful work in the 1820s and 1830s are shown here. Further reference should be made to the Checklist of Books (page 38).

125. (a) Cottages and Trees

Etching and drypoint, platemark dimensions 9.5 × 16.9 (3¾ × 6⅝).

(b) On the Canal, near Birmingham

Etching and drypoint, platemark dimensions 15 × 20.5 (5⅞ × 8¼).
PROV: both bequeathed by J. R. Holliday 1927 (1049'27, 1050'27).
Birmingham Museums and Art Gallery

Cox must have gained considerable experience of printmaking during the publication of his drawing-books, and is quite likely to have worked personally on some of the plates, especially the soft-ground etchings. Further evidence of his activity in this sphere is provided by Solly, who quotes a letter from Lady Sophia Cecil regarding her tuition by Cox, referring to 'the lesson he gave her last year of etching'. This was in 1814, and Solly later cites work done in Wales in 1825 which included 'an etching of a cottage and a pigsty'.

On the Canal, the more interesting of these two etchings, is very faintly inscribed with its title and the monogram signature which Cox seems to have used only in about 1819 (see no. 21). Confirmation of this as a rough date for the etching comes in the shape of the pencil drawing of Hereford Cathedral on the reverse (revealed during conservation work for this exhibition). A number of canal views of industrial Birmingham by Cox have survived, including a sepia *On the Canal* in Birmingham (21'24) and an *Old Canal Bridge, Birmingham*, dated 1810, formerly in the Gilbert Davis collection.

126. County Hall, Hereford 1822 *see p. 126*

Lithograph, published by C. Hullmandel; maximum image 21.7 × 31.2 (8½ × 12¼).
PROV: bequeathed by J. R. Holliday 1927 (1051'27).
Birmingham Museums and Art Gallery

Dated 1822, the success of this print (for which there is a related pencil and chalk drawing in the Fitzwilliam Museum, and a watercolour at Hereford City Art Gallery) may have led to the commission for illustrations to *The Hereford Guide* of 1827 (see next), which also includes a view of the County Hall. The Shire Hall, as it is now known, was a new addition to Hereford's architecture, built in 1817–19 by Sir Robert Smirke.

127. Studies for *The Hereford Guide* *see p. 128*

Pencil, two with grey wash; one 10.4 × 17 (4⅛ × 6⅝), two 10.5 × 7.2 (4⅛ × 2¾), two 6.2 × 8.5 (2⅜ × 3⅜).
PROV: presented by the River Wye Guild (7603/1-5).
EXH: Hereford 1928, (29).
Hereford City Museum and Art Gallery

Five of ten surviving studies for twelve illustrations provided in the third edition of *The Hereford Guide* by W. J. Rees, published in 1827: 'Delineations of the more important Public Buildings . . . which, it is considered, will add not a little to its value'. These were produced in the unusually old-fashioned medium of wood-engraving, 'from Drawings made on the spot by Mr D. Cox', the engraver being Hugh Hughes, a Welsh-born topographer and portraitist, and author of *The Beauties of Cambria* (1823).

128. The High Street Market, Birmingham

Pencil, red chalk and sepia on toned paper 18.3 × 23.8 (7⅛ × 9⅜).
PROV: presented by subscribers to the Birmingham and Midland Institute, before 1881; purchased from the Council of the BMI 1977 (P25'78).
LIT: Solly, p. 59; Hall, pp. 27–8.
Birmingham Museums and Art Gallery

129. Warwick: St Mary's Church, County Hall and Gaol

Watercolour over pencil, with scratching-out 16.1 × 23.5 (6³/₈ × 9¹/₄).
PROV: as above (P28'78).
EXH: Liverpool 1875 (113); BMAG 1890 (244); BMAG 1959 (25).
LIT: Solly, p. 59; Hall, pp. 32, 37–8; Cox, p. 52, pl. 6A.
Birmingham Museums and Art Gallery

Cox contributed five illustrations to *Graphic Illustrations of Warwickshire*, published in 1829, an appropriate commission gained through his friend William Radclyffe, who acted as engraver. Originally published by Beilby, Knott and Beilby, with text by 'Mr Hamper, F.S.A., an antiquary of note then living in Birmingham', the book perhaps reached a wider circulation through the 1862 edition, edited by James Jaffray, with lithographic facsimile plates. The other artists who contributed were de Wint, J. V. Barber, J. D. Harding and William Westall. An amusing letter to Radclyffe, of 22 January 1827, revealing Cox's attention to the detail of the Birmingham scene, is printed by Hall: 'I have this moment recollected that I ought to have made a sketch of some ducks, but if it is to be altered you can do it, and I will touch upon the proof. I still think there can be no objection to the table with the dead poultry.'

The surviving drawings by all the artists are now in the Birmingham collection. That of *Warwick*, in watercolour rather than sepia like the rest, must at

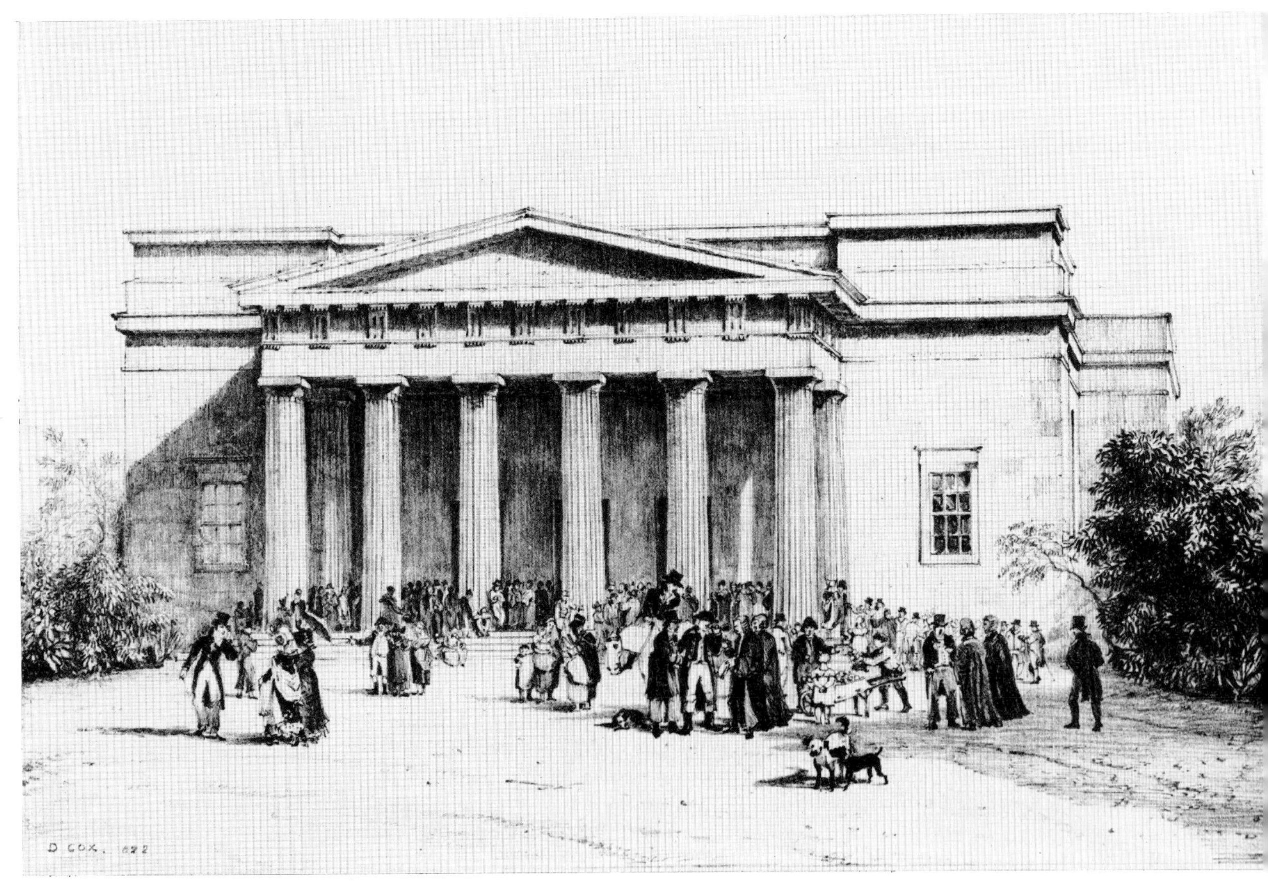

County Hall, Hereford (cat. no. 126)

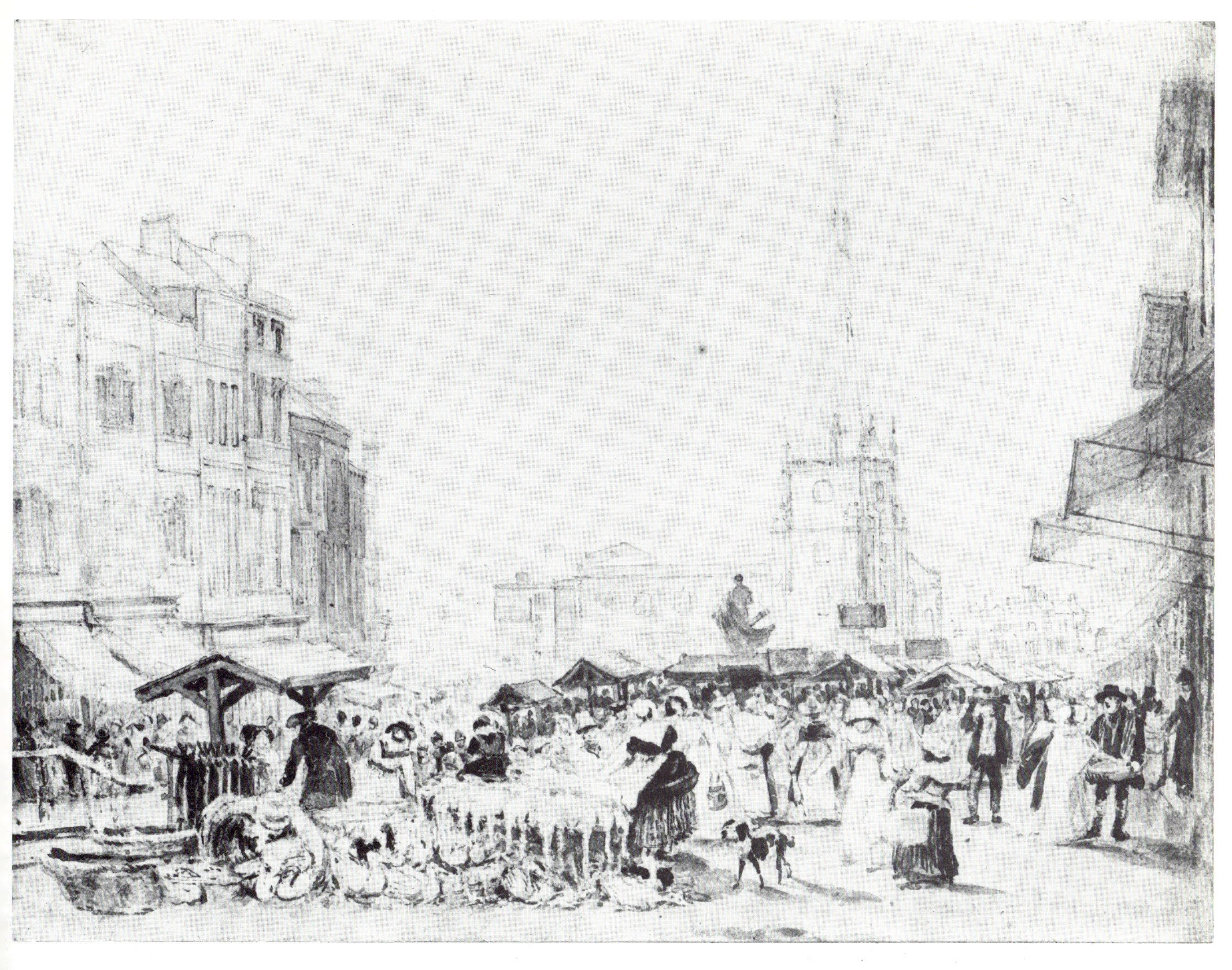

The High Street Market, Birmingham (cat. no. 128)

some time have been substituted in the group; its original sepia found its way into Thomas Wrigley's collection, and is now at Bury Art Gallery.

130. Singham Mahal, Torway, Bejapore, India

(a) Sepia over pencil 12 × 18.3 (4¾ × 7⅛).
(b) Line engraving, by H. Wallis 12 × 18.3 (4¾ × 7⅛).
PROV: bequeathed by J. R. Holliday 1927 (667′27; 1614′27).
Birmingham Museums and Art Gallery

The study and engraving made after a sketch by Capt. R. Elliot, RN, for that author's *Views in the East; comprising India, Canton, and the shores of the Red Sea*, 1833 (Vol. II, plate 15). The working up of amateur travellers' sketches, usually for publication, was quite common in the early 19th century. Copley Fielding and even Turner (in very comparable designs for White's *Views in India*, 1838) did the same, amongst many other artists, and the practice accounts for many apparently implausible subjects that crop up in their work.

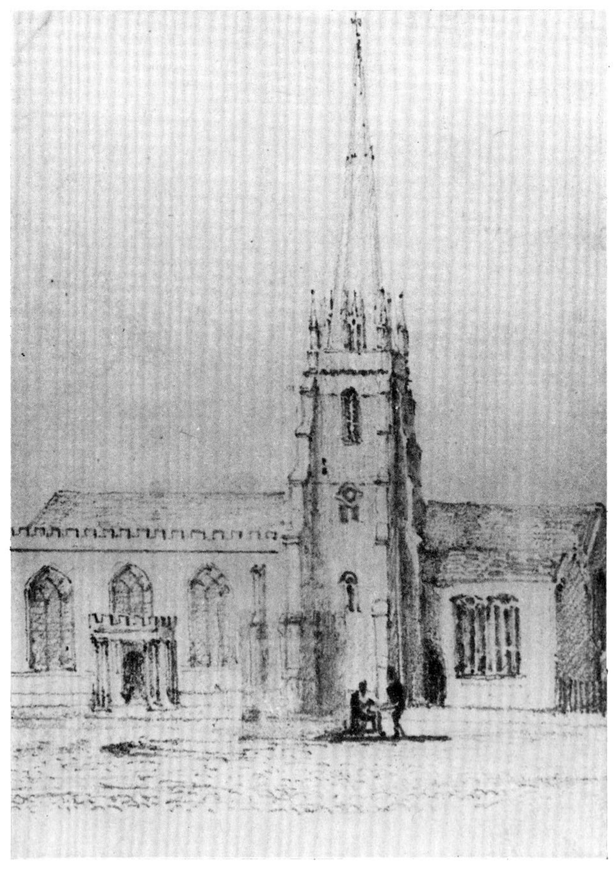

Study for The Hereford Guide (cat. no. 127)

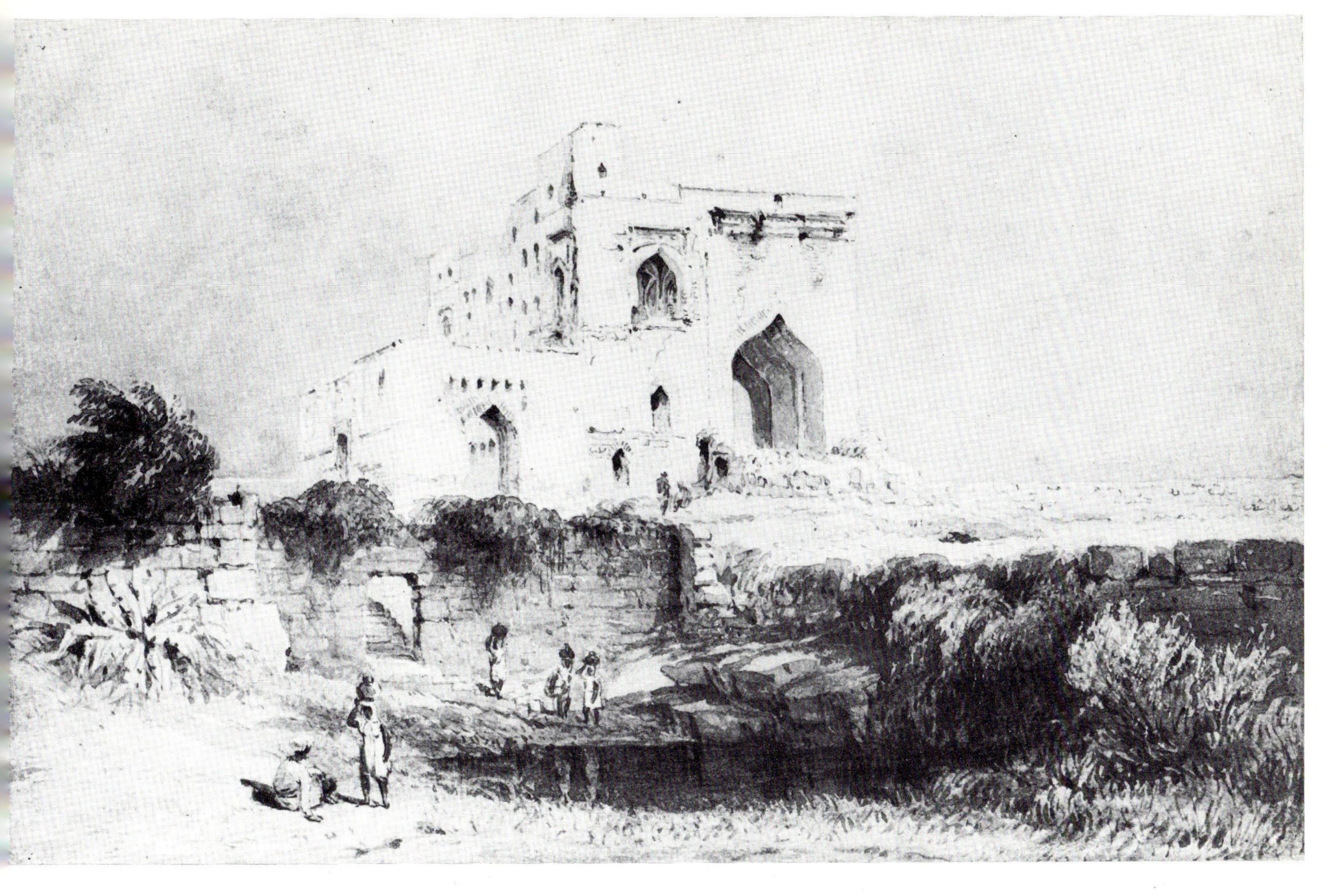

Singham Mahal, Torway, Bejapore, India (cat. no. 130a)

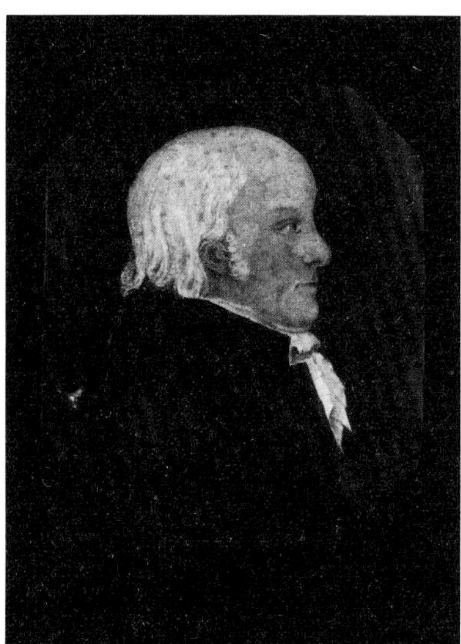

William Johnson, Mayor of Hereford (cat. no. 131)

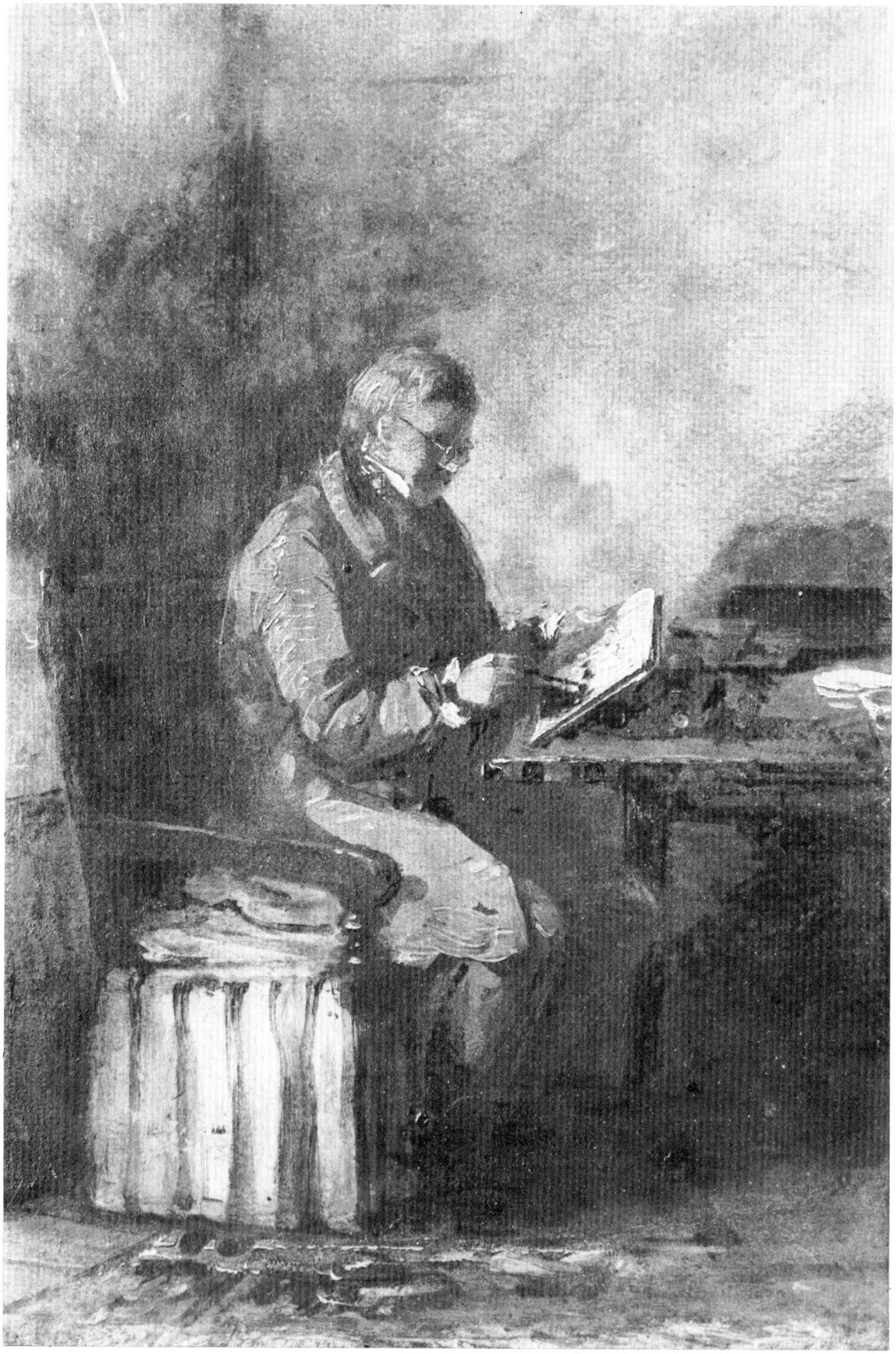

Self-Portrait (?) (cat. no. 132)

10. David Cox the Man

Even his contemporary biographers had to admit that Cox led an essentially uneventful life, its chief milestones being artistic ones. Seldom in the history of art, certainly in British art, can a painter have been so engrossed and yet content in his work. 'Never sparing himself, and never induced for one moment to turn aside into other pursuits, art-work was to him "his being's end and aim"; ease and the allurements of "pleasure" were without attractions to him. Work, always work, was to David Cox true happiness.' (Solly, p. 308)

Yet the image of the man that comes down to us through his work, his letters and the straightforward biographies of Solly and Hall, is not of an austere, dull man permanently stuck in his studio, but of an honest English countryman, ever ready to see or try something new, never afraid of a challenge or short of a word of kindness for those in need, often self-deprecating and frustrated at his own inadequacies, but always sure of being able to return to nature and be moved. No English landscape painter has loved his calling more than David Cox.

131. William Johnson, Mayor of Hereford 1816

Watercolour over pencil on card, trimmed at corners 7.5 × 6.4 (2⅞ × 2½).
PROV: bequeathed by Helen Glinn 1933 (1654).
Hereford City Museum and Art Gallery

A contemporary label on the reverse of the frame, by all appearances in David Cox's hand, reads 'Mayor of the City, 1816 / Portrait of Mr William / Johnson. Proctor Hereford / by David Cox Senior.' If the 'Senior' may be explained by the father's wish to distinguish his work from that of his son, eighteen years old at the time of leaving Hereford, and already probably an artist and drawing-master (he also made at least one lithograph, *Cabbage Lane*, of Hereford), then there seems no reason to doubt this intriguing little portrait to be the sole surviving evidence of Cox's reluctant abilities as a miniaturist.

132. Self-Portrait?

Oil on paper 28.7 × 18.7 (11¼ × 7⅜).
PROV: presented by the Rev. C. H. and Mrs R. F. Bailey.
Hereford City Museum and Art Gallery

Again, a pencil-inscribed label, 'David Cox by Himself', in convincing Hereford period script, is the only circumstantial evidence for this indeed being a self-portrait. Hall (p. 36) speculates as to Cox's possibly painting in oil whilst in Hereford. We must await further investigation to confirm the probable authenticity of what would be the only known self-portrait.

133. Diagram of the artist's palette

Pen and ink 27.3 × 35.5 (10¾ × 14).
PROV: acquired by the present owner 1958.
EXH: BMAG 1959 (161).
LIT: Solly, p. 185.
Private Collection

Showing the arrangement of colours on the artist's palette, this drawing may be compared with a surviving palette and paint-box in the Birmingham collection, and with Cox's own most detailed account of his method of oil painting in a letter of 21 December 1845 to his son (quoted by Solly).

134. Sir John Watson Gordon RA, PRSA (1790–1864): Portrait of David Cox 1855

Oil on canvas 124.5 × 100.3 (49 × 39½).
PROV: David Cox; Birmingham and Midland Institute; transferred to Museums and Art Gallery (P185'78).
EXH: RA 1856 (138); BMAG 1890 (107, repr. frontispiece); BMAG 1959 (154).
LIT: Solly, pp. 236–45; Hall, pp. 167–76; Cox, pp. 106–7, pl. 29; BMAG Oils, p. 63.
Birmingham Museums and Art Gallery

A committee of Cox's friends and admirers was formed in 1855 to present him with his portrait. With Cox's agreement Sir John Watson Gordon was approached, and undertook the commission, provided that Cox gave him sittings in Edinburgh. Despite his bad health, Cox seems to have enjoyed the expedition – his only visit to Scotland – on which he was accompanied by his son. He was not completely impressed, however, by the finished result, remarking that he was sure he never had such a 'long Scotch head' as he had been given. Watson Gordon was delighted with his subject, seeing a great resemblance in Cox's head to Sir Walter Scott's, and in the lower part of the face to Lord Brougham.

The portrait was presented to Cox on 19 November 1855 at a gathering of the subscribers at Metchley Abbey, the Harborne home of Charles Birch, Chairman of the Portrait Committee, and hung at Greenfield House until the artist's death. The subscription was largely local and included many of Cox's patrons, but the presentation volume of signatures (in the Birmingham collection) also contains the names of the painter David Roberts, John Ruskin and the actor W. C. Macready, whose father had employed the young David Cox as a scene-painter's assistant.

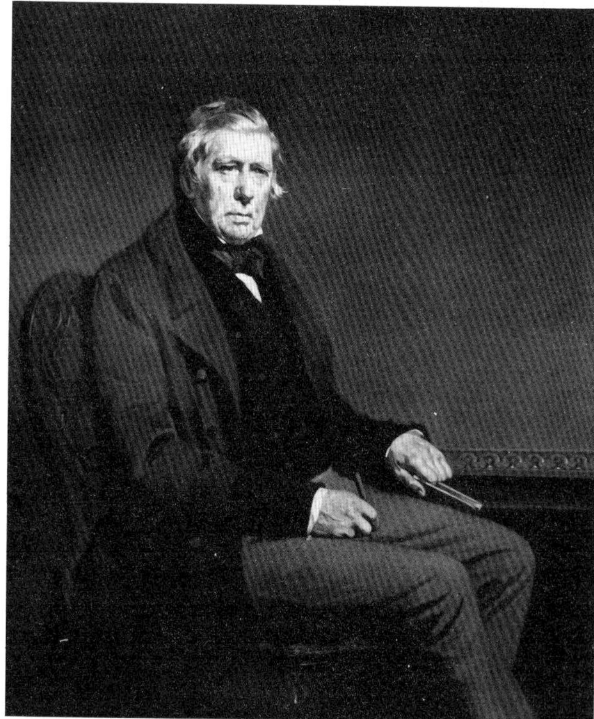

Samuel Bellin (after Watson Gordon), *Portrait of David Cox* (cat. no. 135)

135. Samuel Bellin (1799–1893) after Watson Gordon: Portrait of David Cox

Mezzotint engraving 40.5 × 32.5 (15⅞ × 12¾).
PROV: presented by E. H. Keen (P40′74).
Birmingham Museums and Art Gallery

A copy of this mezzotint was apparently issued to each subscriber to the portrait; it brings out in sharp detail those areas of the painting which have darkened over the years.

136. Sir William Boxall RA (1800–79): Study for portrait of David Cox

Wax crayon and chalks on buff paper 31.3 × 26.2 (12¼ × 10¼).
PROV: presented by the Association of Friends of the Art Gallery 1935 (80′35).
EXH: BMAG 1959 (153).
LIT: Solly, pp. 284–85, 290.
Birmingham Museums and Art Gallery

A preparatory study for the portrait for which Cox sat from 6 June 1856. Exhibited at the RA in 1857 (499), the oil is now in the National Portrait Gallery (see R. Ormond, *Early Victorian Portraits*, Vol. 1, p. 119, and Vol. 2, pl. 218).

137. William Henry Hunt (1790–1864): David Cox and his son playing chess

Pencil 9.5 × 11.5 (3¾ × 4½).
PROV: bequeathed by J. R. Holliday 1927 (895′27).
EXH: BMAG 1959 (156); *William Henry Hunt*, Wolverhampton Art Gallery 1981 (27).
Birmingham Museums and Art Gallery

Cox, with his son David junior, captured in an informal mood by a fellow artist.

138. Peter Hollins (1800–86): Bust of David Cox

White marble 73.5 cm (29 ins) high.
PROV: presented by the Cox Memorial Committee 1868 (2622′85).
EXH: OWCS 1862; BMAG 1959 (155).
LIT: Solly, p. 306; Hall, p. 176; J. Hill & W. Midgley, *The Royal Birmingham Society of Artists*, [1928], pl. 1; Cox, p. 115; R. Gunnis, *Dictionary of British Sculptors* 1953, p. 206.

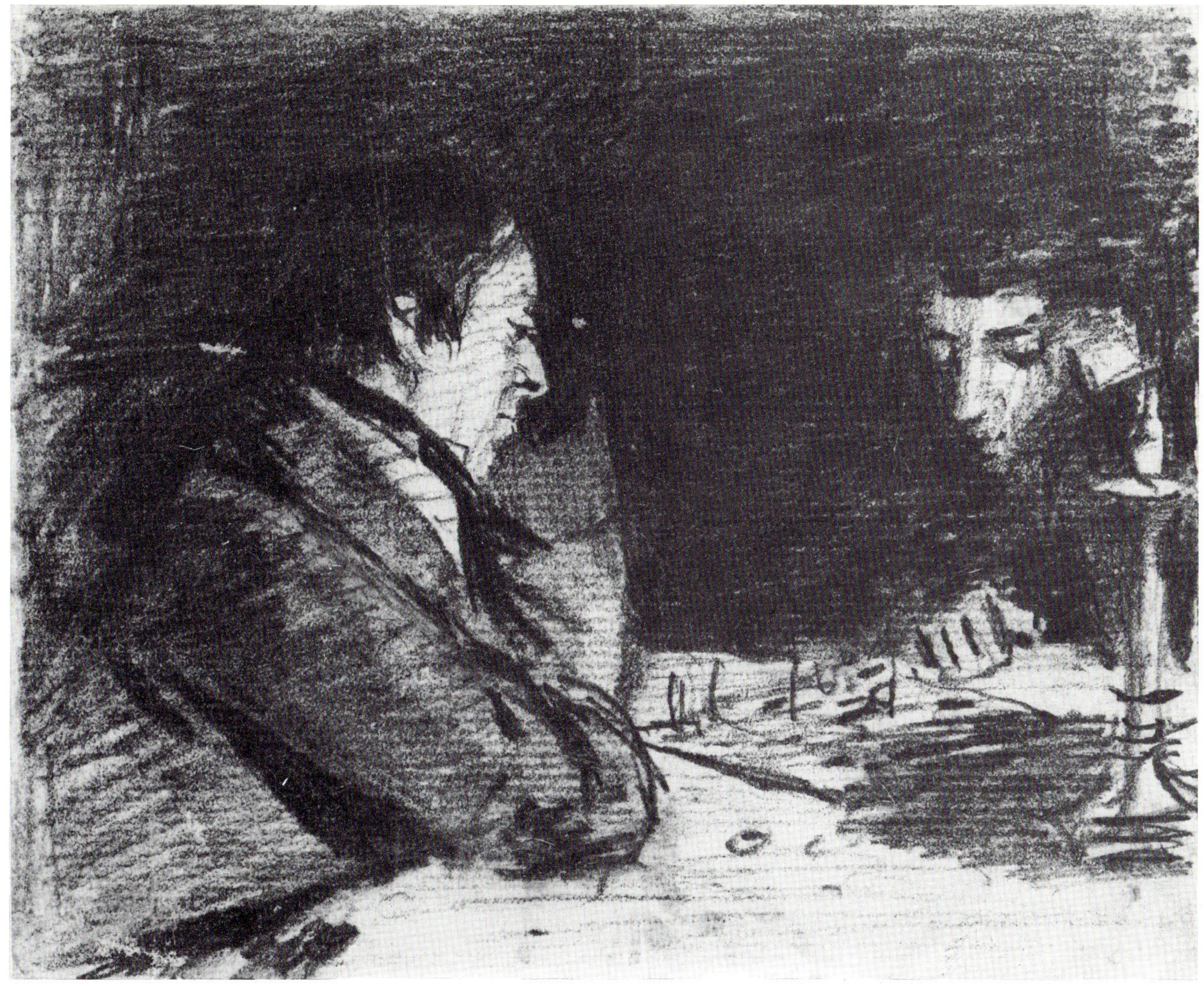

W. H. Hunt, *David Cox and his son playing chess* (cat. no. 137)

Birmingham Museums and Art Gallery

This posthumous bust by Birmingham's leading sculptor was commissioned in 1860 by a group of subscribers, and according to those who knew him, is supposed to be an excellent likeness. In 1862 the Old Water Colour Society accepted the sculptor's offer of displaying the bust as a tribute to Cox in the watercolour exhibition of that year.

139. David Cox, junior (1809–85): Greenfield House, Harborne, the Home of David Cox

see p. 134

Watercolour, with scratching-out 36.7 × 54.5 (14⅜ × 21½).
PROV: presented by H. J. Jennings 1884 (2541'85).
EXH: BMAG 1959 (172).
Birmingham Museums and Art Gallery

Greenfield House was one of the older buildings in

the village of Harborne, probably a farmhouse of the early 18th century. Its brick box-like structure is still discernible today beneath a number of later additions and alterations. Solly describes the house that was Cox's home from 1841 until his death in 1859: 'Greenfield was rather an old-fashioned place when he went to live there. From a desire to be very quiet and retired, he kept the front door facing the road always fastened up, and all comers entered by the garden-door at the back . . . On the ground floor was the parlour or dining-room; on the other side of the passage was a small smoke-room, a front and back kitchen; and up-stairs there were two or three bedrooms, and a long room used as a studio . . . His easel was a large mahogany one, rather solid, and strongly constructed, and one or two simple tables and old chairs completed the furniture. No bric-a-brac or elaborate carvings of any kind. In the winter this studio was very cold. He therefore at that time of year generally transferred his easel and painting apparatus to the dining-room. The house also was very simply furnished, but in his dining-room he had several oil-pictures on the walls.

'The garden was a large one surrounded with trees, and he took great interest in it, often working there himself. He planted a good many young forest trees, which he preferred to any others . . . There was also an avenue of filberts and nut-trees in the garden, and a large willow-bush, of which Cox was immensely proud, having been originally a cutting from *the* willow which grew over Napoleon's tomb at St Helena . . . Cox cultivated broad-leaved plants in his garden, such as rhubarb and different kinds of docks; also Scotch thistles, of which, as well as of hollyhocks, he was especially fond.'

This watercolour must have been made before Cox's death, for the house was thereupon sold, his son continuing to live in London. David junior's reputation as an artist in his own right (he was an Associate of the Old Water Colour Society, and made many British and foreign tours which provided him with exhibits) has necessarily been obscured by his father's work, which his own at first resembled. Later ambitious pieces, however, such as the *Pass of Llanberis* (Victoria and Albert Museum) and a number of French and Swiss panoramic views, were quite removed from Cox senior's style, as he recognised in a letter to a friend: 'The Chamounix gave me the impression of all the suggestive ideas which I had myself despaired of rendering attainable. My father's works were very effective from a very different cause – his direct aim in the open daylight, sense of effect and simpler treatment of the scene as he found it.'

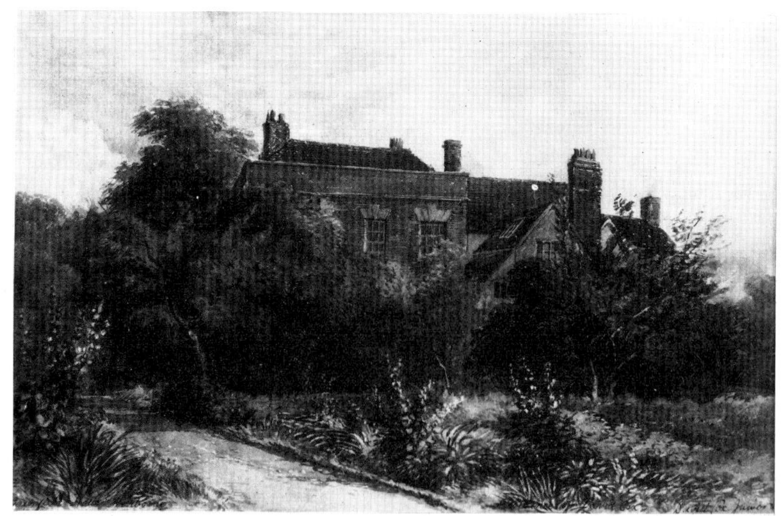

David Cox junior, *Greenfield House, Harborne* (cat. no. 139)

Acknowledgements

It has been a labour of love to re-examine the work of David Cox, and a pleasant surprise to have found such willing co-operation in the task from fellow enthusiasts, collectors, scholars and curators.

I have received much useful information from private collectors, some of whom have been prevailed upon to fill important gaps in the exhibition. I should like to express my gratitude to the directors and staff of the many institutions which I have visited, and which have eased the task of collecting information and borrowing the works within their care. Amongst these, I should particularly like to thank Ann Whyte, Aberdeen Art Gallery; Andy Ashton, Bury Art Gallery; David Scrase, Fitzwilliam Museum, Cambridge; Peter Day, Keeper of the Devonshire Collections, Chatsworth; Roger Dodsworth, Dudley Art Gallery; Clara Young, Dundee City Art Gallery; Duncan Bull, National Gallery of Scotland, Edinburgh; Hilary Macartney, formerly of Glasgow Art Gallery; Anne Sandford, Hereford City Museum and Art Gallery; Alexander Robertson, Leeds City Art Galleries; Mary Bennett and Edward Morris, Walker Art Gallery, Liverpool; John Rowlands, Lindsay Stainton and Hilary Williams, Department of Prints and Drawings, British Museum; William Bradford, Courtauld Institute Galleries; Malcolm Fry and Michael Spender, Royal Society of Painters in Water-Colours; Jonathan Mason, Tate Gallery; Michael Kauffmann and John Murdoch, Victoria and Albert Museum; Jane Farrington, Manchester City Art Gallery; Craig Hartley, Whitworth Art Gallery, University of Manchester; Andrew Greg, Laing Art Gallery, Newcastle-upon-Tyne; Jon Whiteley, Ashmolean Museum, Oxford; Lucy Wood, Lady Lever Art Gallery, Port Sunlight; Stephen Sartin, Harris Museum and Art Gallery, Preston; Peter Vigurs and Sarah Richardson, Wolverhampton Art Gallery; and Zoë Capernaros, Worcester City Museum and Art Gallery. As always, unstinting help has come from Patrick Baird and others at the Central Reference Library, Birmingham, and from the staff of the University Library, Cambridge.

I should also like to express personal thanks for hospitality and assistance in offering unlimited use of family archive material to Canon and Mrs J. G. Grimwade, and Mr and Mrs J. Hills. Further debts of gratitude I owe to Jim Berrow, Peter Bicknell, Sir Trenchard Cox, Anthony Reed, David Temperley and Glennys Wild.

Most of all, may I acknowledge the support and good humour displayed by my long-suffering colleagues at Birmingham, especially those in the Art Departments. An equal share in the success of the exhibition, if not in the shortcomings of this catalogue, is the only adequate reward for the constant encouragement and unflagging enthusiasm of Richard Lockett.

Other members of staff have made important contributions – Sue Kruszynski has typed the manuscript under extreme pressure, David Bailey has produced the excellent photographs, Stewart Meese, Moira Twist and Terry Huguenin have performed miracles of conservation, and Peter Butler and Bruce Barron have provided the crucial technical support; to all of them our grateful thanks.

STEPHEN WILDMAN

Photographs: In all cases, photographs were supplied by the institutions and by individual lenders to the exhibition. The colour plates of items in the Birmingham collection were taken by Cecil Reilly, and the others by Richard Hammonds and Mr H. Read. We are very grateful to Central Independent Television for financial assistance towards producing the colour plates.

Index of Lenders

The Authors

STEPHEN WILDMAN read English and History of Art at Queens' College, Cambridge, graduating with first class honours in 1974 and becoming a Research Fellow of his college in 1976. In 1980 he took up the appointment as Deputy Keeper of Fine Art at Birmingham Museums and Art Gallery, with special responsibility for the Prints and Drawings Collection. In the same year he organised (with Duncan Robinson) the *Morris & Company in Cambridge* exhibition at the Fitzwilliam Museum. He has published several articles on British art and architectural history of the 19th century and is currently a Regional Secretary of the Victorian Society.

JOHN MURDOCH's first appointment was as Assistant Keeper of Fine Art at Birmingham Museums and Art Gallery. He then became Assistant Keeper of Paintings at the Victoria and Albert Museum, of which Department he is now Deputy Keeper. Amongst his publications are *Forty-two British Watercolours from the Victoria and Albert Museum* (1977), *Byron* (1974, the exhibition organised jointly with Anthony Burton) and, with other authors, *The English Miniature* (1982).

RICHARD LOCKETT became a Lecturer at Birmingham University in 1968 and a member of the staff of the Barber Institute of Fine Arts. In 1979 he moved to the City Museums and Art Gallery to become Keeper of Fine Art. He has selected two major touring exhibitions from the Birmingham Collection, the first in 1980–81 for the Arts Council, and the second in 1982–83 for the British Council. He is currently working on the life of the 19th-century watercolour painter Samuel Prout FSA.